Th ... Lee

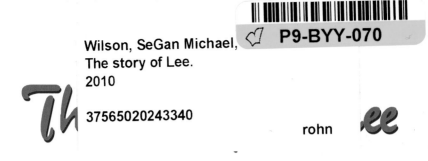

rohn

The Story of Lee

Volume 1

by Seán Michael Wilson
& Chie Kutsuwada

ISBN: 978-1-56163-594-8
© 2010 Seán Michael Wilson & Chie Kutsuwada
Library of Congress Control Number: 2010941038
Scott Walker, "The War Is Over" © 1970 Philips Records
The Clientele, various songs © 2000, 2003, 2005, 2007 Merge Records
1st printing, December 2010

Comicslit is an imprint
and trademark of

NANTIER · BEALL · MINOUSTCHINE
Publishing inc.
new york

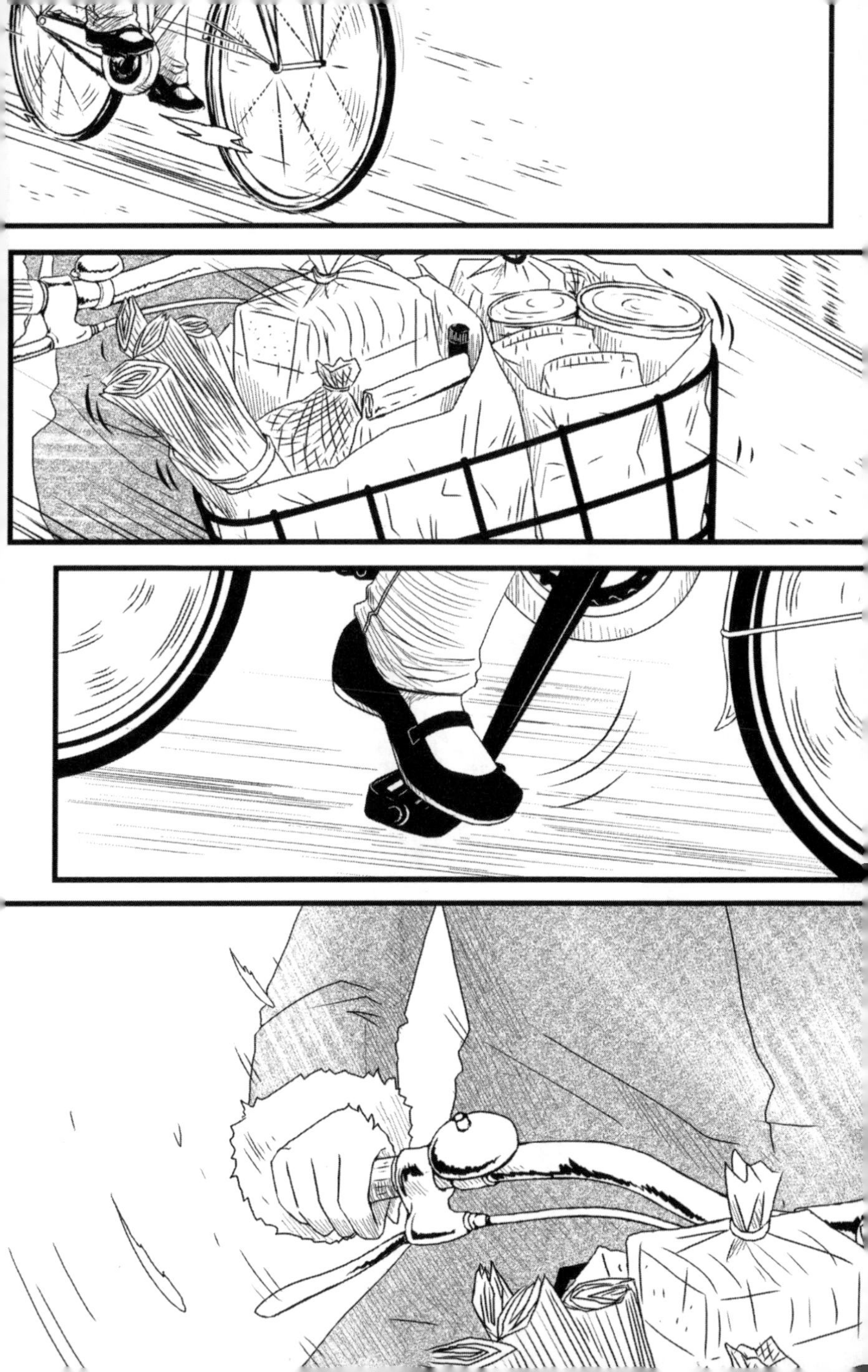

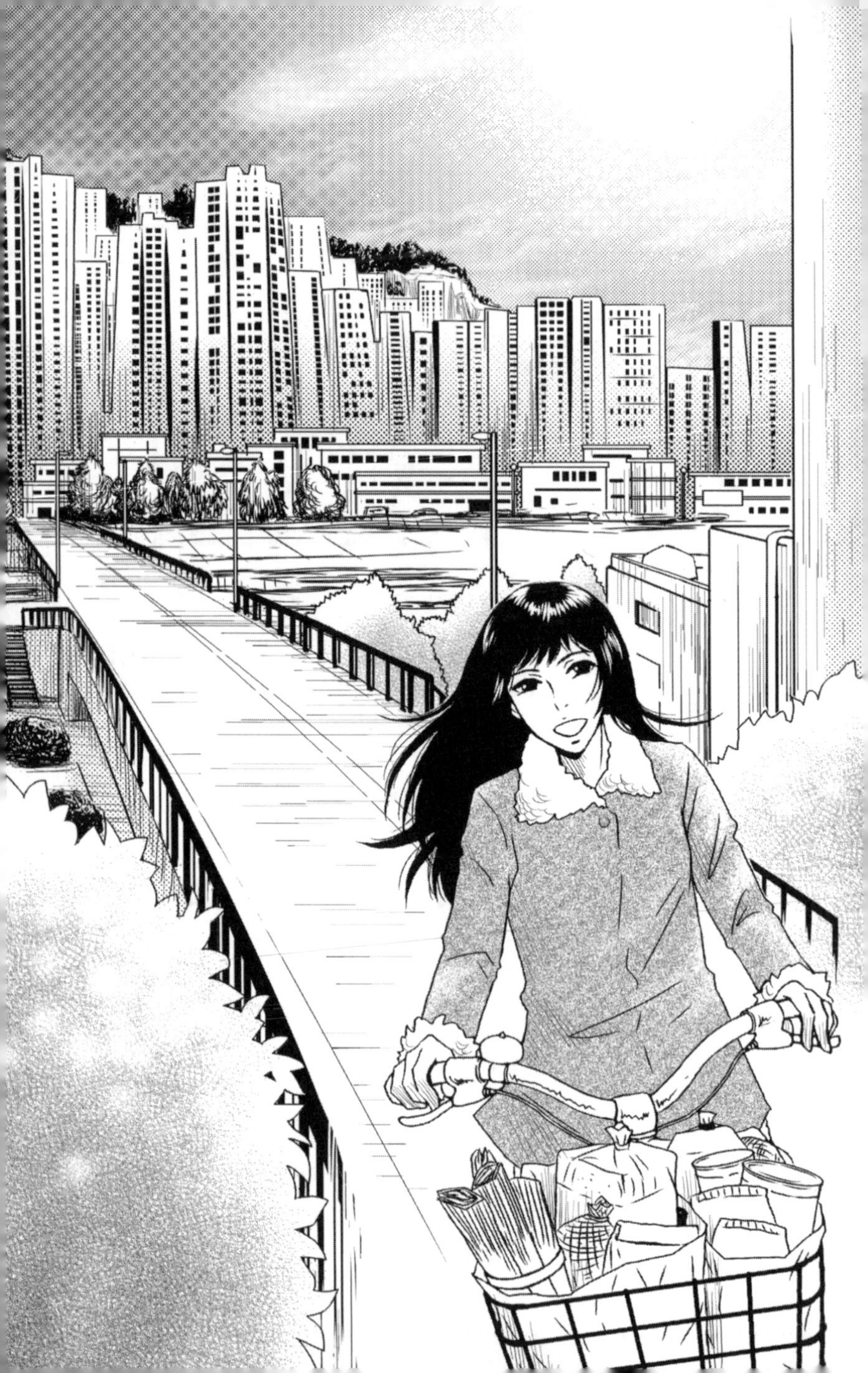

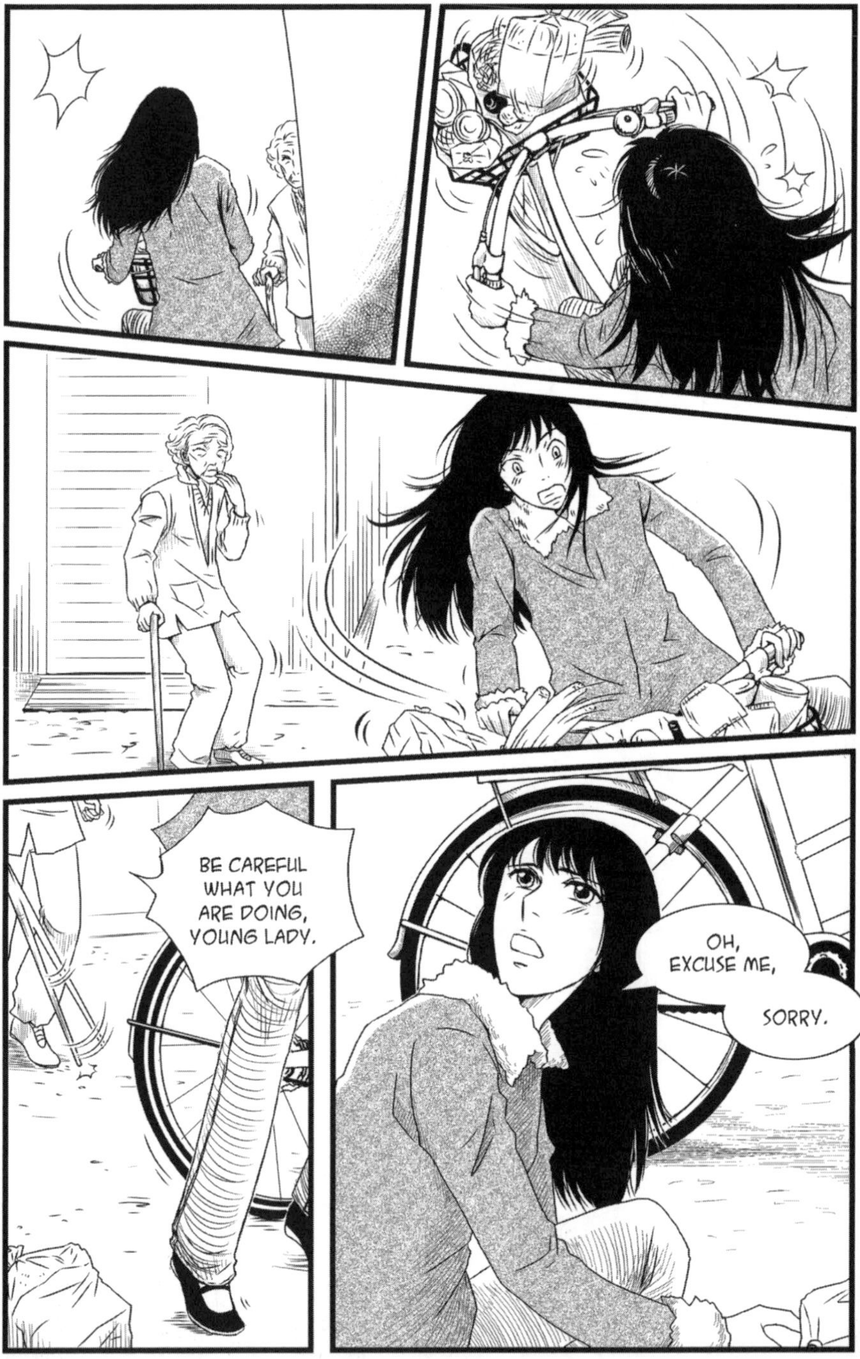
BE CAREFUL WHAT YOU ARE DOING, YOUNG LADY.
OH, EXCUSE ME,
SORRY.

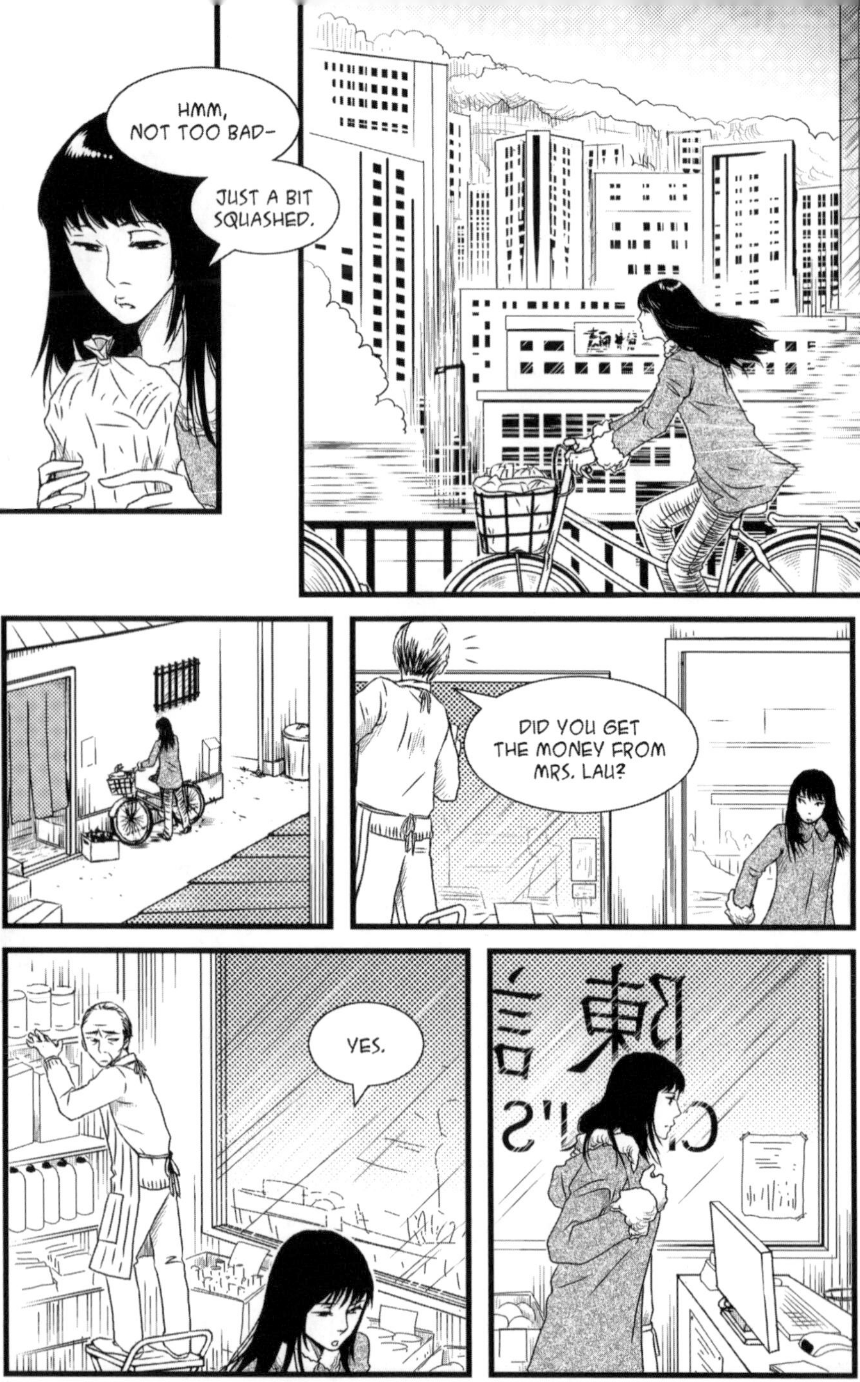
HMM, NOT TOO BAD-
JUST A BIT SQUASHED.
DID YOU GET THE MONEY FROM MRS. LAU?
YES.

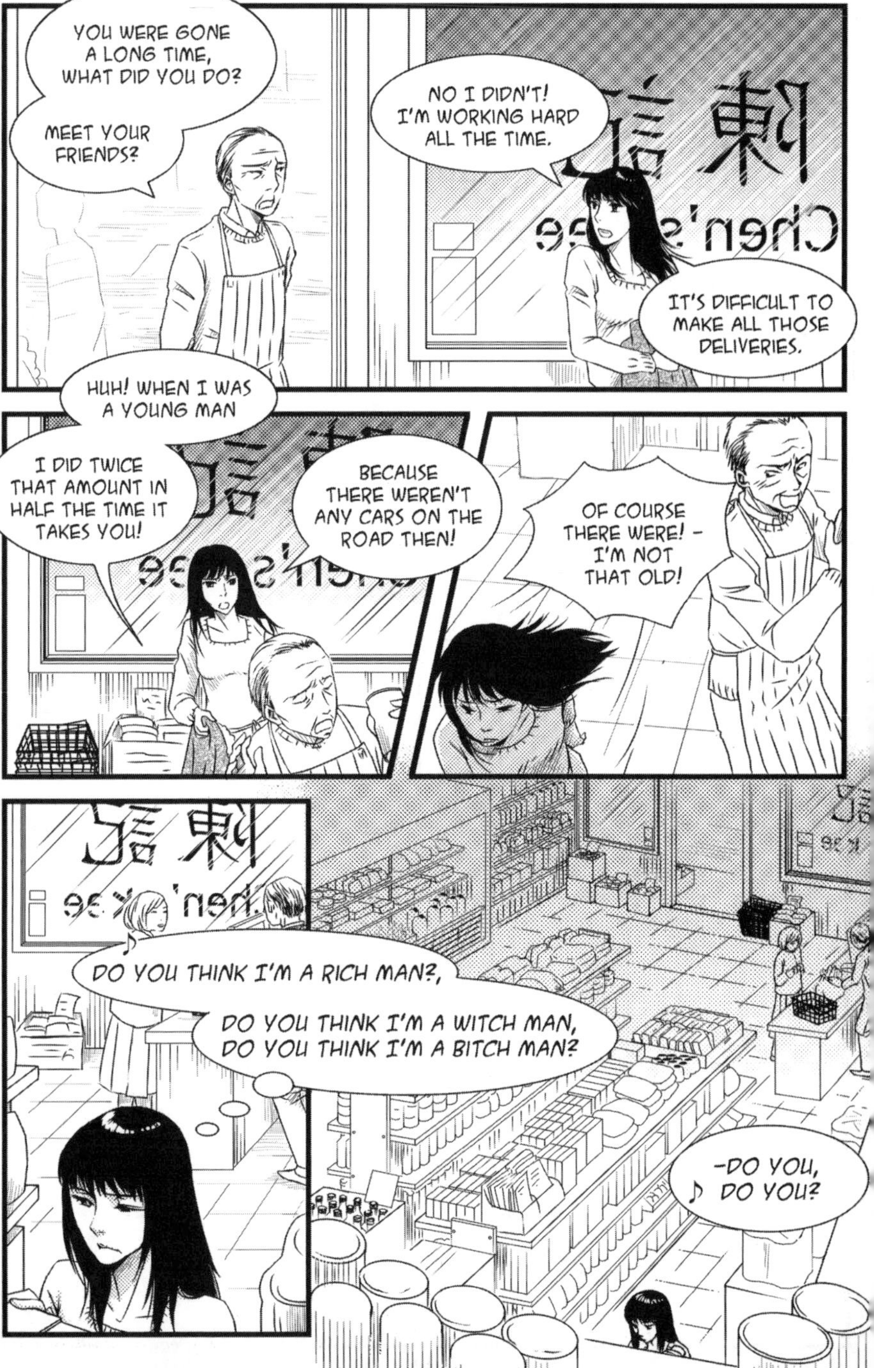
YOU WERE GONE A LONG TIME, WHAT DID YOU DO?
MEET YOUR FRIENDS?
NO I DIDN'T! I'M WORKING HARD ALL THE TIME.
IT'S DIFFICULT TO MAKE ALL THOSE DELIVERIES.
HUH! WHEN I WAS A YOUNG MAN
I DID TWICE THAT AMOUNT IN HALF THE TIME IT TAKES YOU!
BECAUSE THERE WEREN'T ANY CARS ON THE ROAD THEN!
OF COURSE THERE WERE! - I'M NOT THAT OLD!
DO YOU THINK I'M A RICH MAN?,
DO YOU THINK I'M A WITCH MAN, DO YOU THINK I'M A BITCH MAN?
-DO YOU, ♪ DO YOU?

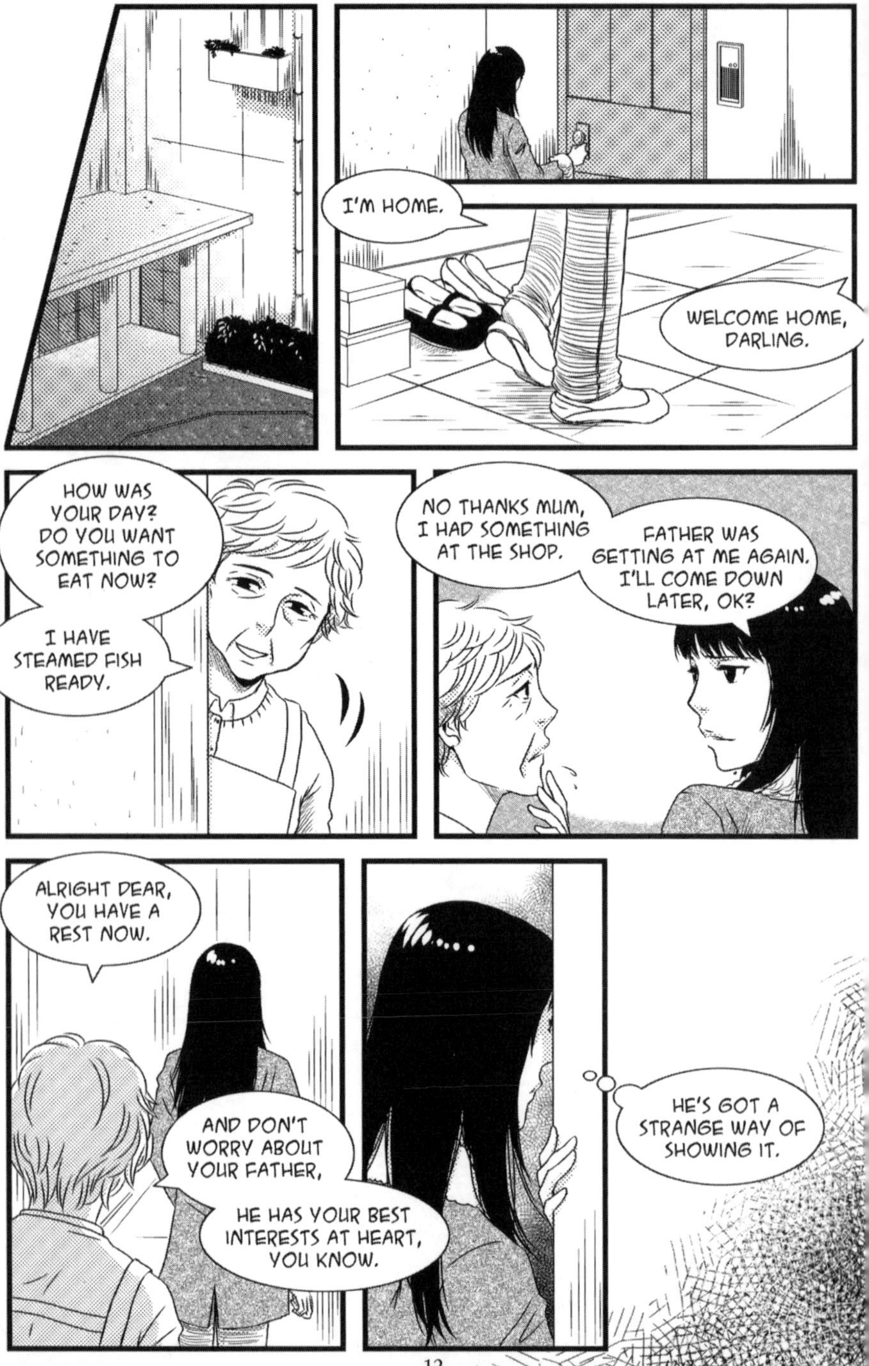
I'M HOME.
WELCOME HOME, DARLING.
HOW WAS YOUR DAY? DO YOU WANT SOMETHING TO EAT NOW?
I HAVE STEAMED FISH READY.
NO THANKS MUM, I HAD SOMETHING AT THE SHOP.
FATHER WAS GETTING AT ME AGAIN. I'LL COME DOWN LATER, OK?
ALRIGHT DEAR, YOU HAVE A REST NOW.
AND DON'T WORRY ABOUT YOUR FATHER,
HE HAS YOUR BEST INTERESTS AT HEART, YOU KNOW.
HE'S GOT A STRANGE WAY OF SHOWING IT.

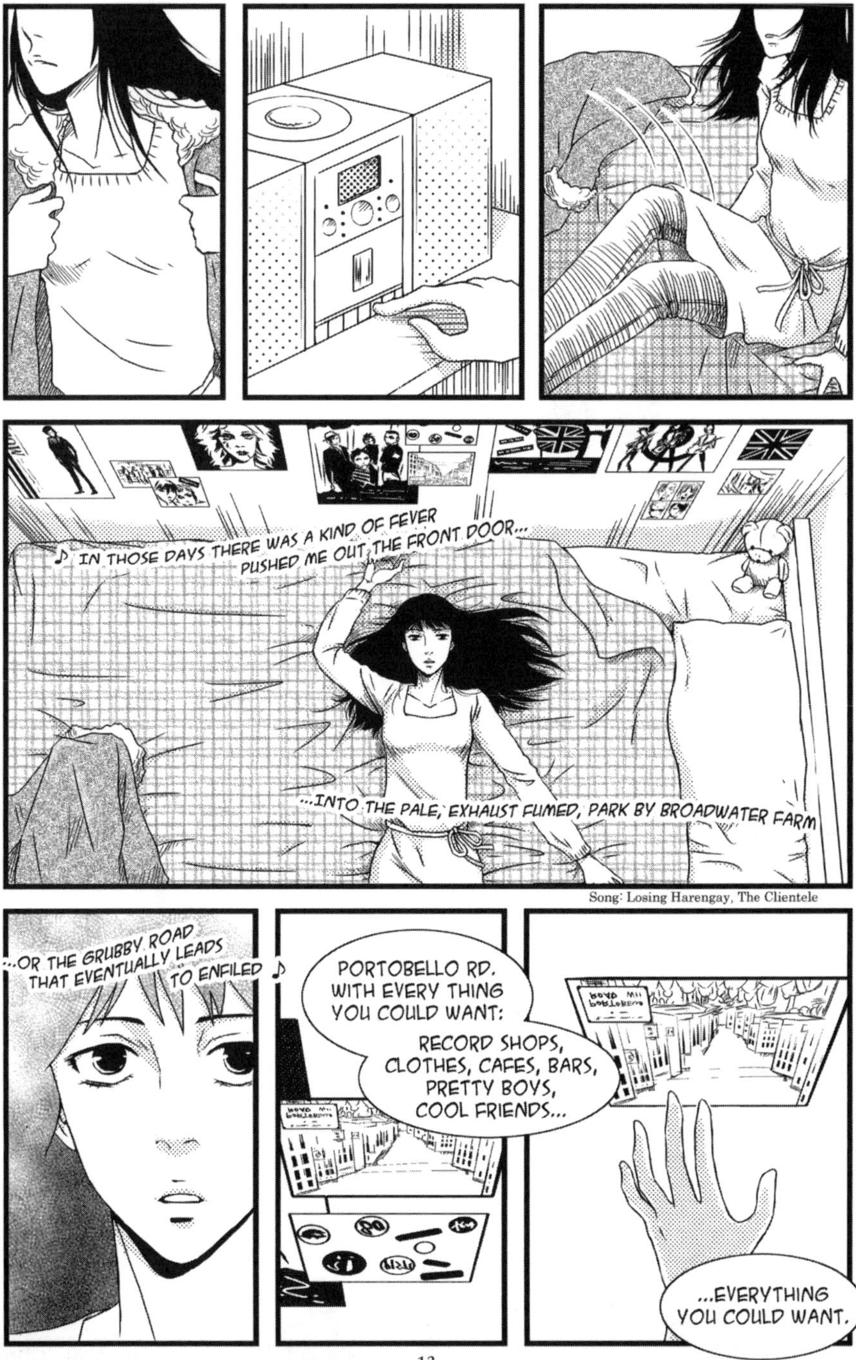
♪ IN THOSE DAYS THERE WAS A KIND OF FEVER
PUSHED ME OUT THE FRONT DOOR...
...INTO THE PALE, EXHAUST FUMED, PARK BY BROADWATER FARM
...OR THE GRUBBY ROAD THAT EVENTUALLY LEADS TO ENFILED ♪
PORTOBELLO RD. WITH EVERY THING YOU COULD WANT:
RECORD SHOPS, CLOTHES, CAFES, BARS, PRETTY BOYS, COOL FRIENDS...
...EVERYTHING YOU COULD WANT.

Song: Losing Harengay, The Clientele

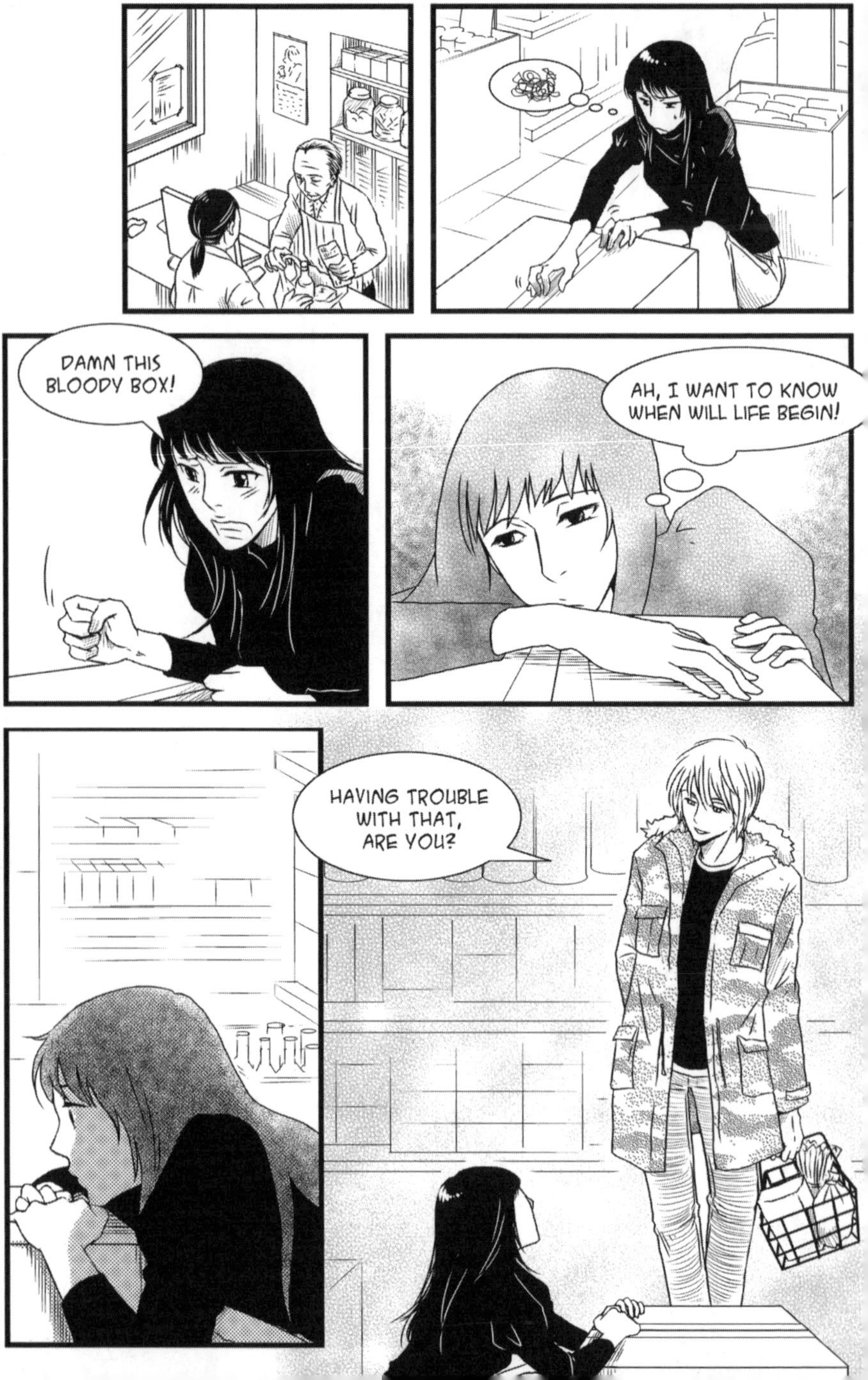
DAMN THIS BLOODY BOX!
AH, I WANT TO KNOW WHEN WILL LIFE BEGIN!
HAVING TROUBLE WITH THAT, ARE YOU?

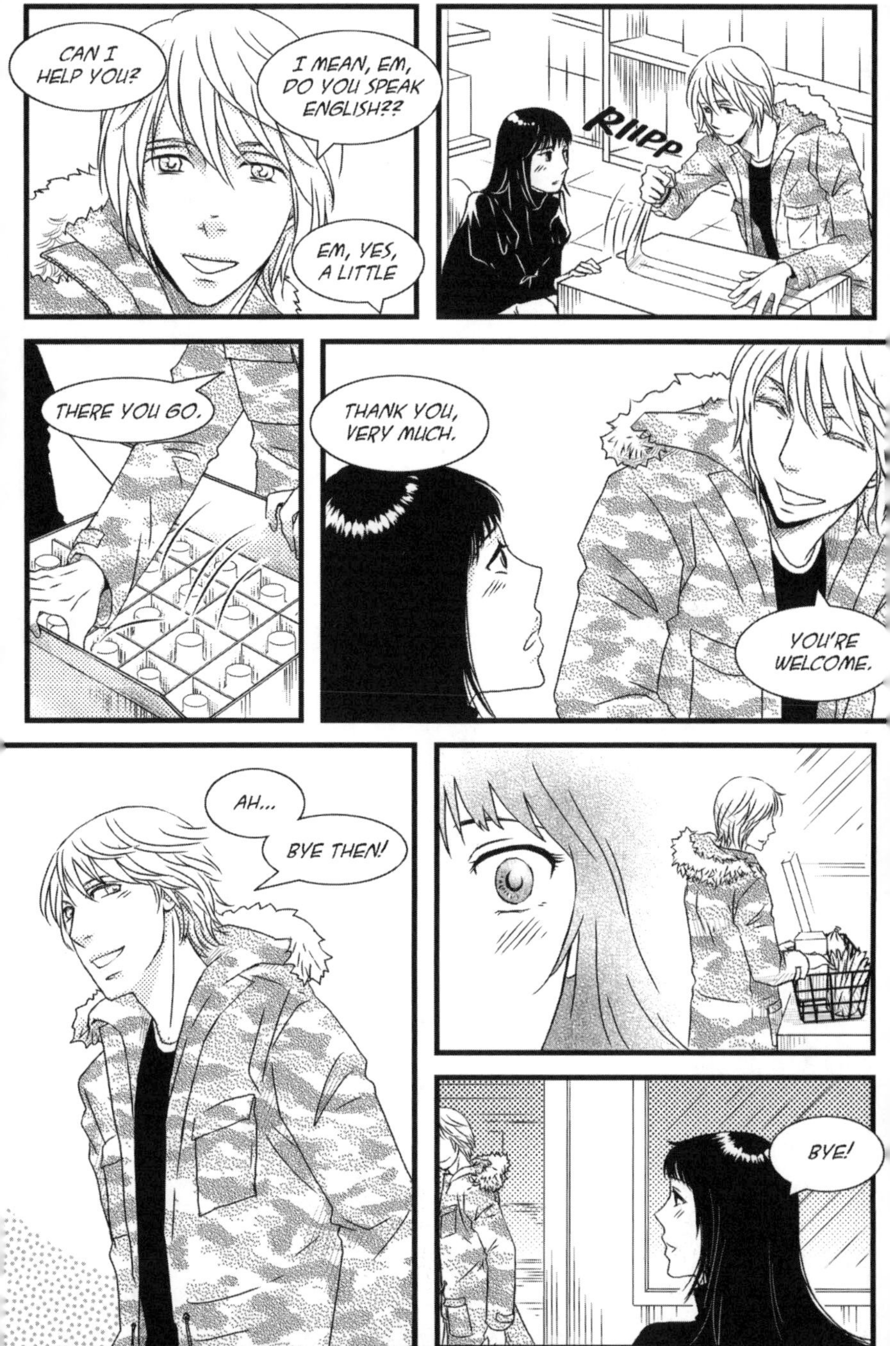
CAN I HELP YOU?
I MEAN, EM, DO YOU SPEAK ENGLISH??
EM, YES, A LITTLE
RIIPP
THERE YOU GO.
THANK YOU, VERY MUCH.
YOU'RE WELCOME.
AH...
BYE THEN!
BYE!

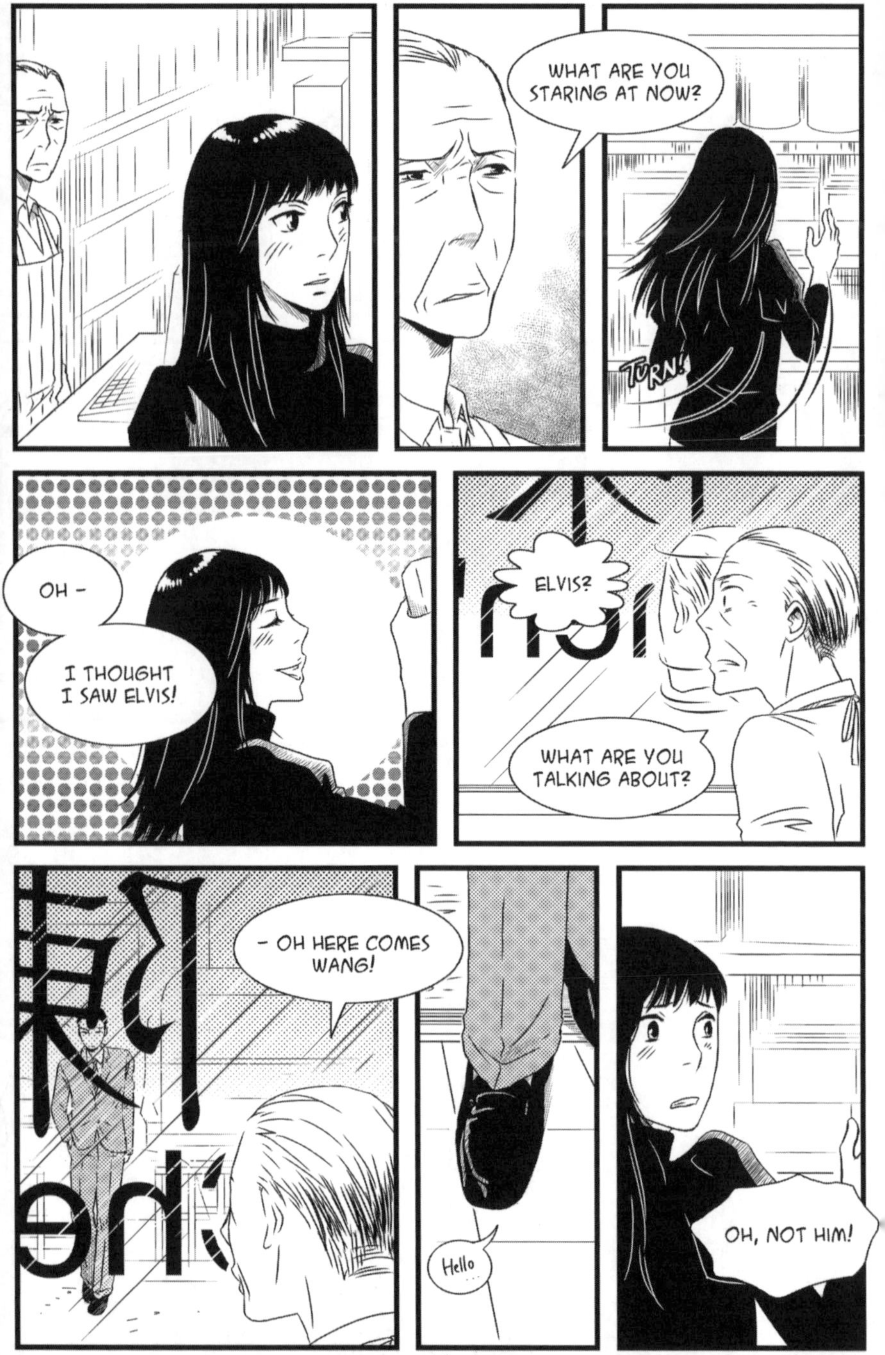
WHAT ARE YOU STARING AT NOW?
TURN!
OH -
I THOUGHT I SAW ELVIS!
ELVIS?
WHAT ARE YOU TALKING ABOUT?
- OH HERE COMES WANG!
Hello ...
OH, NOT HIM!

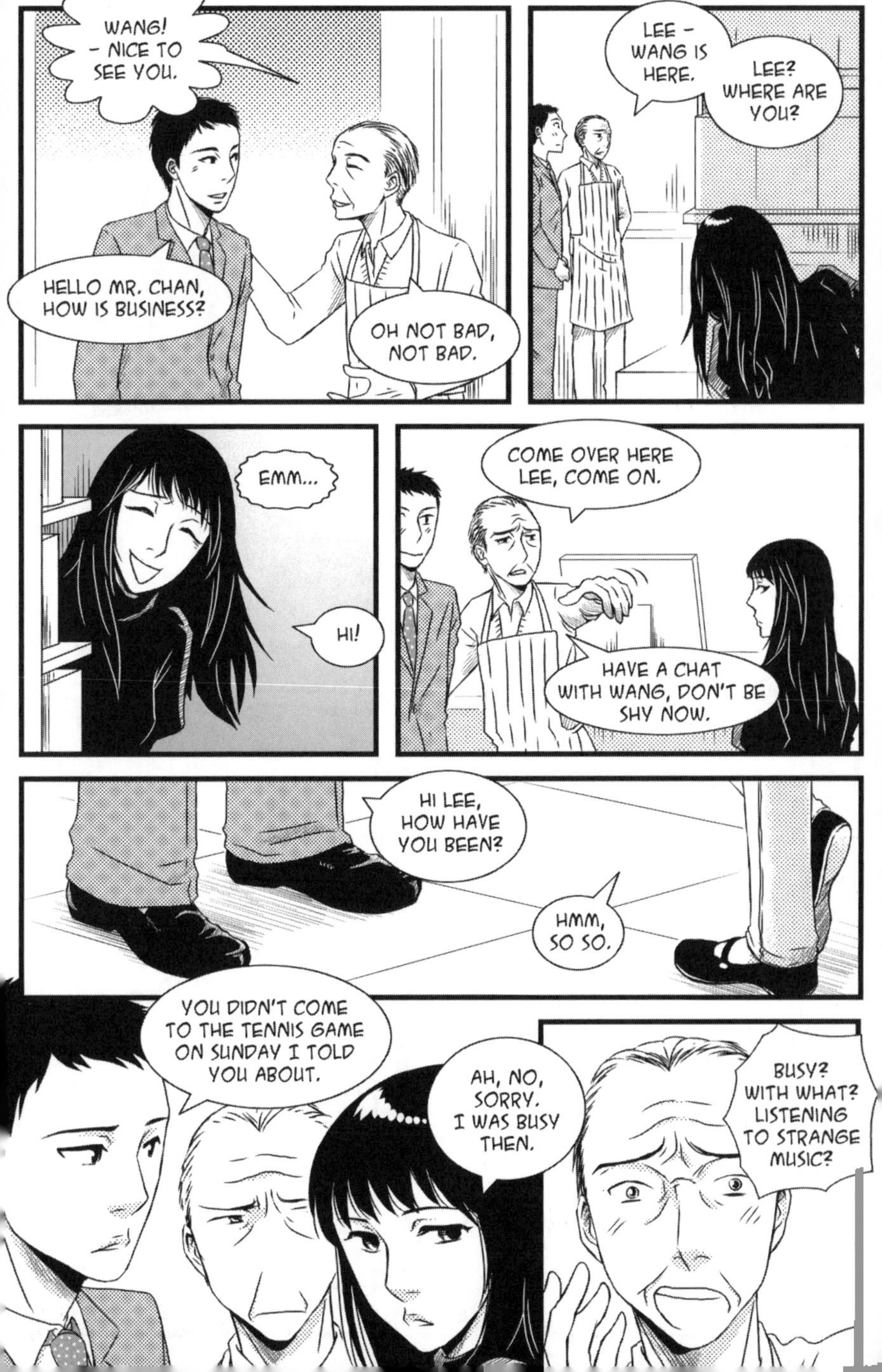
WANG! - NICE TO SEE YOU.
HELLO MR. CHAN, HOW IS BUSINESS?
OH NOT BAD, NOT BAD.
LEE - WANG IS HERE.
LEE? WHERE ARE YOU?
EMM...
HI!
COME OVER HERE LEE, COME ON.
HAVE A CHAT WITH WANG, DON'T BE SHY NOW.
HI LEE, HOW HAVE YOU BEEN?
HMM, SO SO.
YOU DIDN'T COME TO THE TENNIS GAME ON SUNDAY I TOLD YOU ABOUT.
AH, NO, SORRY. I WAS BUSY THEN.
BUSY? WITH WHAT? LISTENING TO STRANGE MUSIC?

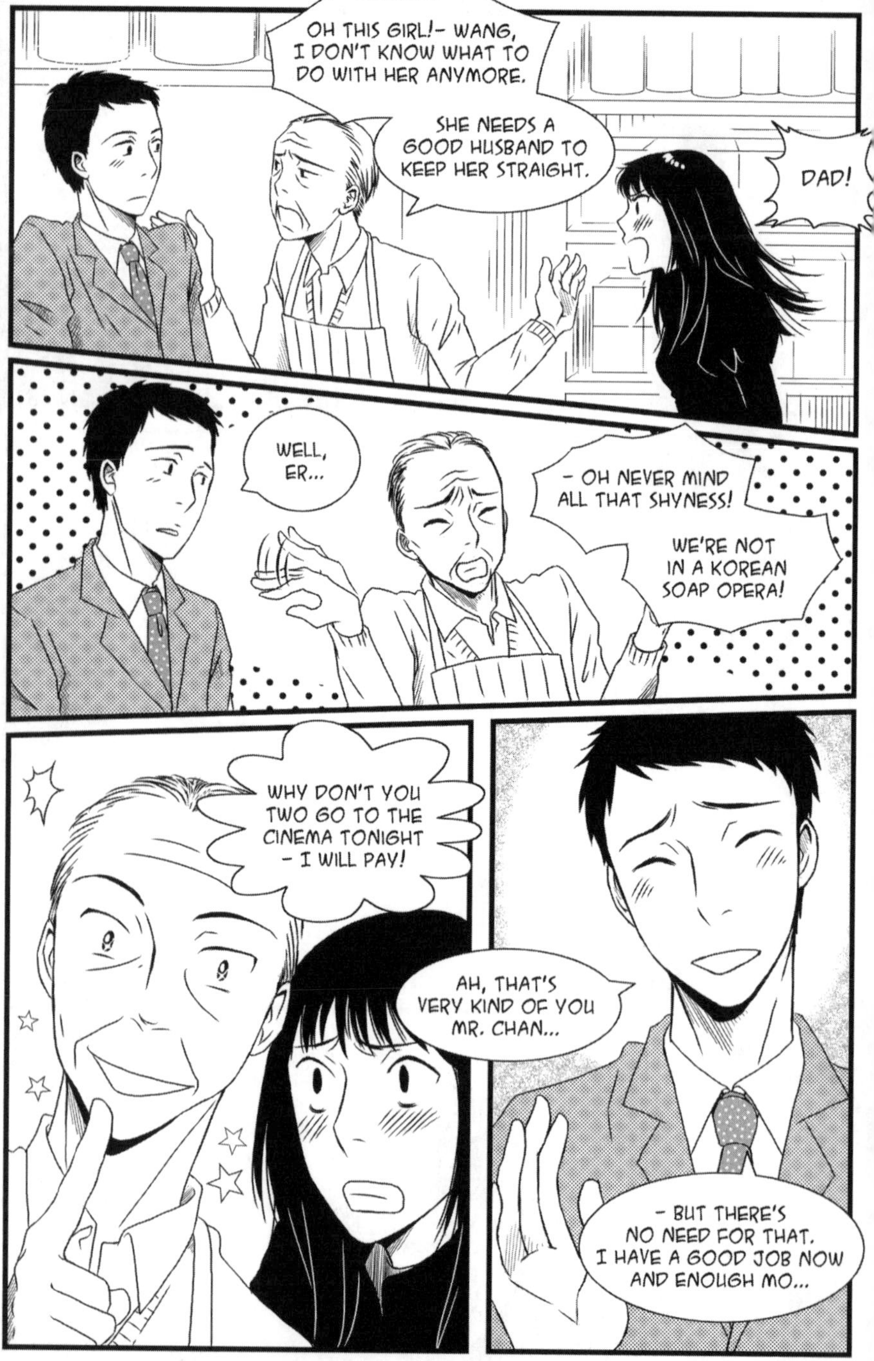
OH THIS GIRL!- WANG, I DON'T KNOW WHAT TO DO WITH HER ANYMORE.
SHE NEEDS A GOOD HUSBAND TO KEEP HER STRAIGHT.
DAD!
WELL, ER...
- OH NEVER MIND ALL THAT SHYNESS!
WE'RE NOT IN A KOREAN SOAP OPERA!
WHY DON'T YOU TWO GO TO THE CINEMA TONIGHT - I WILL PAY!
AH, THAT'S VERY KIND OF YOU MR. CHAN...
- BUT THERE'S NO NEED FOR THAT. I HAVE A GOOD JOB NOW AND ENOUGH MO...

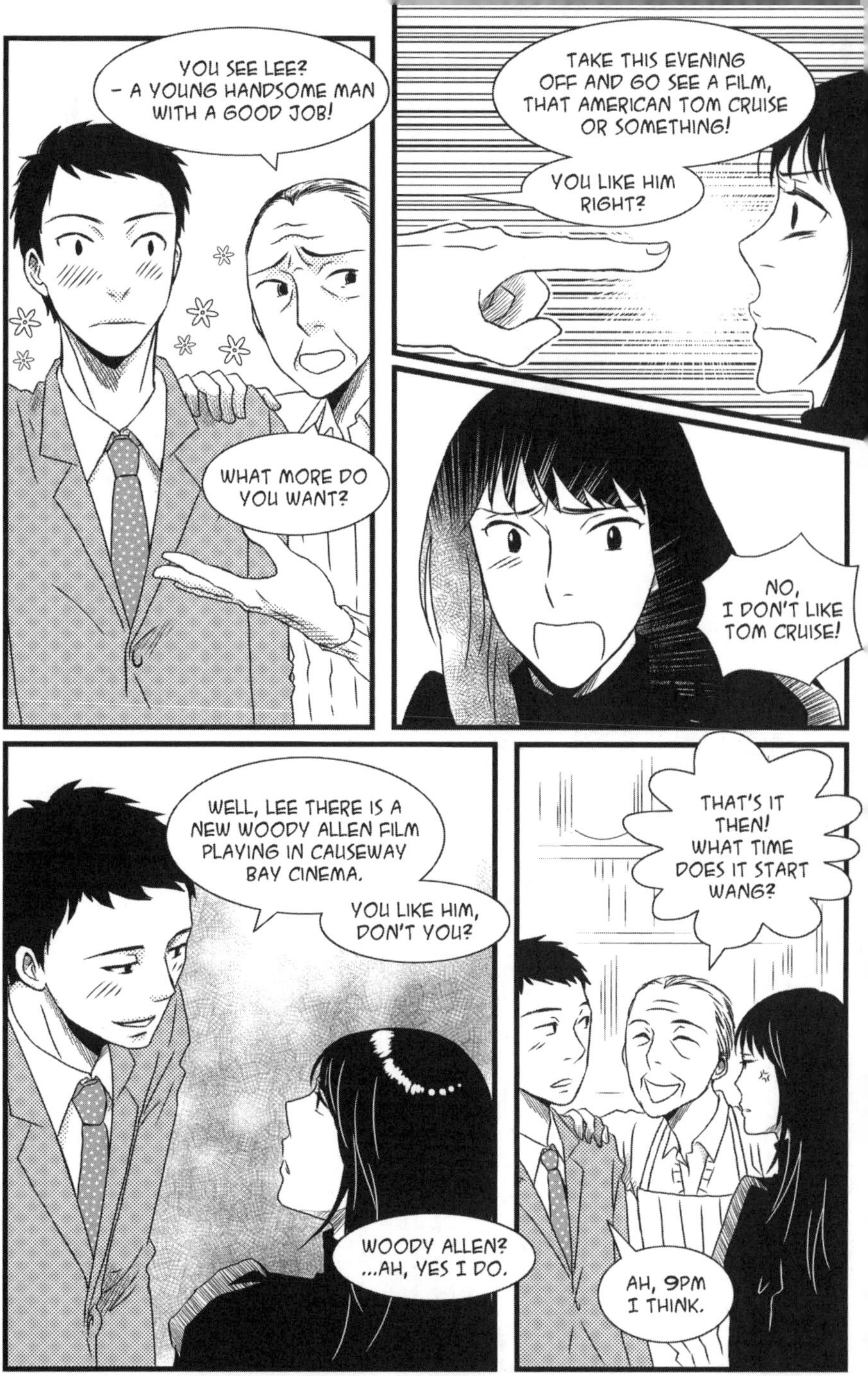
YOU SEE LEE? - A YOUNG HANDSOME MAN WITH A GOOD JOB!
WHAT MORE DO YOU WANT?
TAKE THIS EVENING OFF AND GO SEE A FILM, THAT AMERICAN TOM CRUISE OR SOMETHING!
YOU LIKE HIM RIGHT?
NO, I DON'T LIKE TOM CRUISE!
WELL, LEE THERE IS A NEW WOODY ALLEN FILM PLAYING IN CAUSEWAY BAY CINEMA.
YOU LIKE HIM, DON'T YOU?
WOODY ALLEN? ...AH, YES I DO.
THAT'S IT THEN! WHAT TIME DOES IT START WANG?
AH, 9PM I THINK.

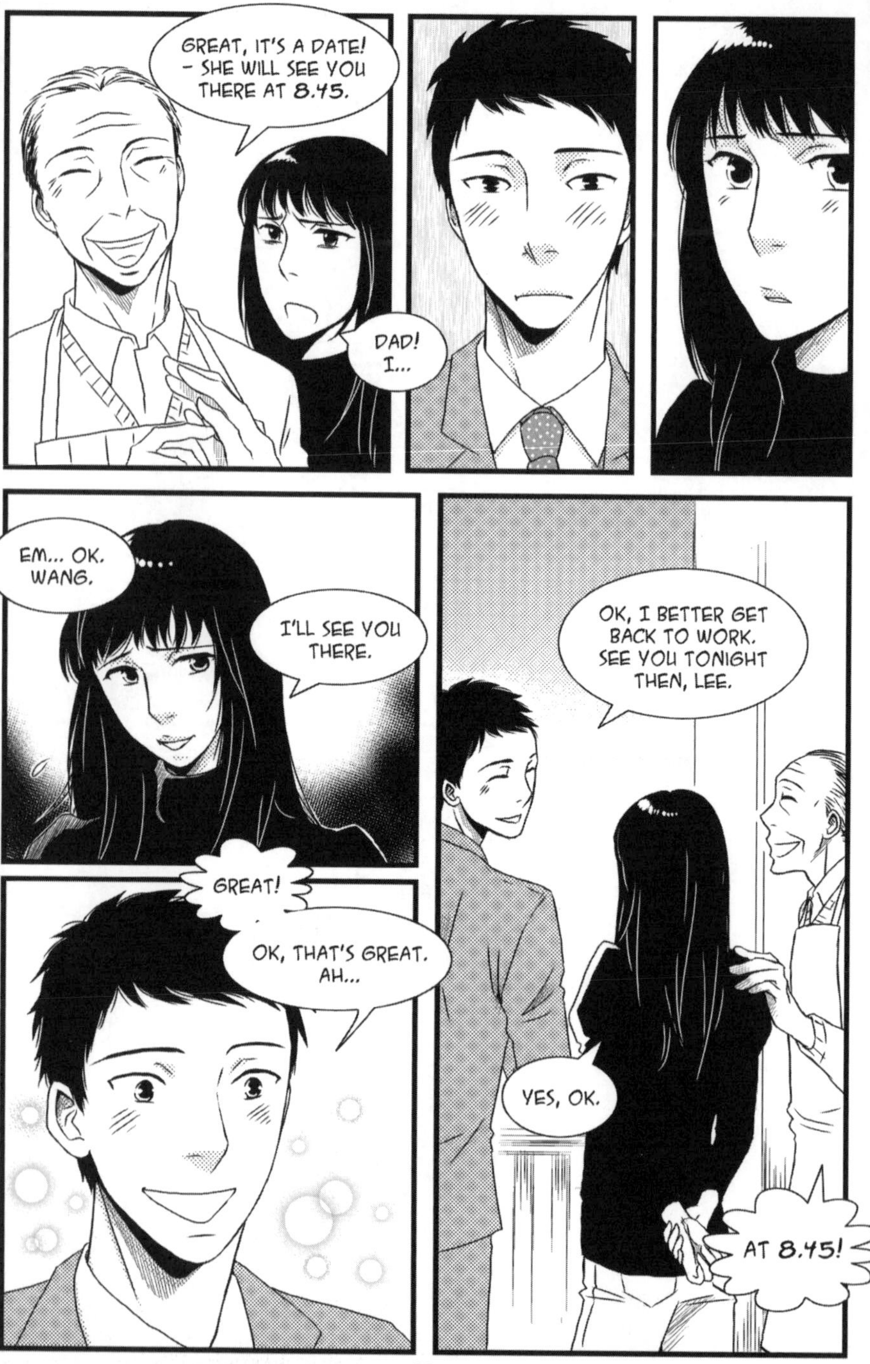
GREAT, IT'S A DATE! - SHE WILL SEE YOU THERE AT 8.45.
DAD! I...
EM... OK. WANG.
I'LL SEE YOU THERE.
GREAT!
OK, THAT'S GREAT. AH...
OK, I BETTER GET BACK TO WORK. SEE YOU TONIGHT THEN, LEE.
YES, OK.
AT 8.45!

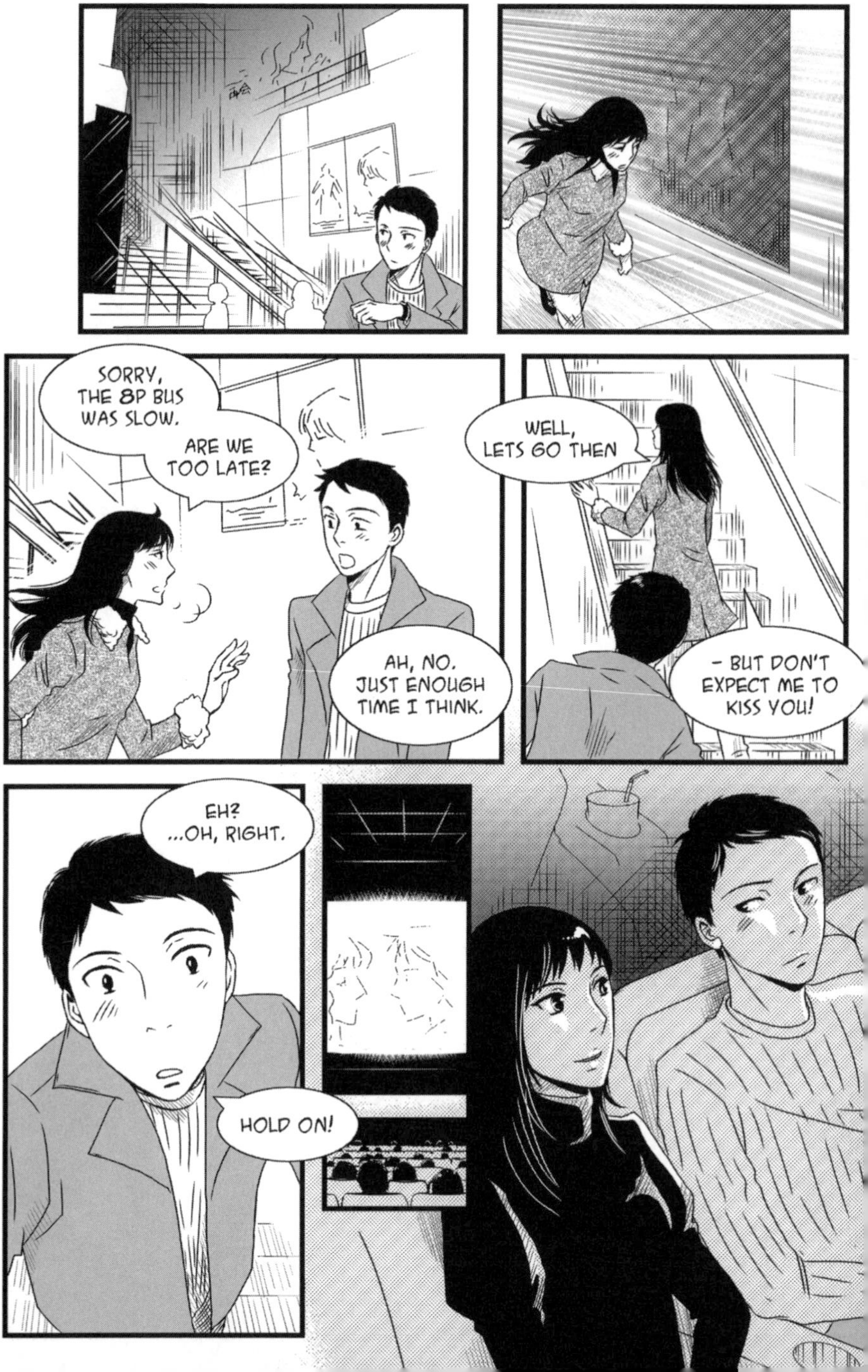
SORRY,
THE 8P BUS
WAS SLOW.
ARE WE
TOO LATE?
AH, NO.
JUST ENOUGH
TIME I THINK.
WELL,
LETS GO THEN
- BUT DON'T
EXPECT ME TO
KISS YOU!
EH?
...OH, RIGHT.
HOLD ON!

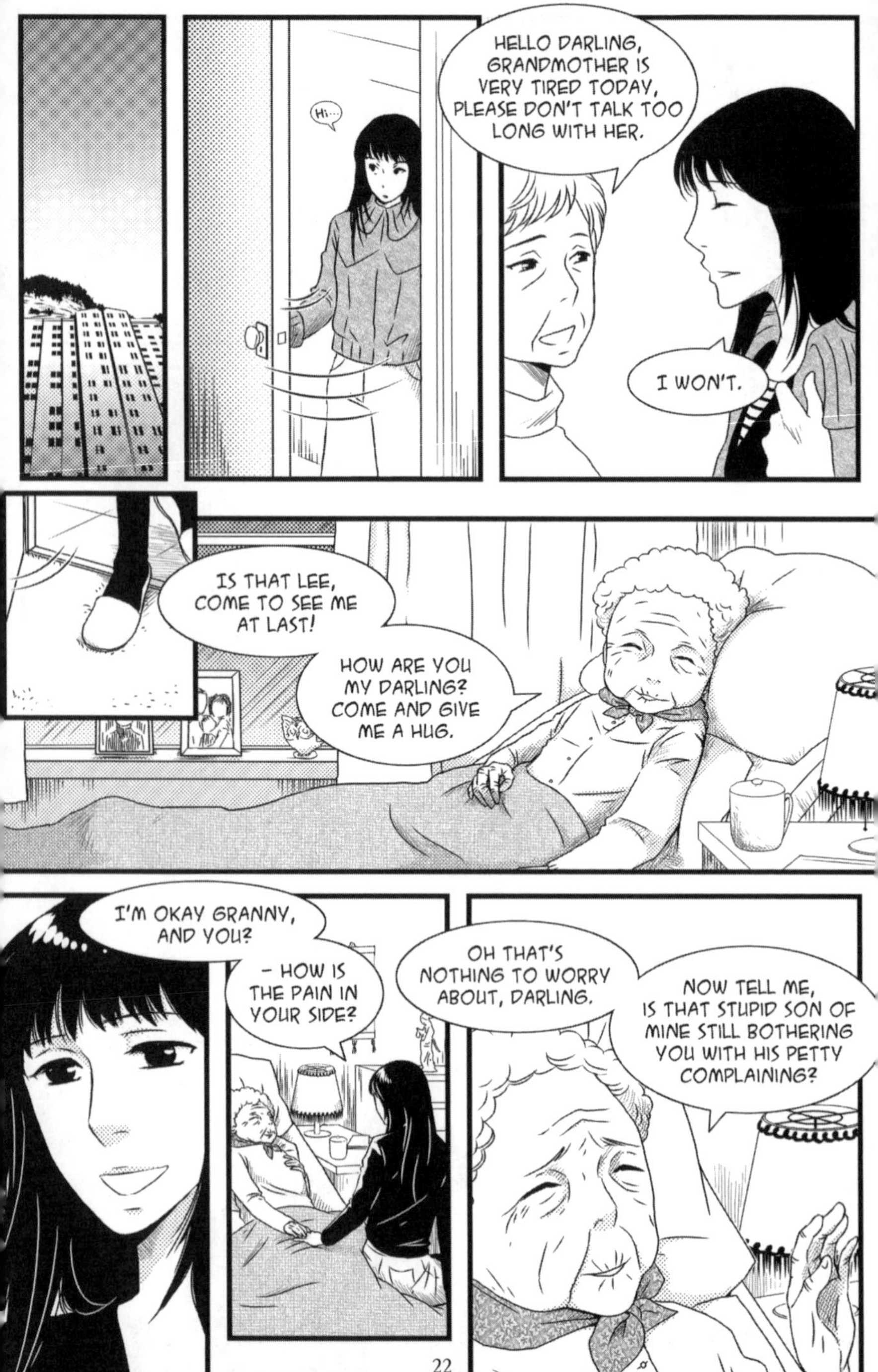
Hi...
HELLO DARLING, GRANDMOTHER IS VERY TIRED TODAY, PLEASE DON'T TALK TOO LONG WITH HER.
I WON'T.
IS THAT LEE, COME TO SEE ME AT LAST!
HOW ARE YOU MY DARLING? COME AND GIVE ME A HUG.
I'M OKAY GRANNY, AND YOU?
- HOW IS THE PAIN IN YOUR SIDE?
OH THAT'S NOTHING TO WORRY ABOUT, DARLING.
NOW TELL ME, IS THAT STUPID SON OF MINE STILL BOTHERING YOU WITH HIS PETTY COMPLAINING?

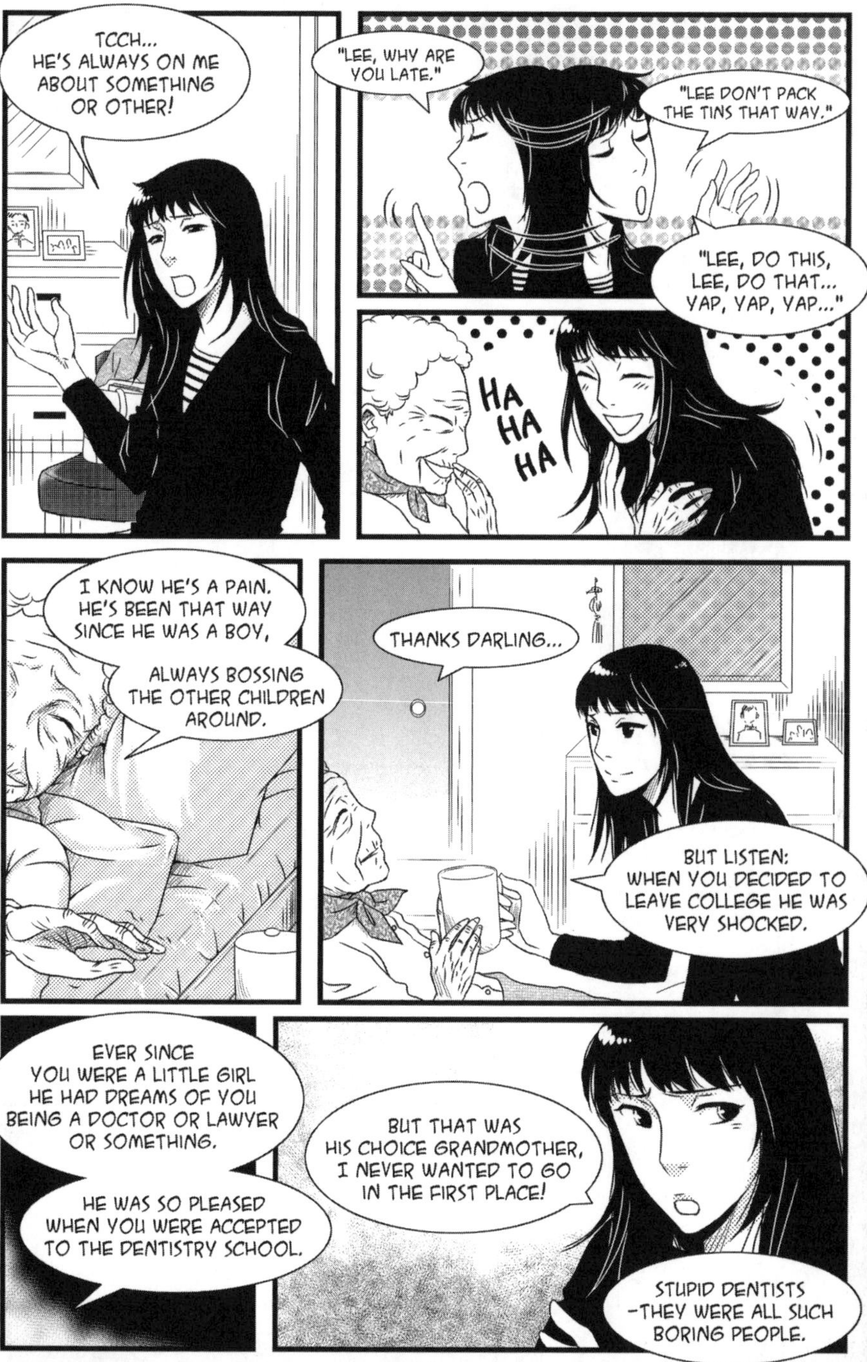
TCCH...
HE'S ALWAYS ON ME ABOUT SOMETHING OR OTHER!
"LEE, WHY ARE YOU LATE."
"LEE DON'T PACK THE TINS THAT WAY."
"LEE, DO THIS, LEE, DO THAT... YAP, YAP, YAP..."
HA HA HA
I KNOW HE'S A PAIN. HE'S BEEN THAT WAY SINCE HE WAS A BOY,
ALWAYS BOSSING THE OTHER CHILDREN AROUND.
THANKS DARLING...
BUT LISTEN: WHEN YOU DECIDED TO LEAVE COLLEGE HE WAS VERY SHOCKED.
EVER SINCE YOU WERE A LITTLE GIRL HE HAD DREAMS OF YOU BEING A DOCTOR OR LAWYER OR SOMETHING.
HE WAS SO PLEASED WHEN YOU WERE ACCEPTED TO THE DENTISTRY SCHOOL.
BUT THAT WAS HIS CHOICE GRANDMOTHER, I NEVER WANTED TO GO IN THE FIRST PLACE!
STUPID DENTISTS -THEY WERE ALL SUCH BORING PEOPLE.

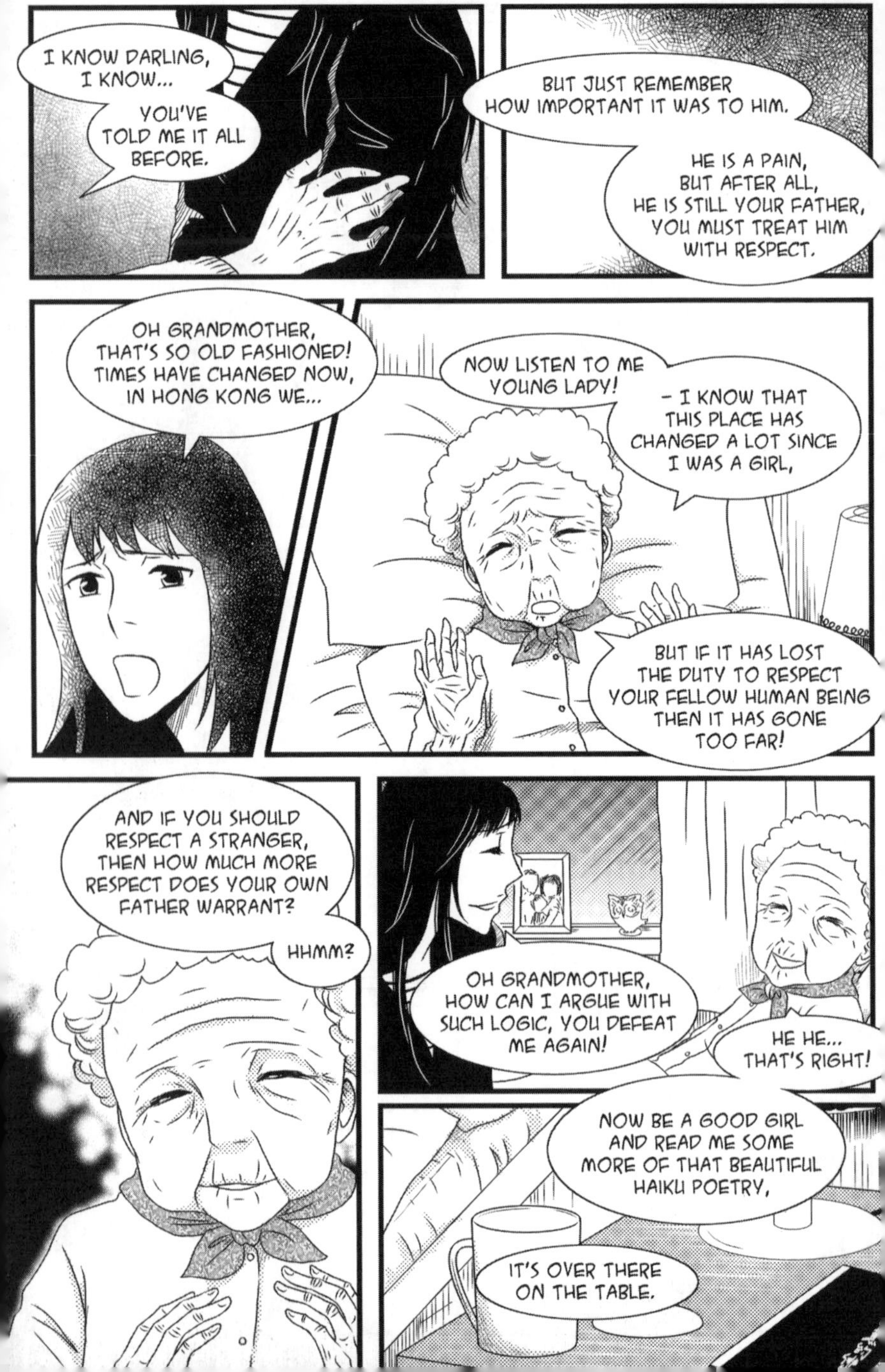
I KNOW DARLING, I KNOW...
YOU'VE TOLD ME IT ALL BEFORE.
BUT JUST REMEMBER HOW IMPORTANT IT WAS TO HIM.
HE IS A PAIN, BUT AFTER ALL, HE IS STILL YOUR FATHER, YOU MUST TREAT HIM WITH RESPECT.
OH GRANDMOTHER, THAT'S SO OLD FASHIONED! TIMES HAVE CHANGED NOW, IN HONG KONG WE...
NOW LISTEN TO ME YOUNG LADY!
- I KNOW THAT THIS PLACE HAS CHANGED A LOT SINCE I WAS A GIRL,
BUT IF IT HAS LOST THE DUTY TO RESPECT YOUR FELLOW HUMAN BEING THEN IT HAS GONE TOO FAR!
AND IF YOU SHOULD RESPECT A STRANGER, THEN HOW MUCH MORE RESPECT DOES YOUR OWN FATHER WARRANT?
HHMM?
OH GRANDMOTHER, HOW CAN I ARGUE WITH SUCH LOGIC, YOU DEFEAT ME AGAIN!
HE HE... THAT'S RIGHT!
NOW BE A GOOD GIRL AND READ ME SOME MORE OF THAT BEAUTIFUL HAIKU POETRY,
IT'S OVER THERE ON THE TABLE.

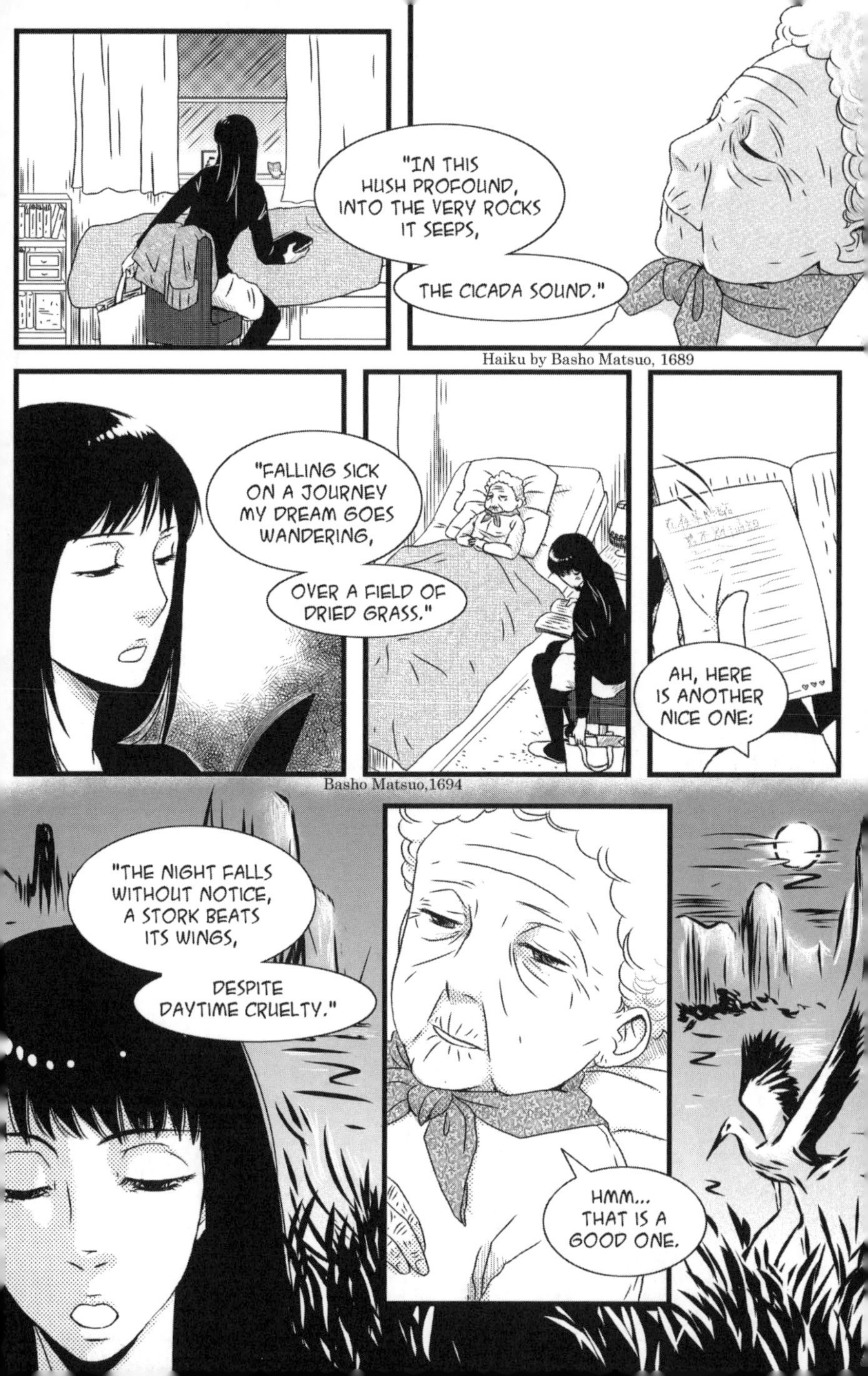
"IN THIS HUSH PROFOUND, INTO THE VERY ROCKS IT SEEPS,
THE CICADA SOUND."
Haiku by Basho Matsuo, 1689
"FALLING SICK ON A JOURNEY MY DREAM GOES WANDERING,
OVER A FIELD OF DRIED GRASS."
AH, HERE IS ANOTHER NICE ONE:
Basho Matsuo,1694
"THE NIGHT FALLS WITHOUT NOTICE, A STORK BEATS ITS WINGS,
DESPITE DAYTIME CRUELTY."
HMM... THAT IS A GOOD ONE.

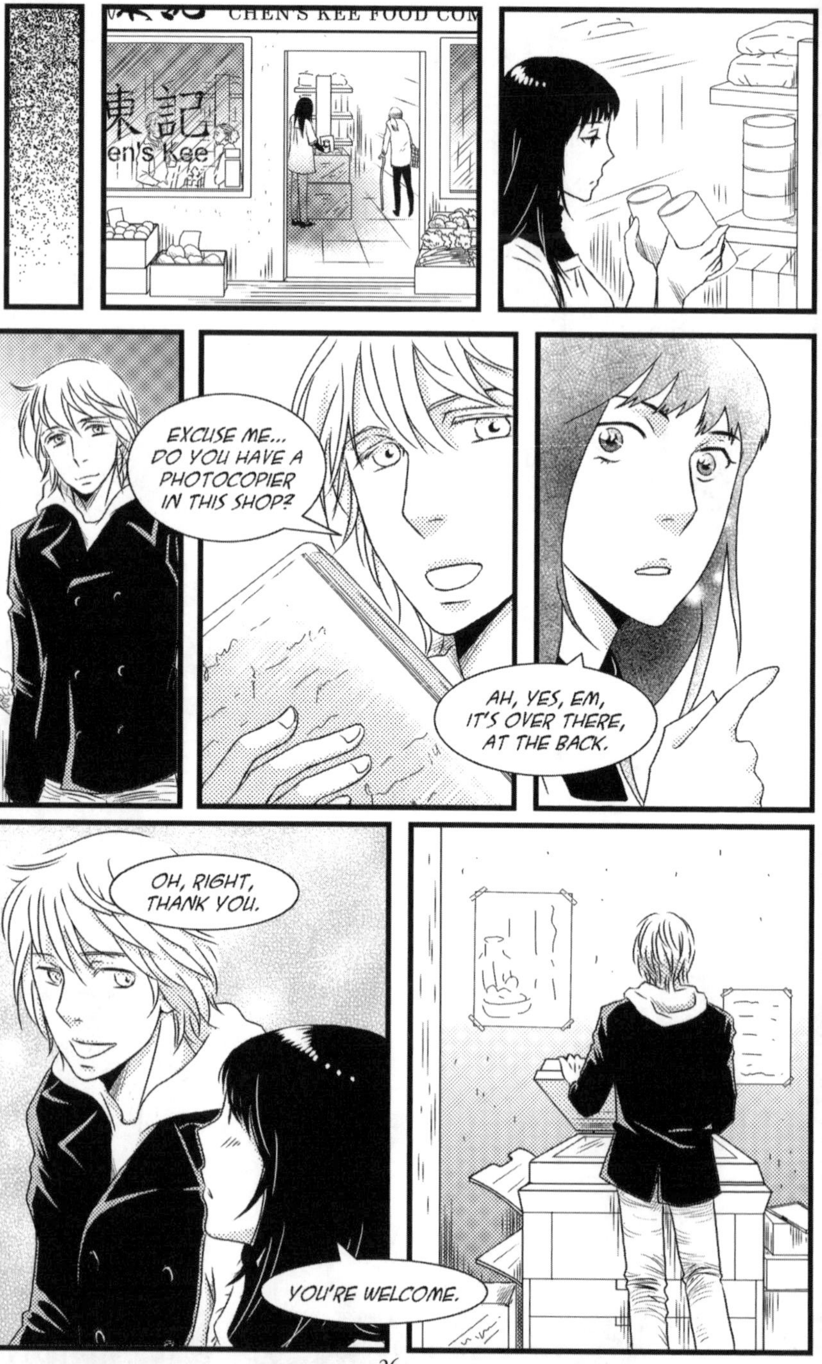
CHEN'S KEE FOOD CO
陳記
en's Kee
EXCUSE ME... DO YOU HAVE A PHOTOCOPIER IN THIS SHOP?
AH, YES, EM, IT'S OVER THERE, AT THE BACK.
OH, RIGHT, THANK YOU.
YOU'RE WELCOME.

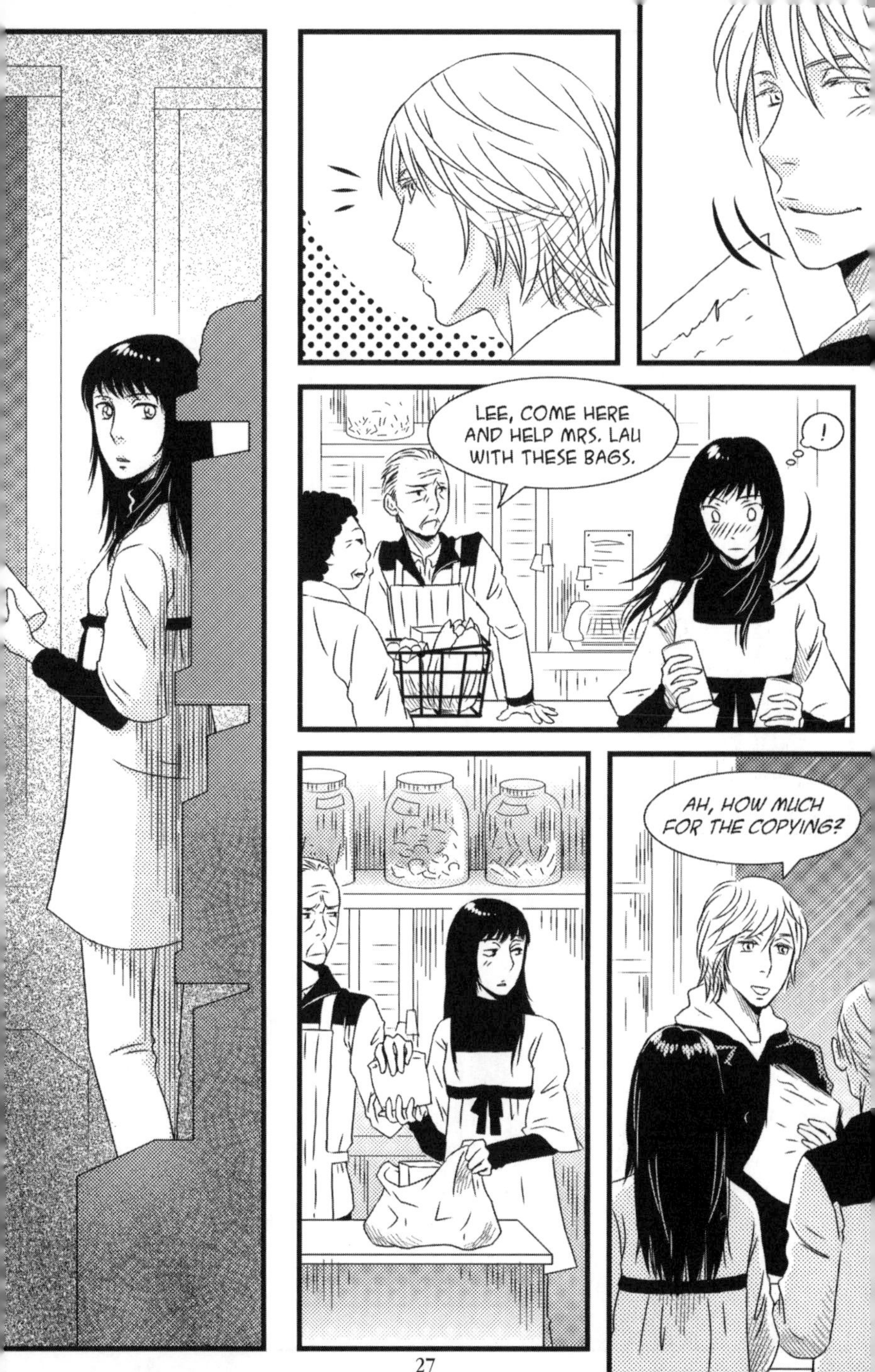
LEE, COME HERE AND HELP MRS. LAU WITH THESE BAGS.
!
AH, HOW MUCH FOR THE COPYING?

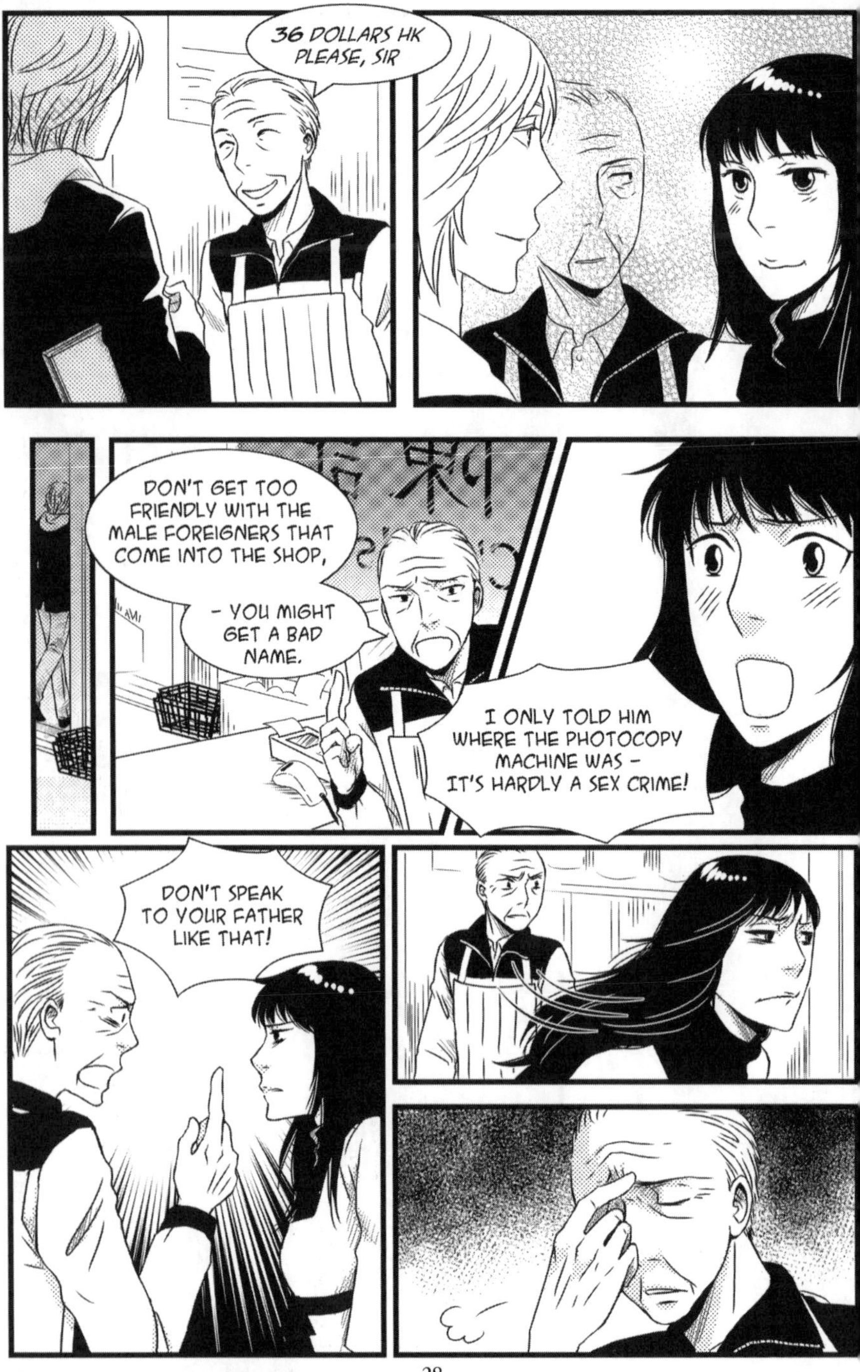
36 DOLLARS HK PLEASE, SIR
DON'T GET TOO FRIENDLY WITH THE MALE FOREIGNERS THAT COME INTO THE SHOP,
- YOU MIGHT GET A BAD NAME.
I ONLY TOLD HIM WHERE THE PHOTOCOPY MACHINE WAS - IT'S HARDLY A SEX CRIME!
DON'T SPEAK TO YOUR FATHER LIKE THAT!

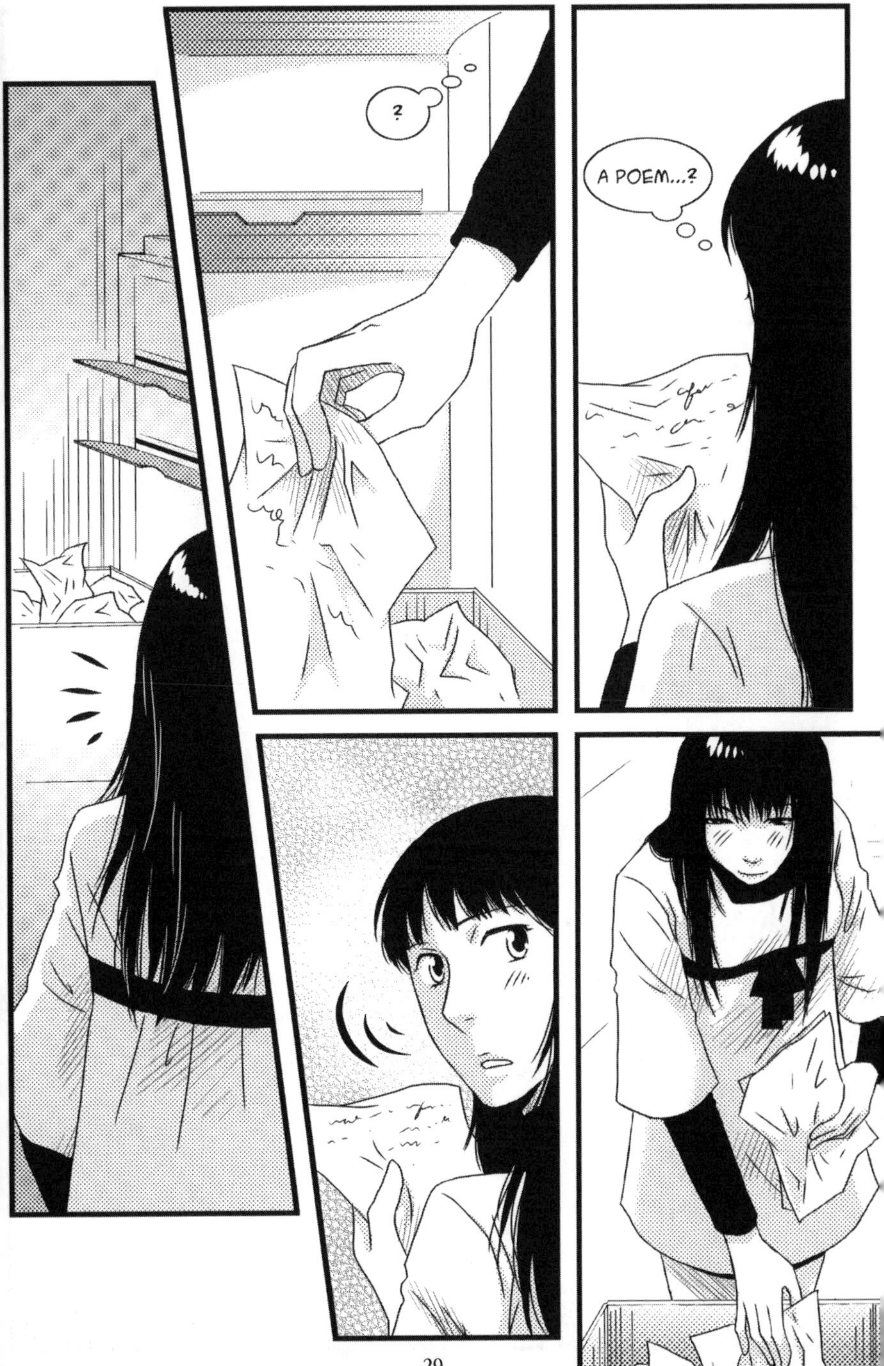
?
A POEM...?

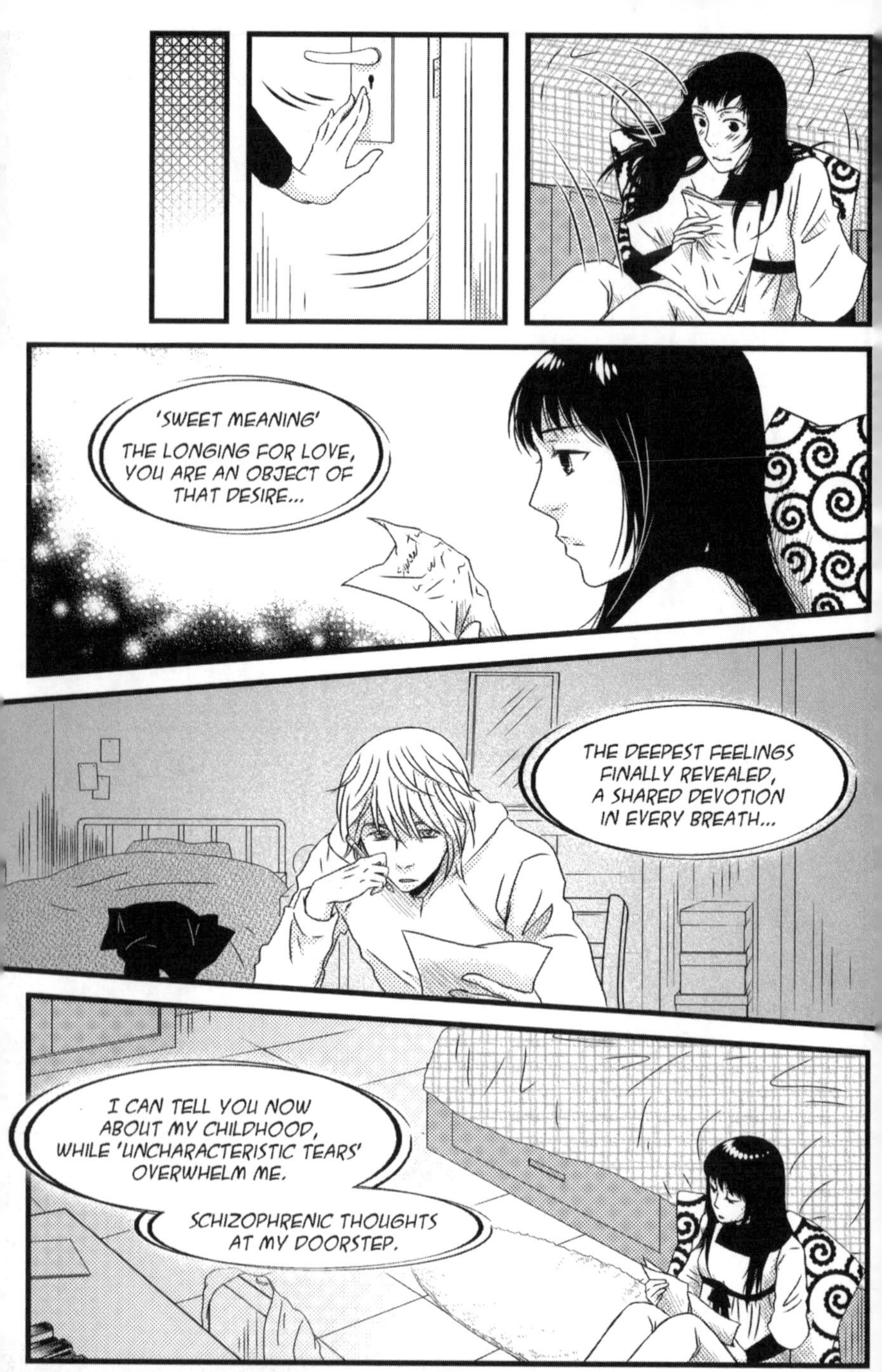
'SWEET MEANING'
THE LONGING FOR LOVE, YOU ARE AN OBJECT OF THAT DESIRE...
THE DEEPEST FEELINGS FINALLY REVEALED, A SHARED DEVOTION IN EVERY BREATH...
I CAN TELL YOU NOW ABOUT MY CHILDHOOD, WHILE 'UNCHARACTERISTIC TEARS' OVERWHELM ME.
SCHIZOPHRENIC THOUGHTS AT MY DOORSTEP.

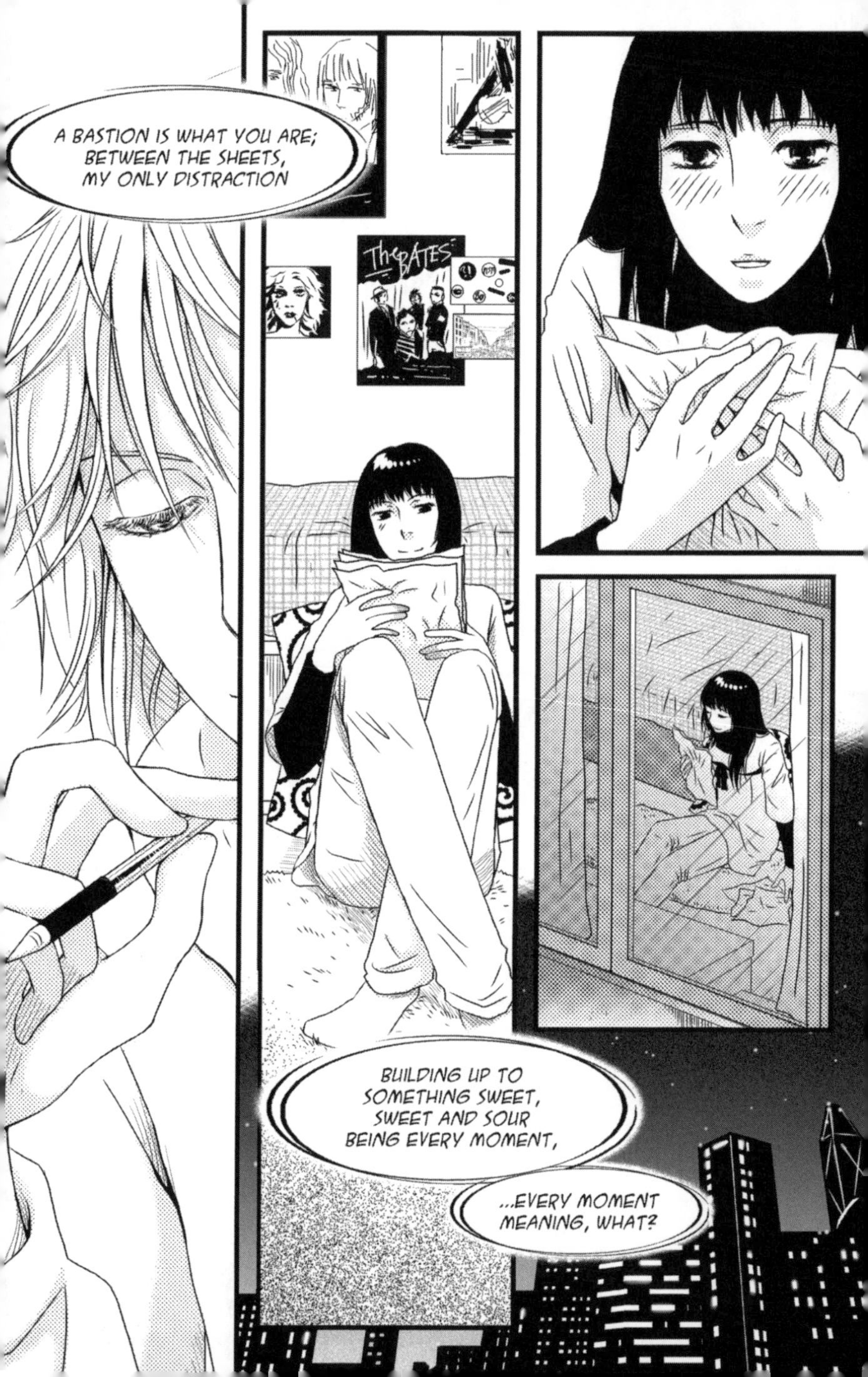
A BASTION IS WHAT YOU ARE; BETWEEN THE SHEETS, MY ONLY DISTRACTION
The BATES
BUILDING UP TO SOMETHING SWEET, SWEET AND SOUR BEING EVERY MOMENT,
...EVERY MOMENT MEANING, WHAT?

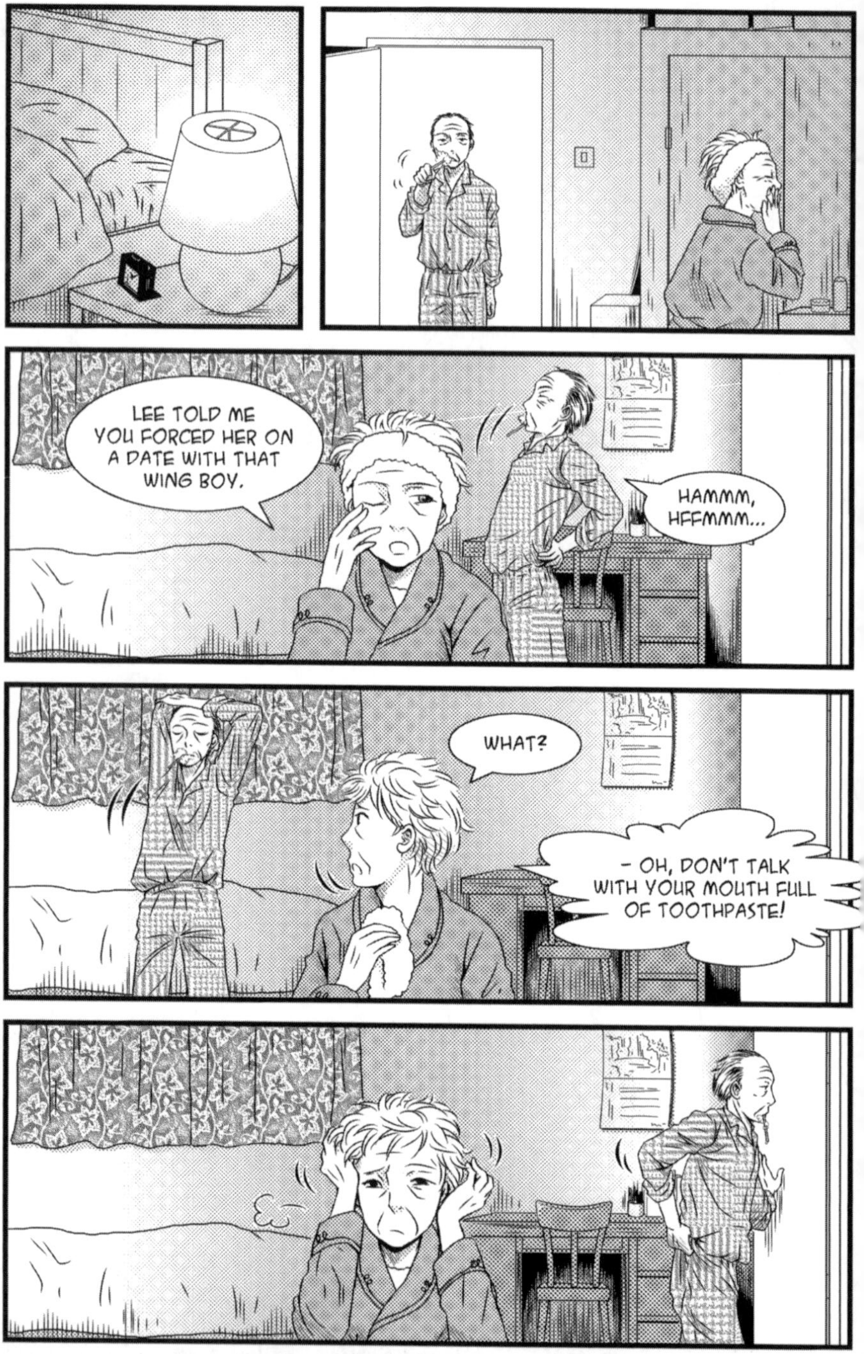
LEE TOLD ME YOU FORCED HER ON A DATE WITH THAT WING BOY.
HAMMM, HFFMMM...
WHAT?
- OH, DON'T TALK WITH YOUR MOUTH FULL OF TOOTHPASTE!

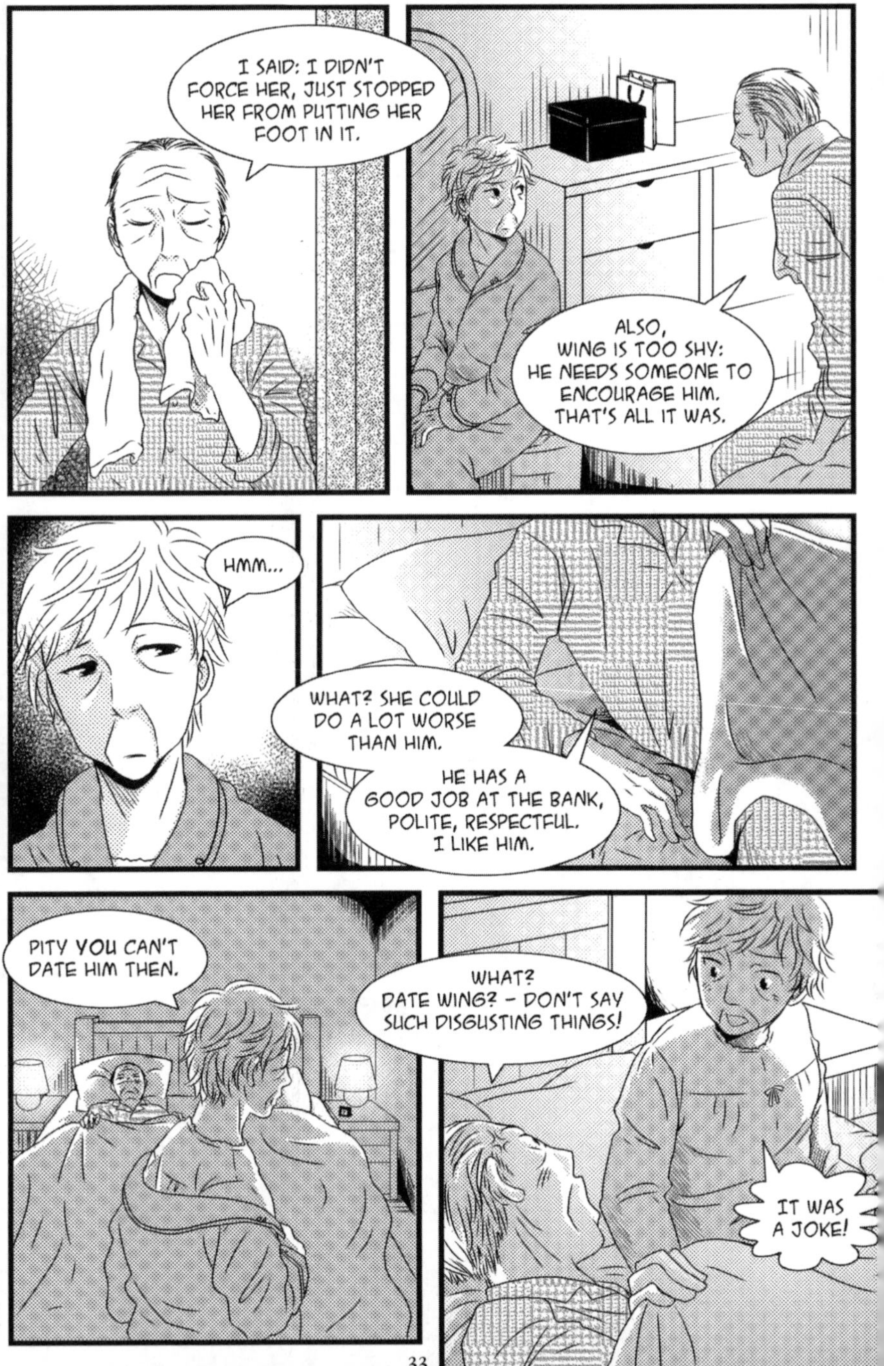
I SAID: I DIDN'T FORCE HER, JUST STOPPED HER FROM PUTTING HER FOOT IN IT.
ALSO, WING IS TOO SHY: HE NEEDS SOMEONE TO ENCOURAGE HIM. THAT'S ALL IT WAS.
HMM...
WHAT? SHE COULD DO A LOT WORSE THAN HIM.
HE HAS A GOOD JOB AT THE BANK, POLITE, RESPECTFUL. I LIKE HIM.
PITY YOU CAN'T DATE HIM THEN.
WHAT? DATE WING? - DON'T SAY SUCH DISGUSTING THINGS!
IT WAS A JOKE!

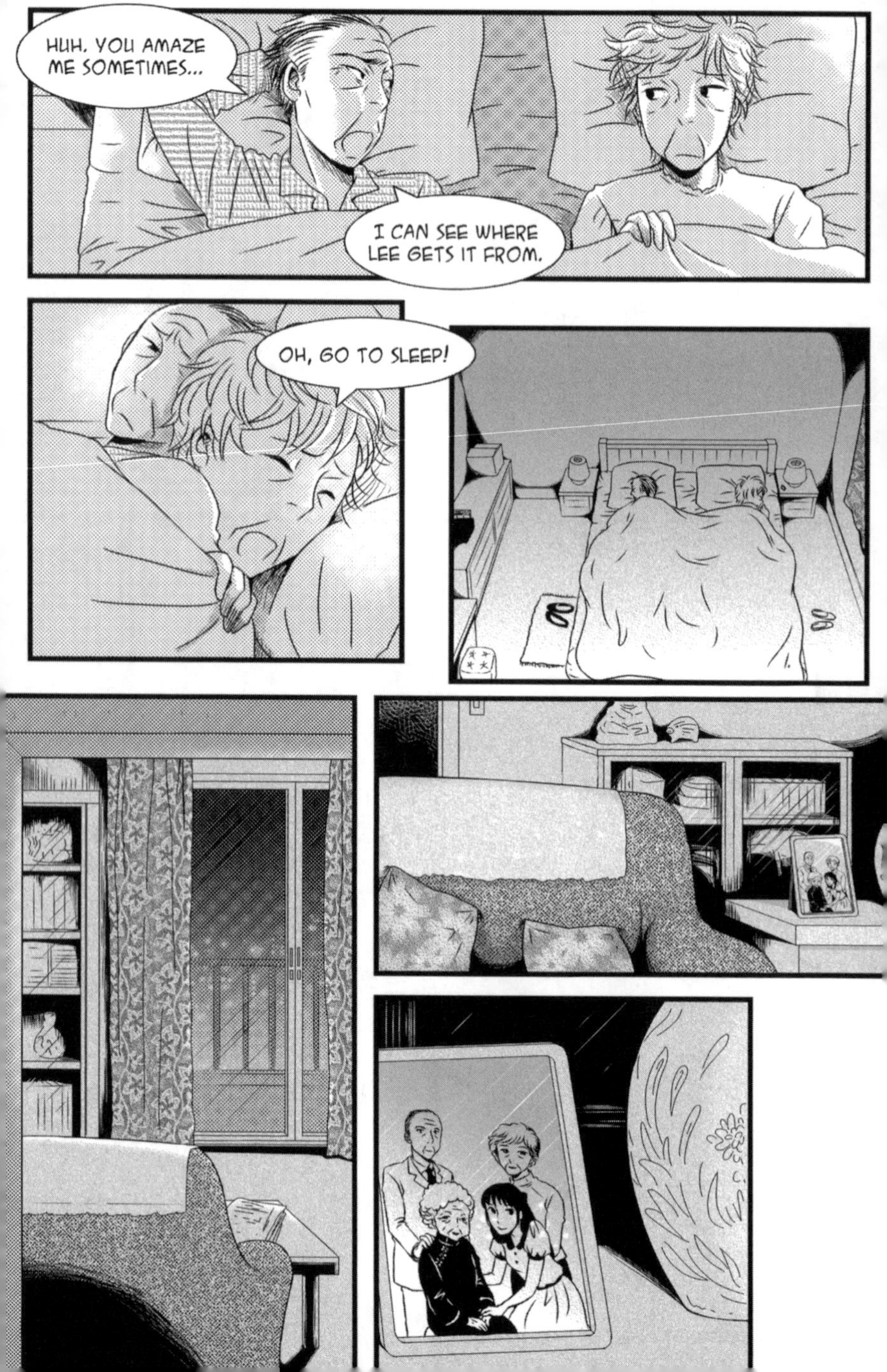
HUH. YOU AMAZE ME SOMETIMES...
I CAN SEE WHERE LEE GETS IT FROM.
OH, GO TO SLEEP!

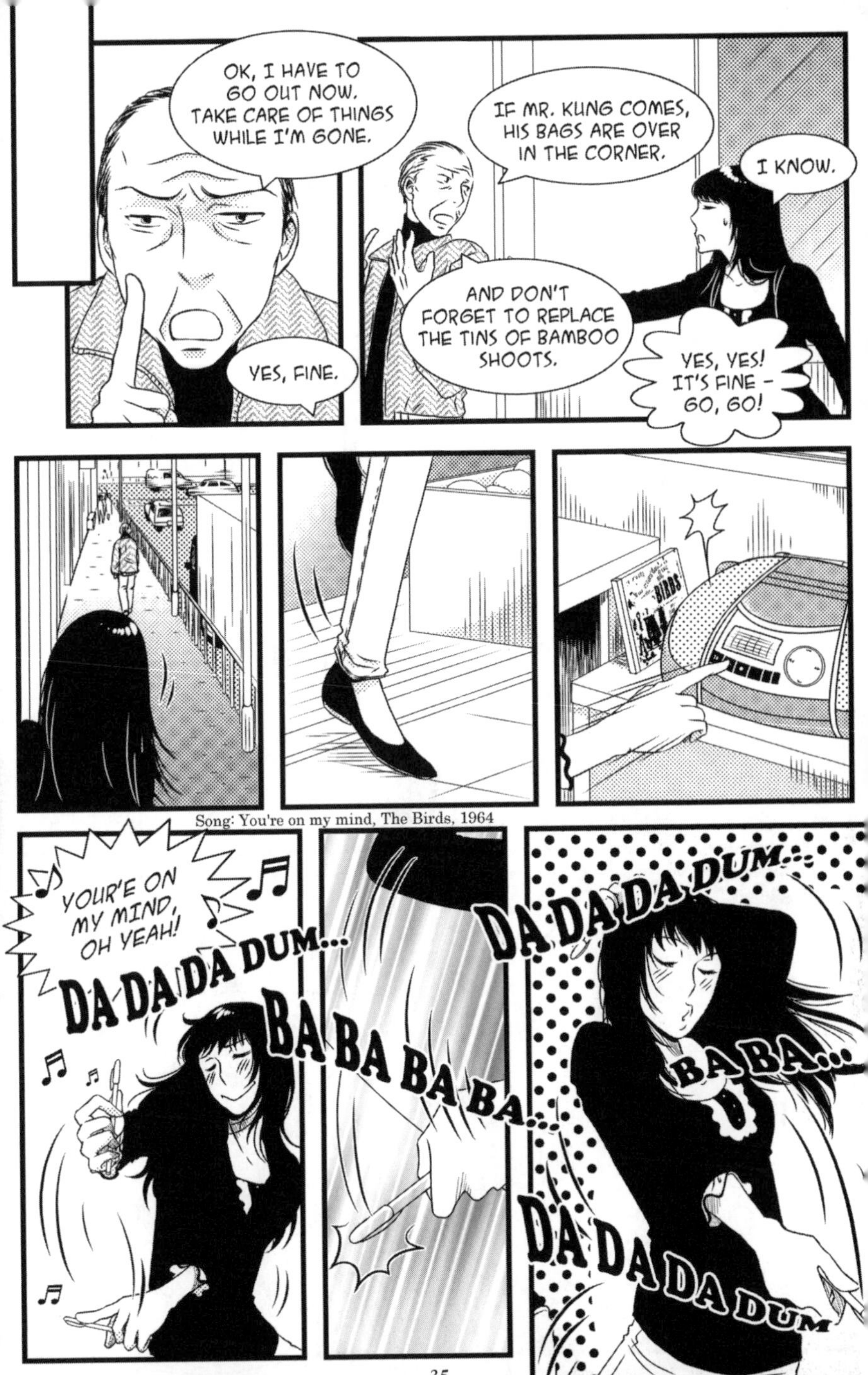

OK, I HAVE TO GO OUT NOW. TAKE CARE OF THINGS WHILE I'M GONE.
YES, FINE.
IF MR. KUNG COMES, HIS BAGS ARE OVER IN THE CORNER.
I KNOW.
AND DON'T FORGET TO REPLACE THE TINS OF BAMBOO SHOOTS.
YES, YES! IT'S FINE - GO, GO!
BIRDS
YOUR'E ON MY MIND, OH YEAH!
DA DA DA DUM...
BA BA BA BA...
DA DA DA DUM...
BA BA...
DA DA DA DA DUM

Song: You're on my mind, The Birds, 1964

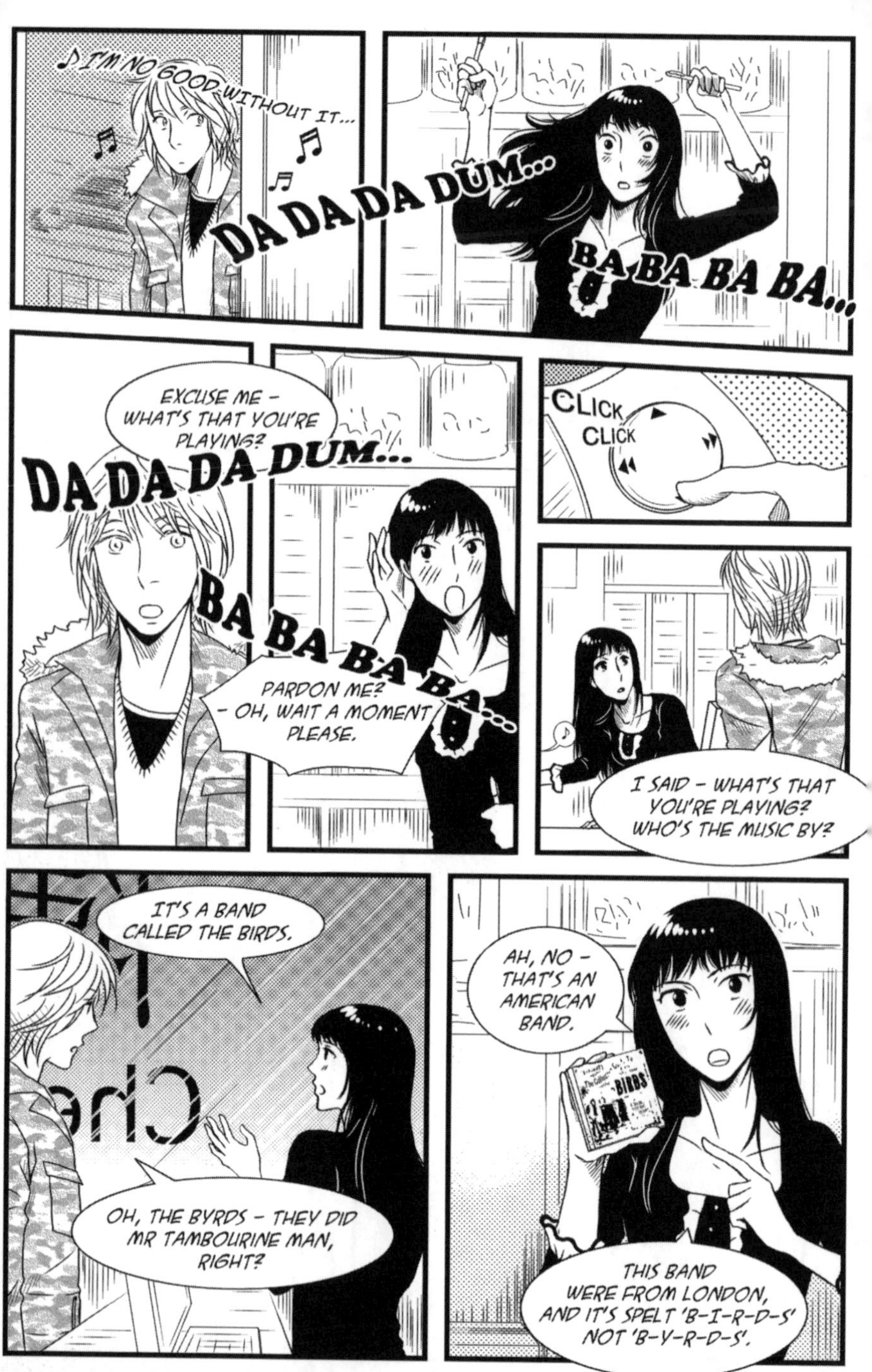
♪I'M NO GOOD WITHOUT IT...
DA DA DA DA DUM...
BA BA BA BA...
EXCUSE ME - WHAT'S THAT YOU'RE PLAYING?
DA DA DA DUM...
BA BA BA BA...
PARDON ME? - OH, WAIT A MOMENT PLEASE.
CLICK
CLICK
I SAID - WHAT'S THAT YOU'RE PLAYING? WHO'S THE MUSIC BY?
IT'S A BAND CALLED THE BIRDS.
OH, THE BYRDS - THEY DID MR TAMBOURINE MAN, RIGHT?
AH, NO - THAT'S AN AMERICAN BAND.
BIRDS
THIS BAND WERE FROM LONDON, AND IT'S SPELT 'B-I-R-D-S' NOT 'B-Y-R-D-S'.

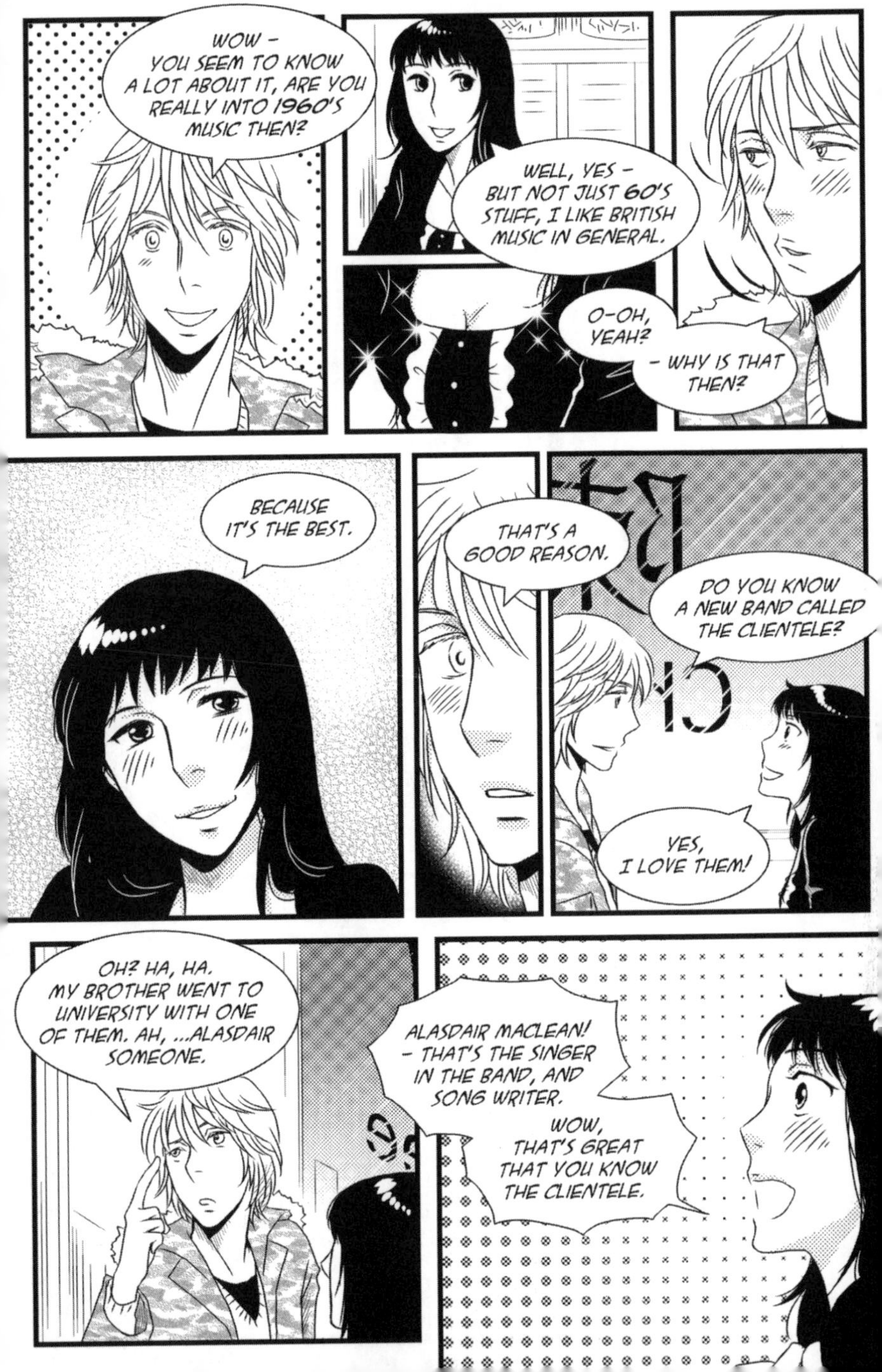
WOW - YOU SEEM TO KNOW A LOT ABOUT IT, ARE YOU REALLY INTO 1960'S MUSIC THEN?
WELL, YES - BUT NOT JUST 60'S STUFF, I LIKE BRITISH MUSIC IN GENERAL.
O-OH, YEAH?
- WHY IS THAT THEN?
BECAUSE IT'S THE BEST.
THAT'S A GOOD REASON.
DO YOU KNOW A NEW BAND CALLED THE CLIENTELE?
YES, I LOVE THEM!
OH? HA, HA. MY BROTHER WENT TO UNIVERSITY WITH ONE OF THEM. AH, ...ALASDAIR SOMEONE.
ALASDAIR MACLEAN! - THAT'S THE SINGER IN THE BAND, AND SONG WRITER.
WOW, THAT'S GREAT THAT YOU KNOW THE CLIENTELE.

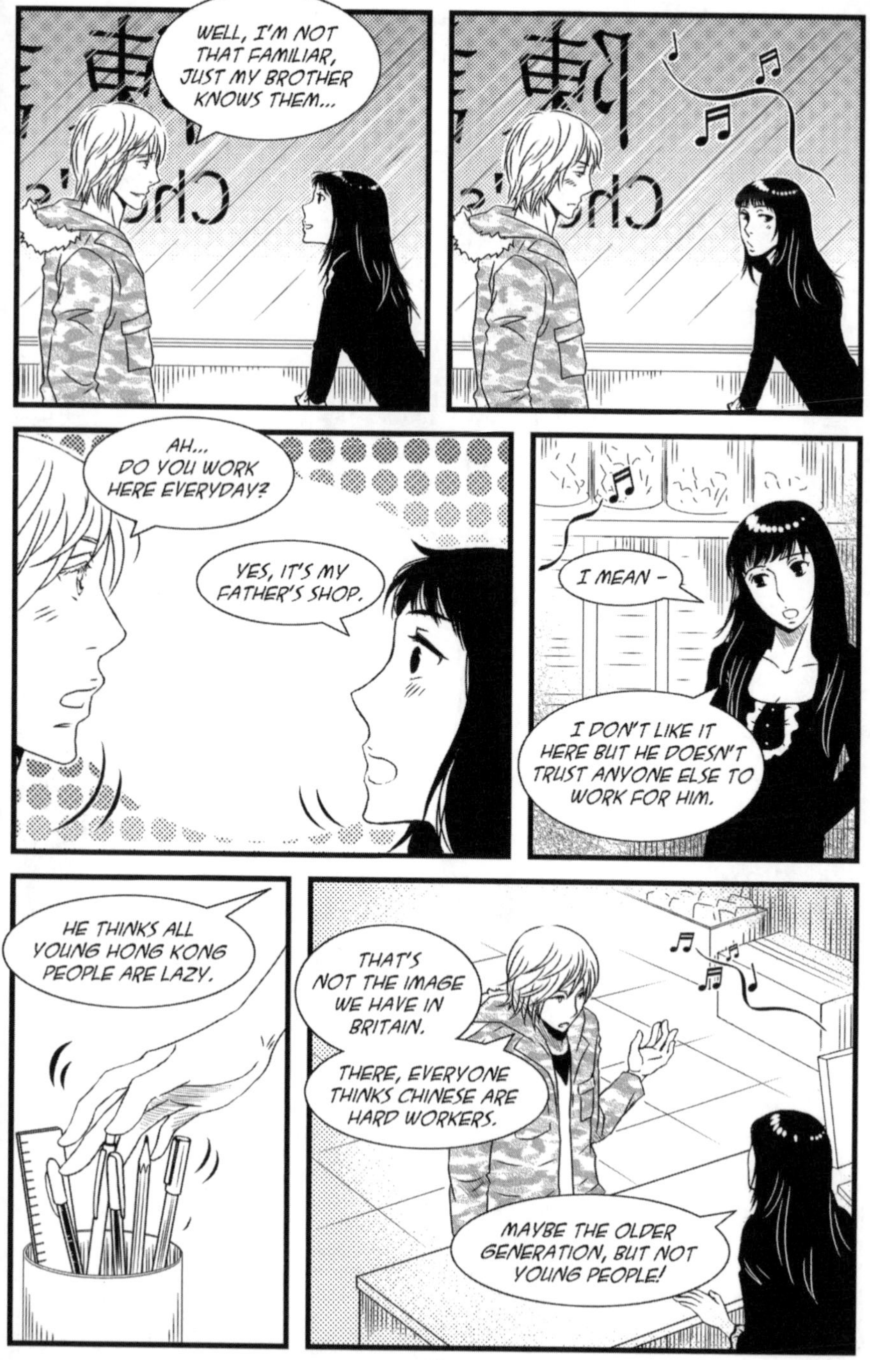
WELL, I'M NOT THAT FAMILIAR, JUST MY BROTHER KNOWS THEM...
AH... DO YOU WORK HERE EVERYDAY?
YES, IT'S MY FATHER'S SHOP.
I MEAN -
I DON'T LIKE IT HERE BUT HE DOESN'T TRUST ANYONE ELSE TO WORK FOR HIM.
HE THINKS ALL YOUNG HONG KONG PEOPLE ARE LAZY.
THAT'S NOT THE IMAGE WE HAVE IN BRITAIN.
THERE, EVERYONE THINKS CHINESE ARE HARD WORKERS.
MAYBE THE OLDER GENERATION, BUT NOT YOUNG PEOPLE!

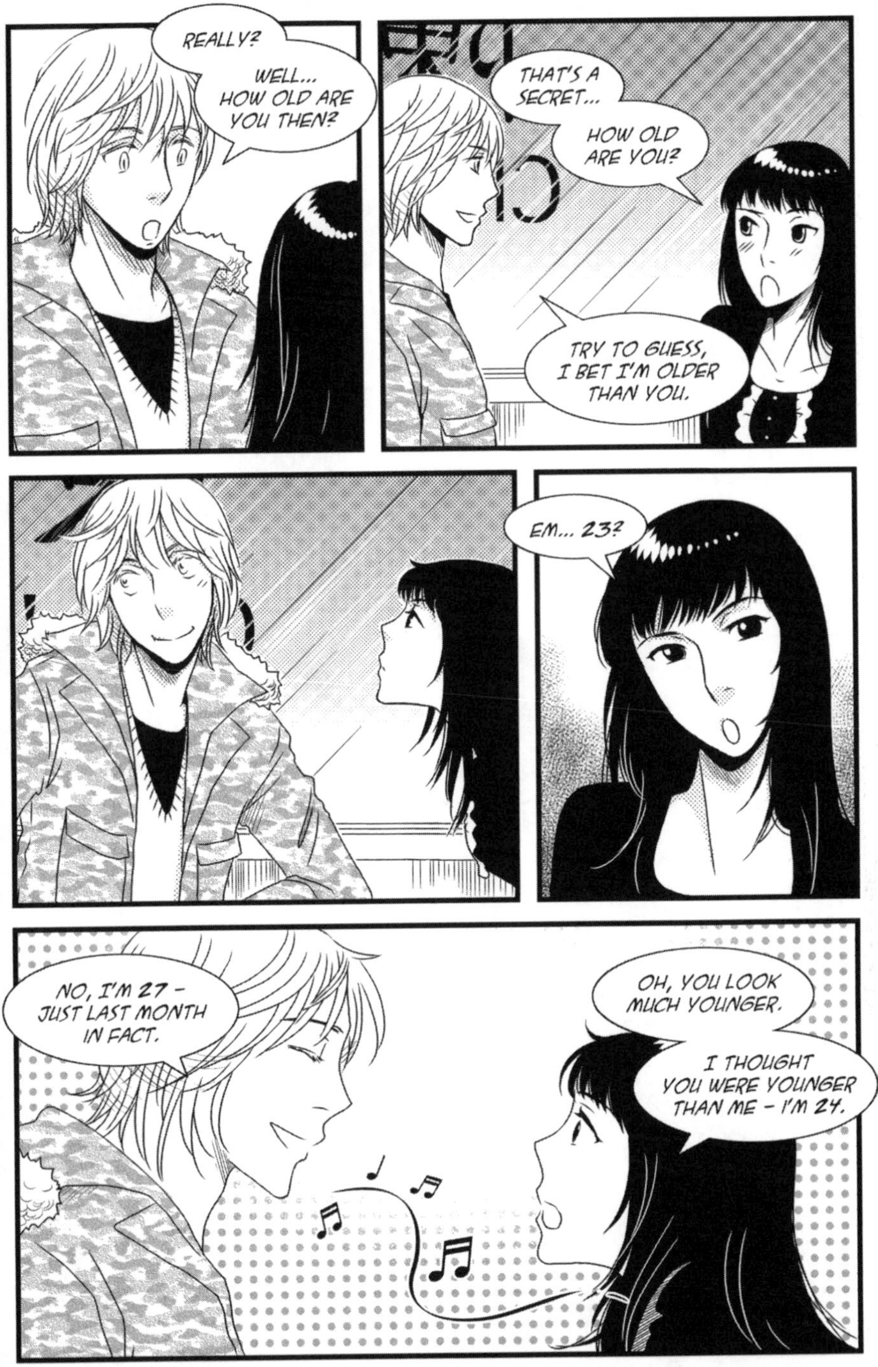
REALLY?
WELL... HOW OLD ARE YOU THEN?
THAT'S A SECRET...
HOW OLD ARE YOU?
TRY TO GUESS, I BET I'M OLDER THAN YOU.
EM... 23?
NO, I'M 27 - JUST LAST MONTH IN FACT.
OH, YOU LOOK MUCH YOUNGER.
I THOUGHT YOU WERE YOUNGER THAN ME - I'M 24.

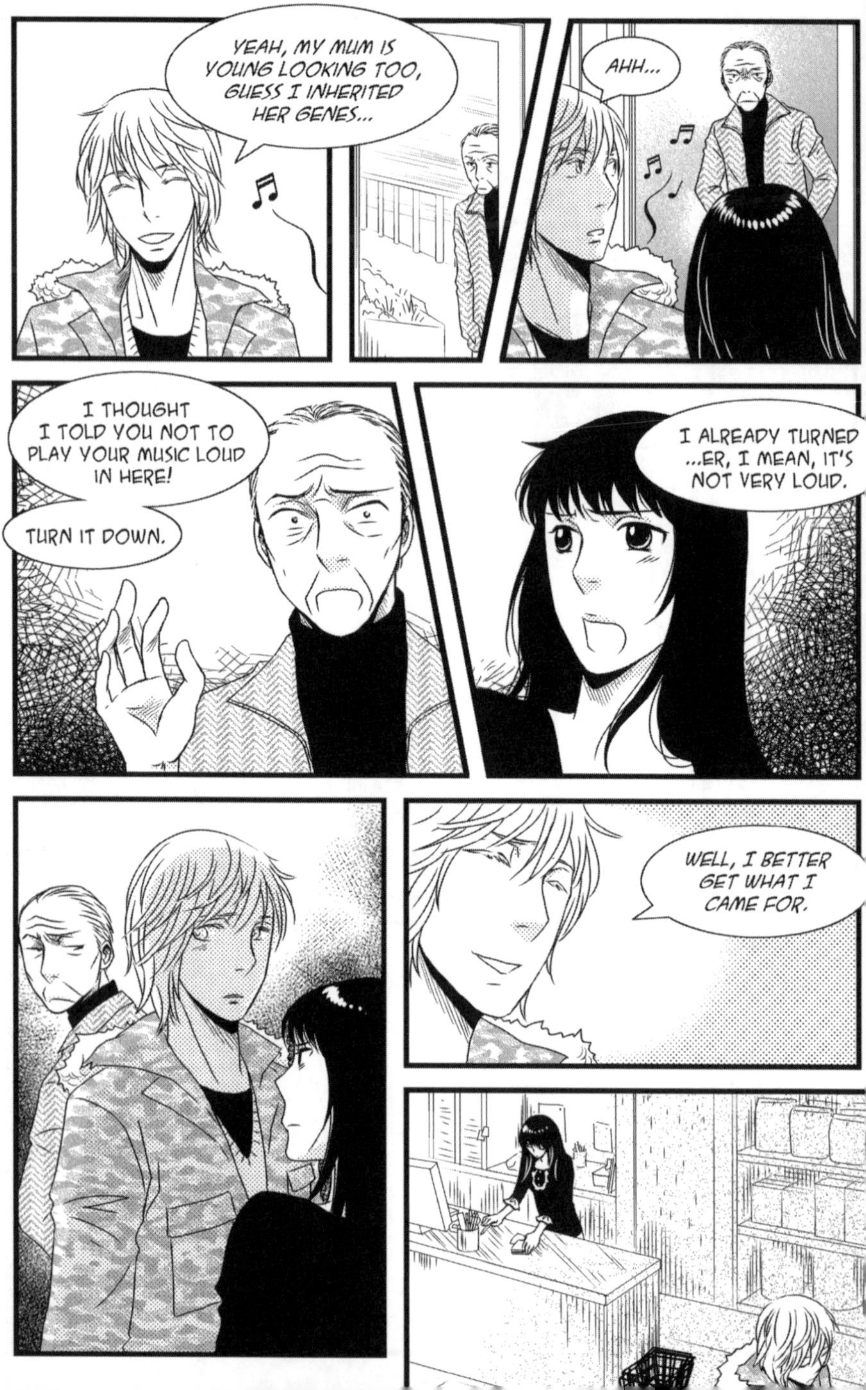
YEAH, MY MUM IS YOUNG LOOKING TOO, GUESS I INHERITED HER GENES...
AHH...
I THOUGHT I TOLD YOU NOT TO PLAY YOUR MUSIC LOUD IN HERE!
TURN IT DOWN.
I ALREADY TURNED ...ER, I MEAN, IT'S NOT VERY LOUD.
WELL, I BETTER GET WHAT I CAME FOR.

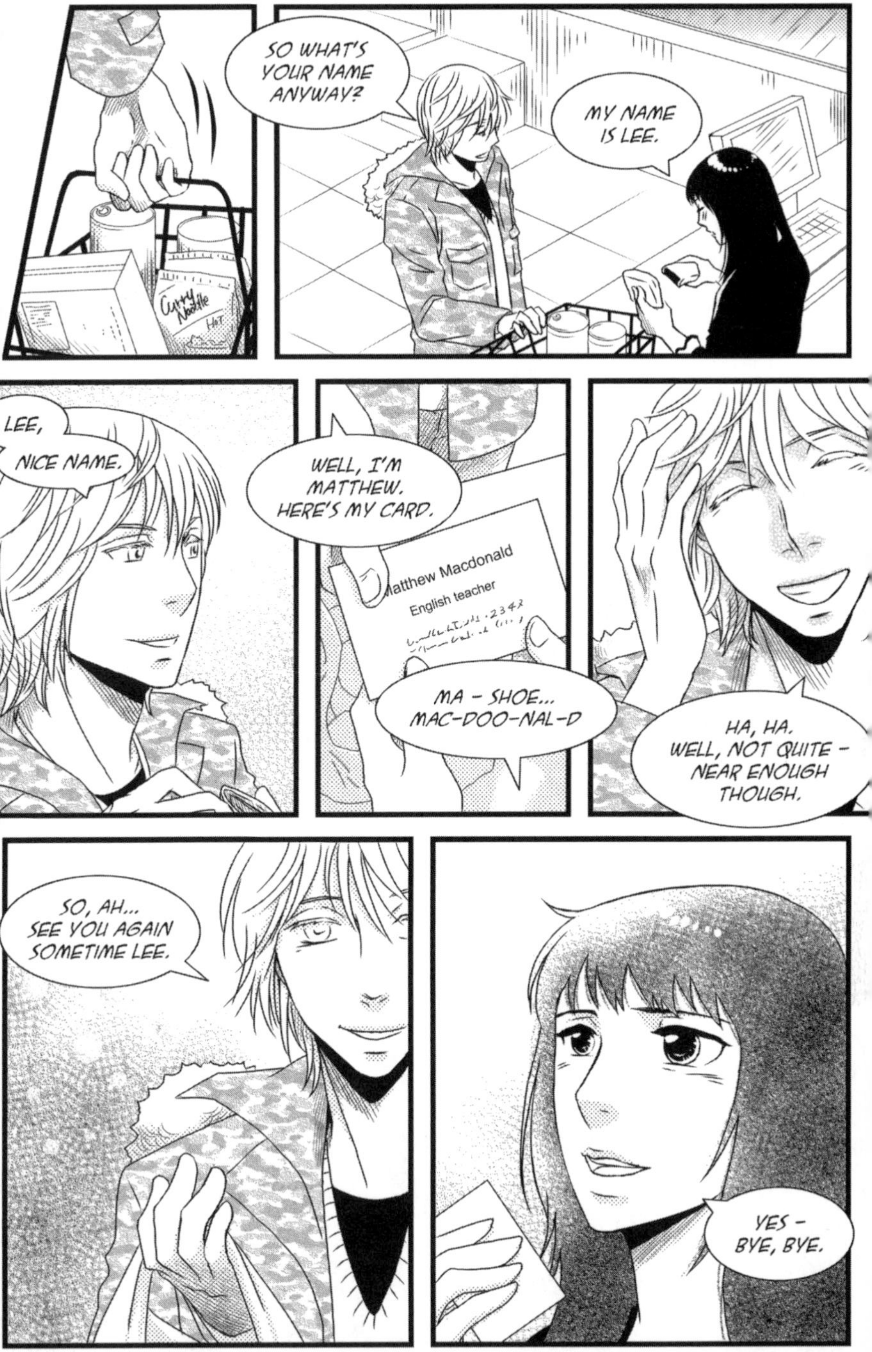
SO WHAT'S YOUR NAME ANYWAY?
MY NAME IS LEE.
LEE,
NICE NAME.
WELL, I'M MATTHEW. HERE'S MY CARD.
Matthew Macdonald
English teacher
MA - SHOE... MAC-DOO-NAL-D
HA, HA. WELL, NOT QUITE - NEAR ENOUGH THOUGH.
SO, AH... SEE YOU AGAIN SOMETIME LEE.
YES - BYE, BYE.

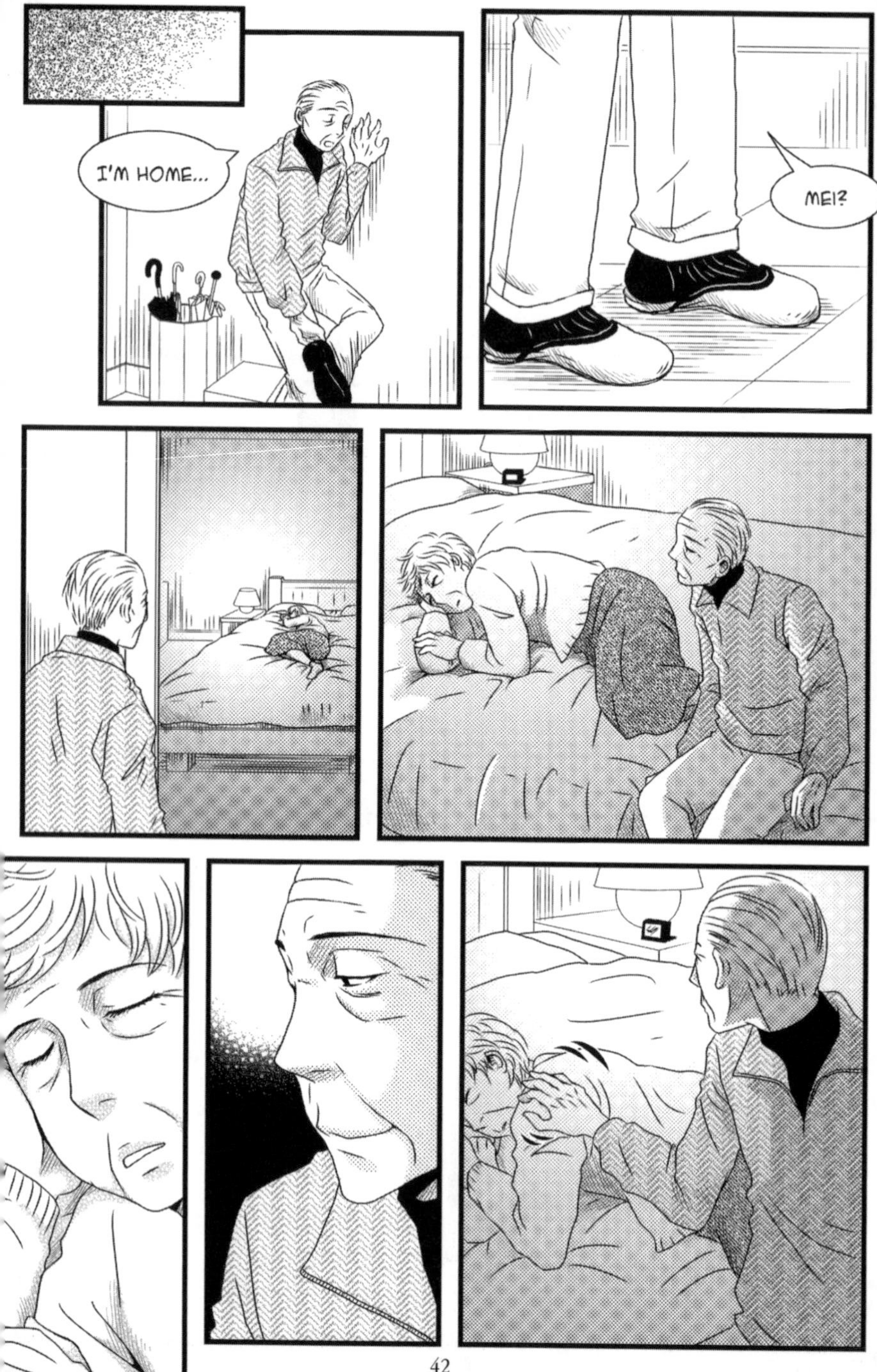
I'M HOME...
MEI?

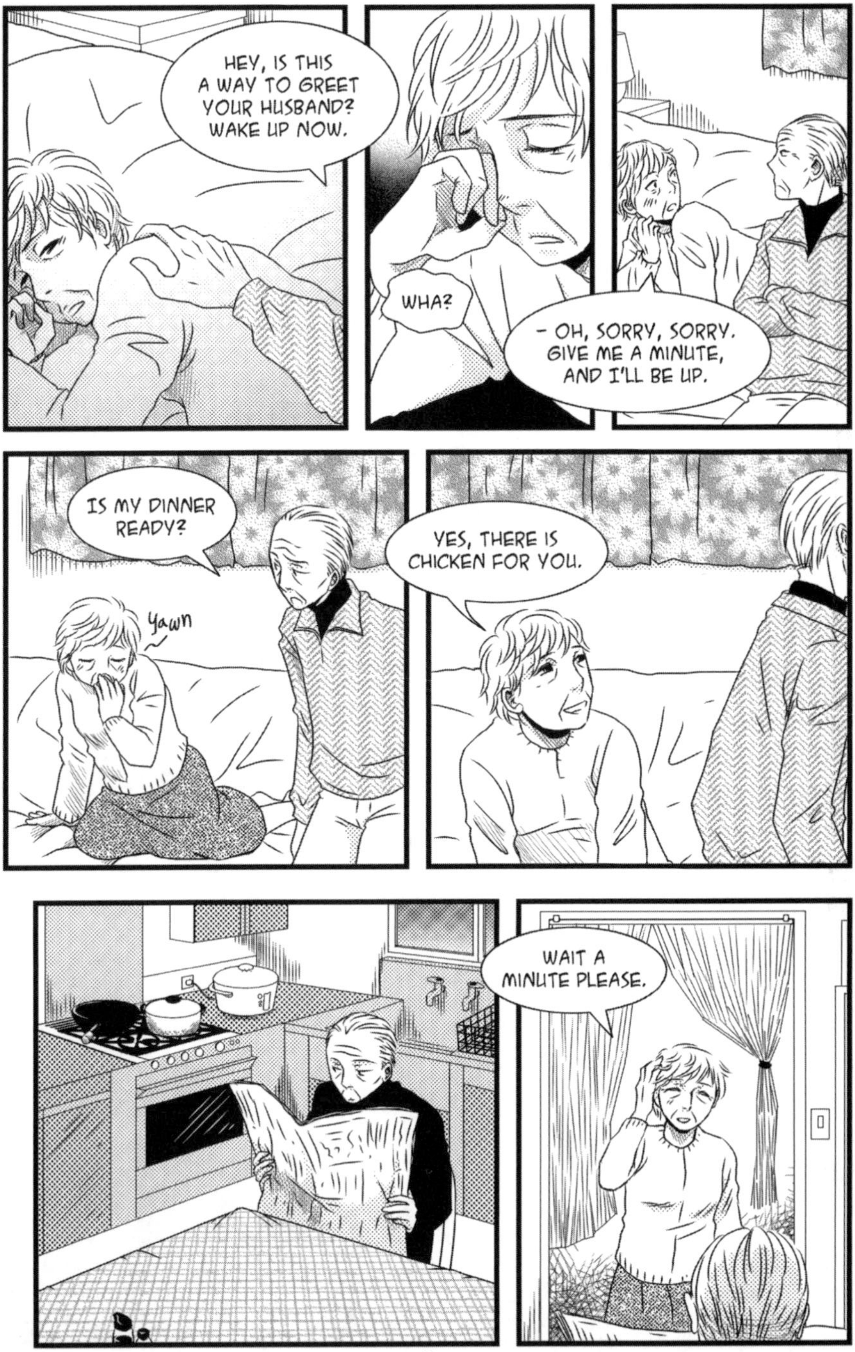
HEY, IS THIS A WAY TO GREET YOUR HUSBAND? WAKE UP NOW.
WHA?
- OH, SORRY, SORRY. GIVE ME A MINUTE, AND I'LL BE UP.
IS MY DINNER READY?
Yawn
YES, THERE IS CHICKEN FOR YOU.
WAIT A MINUTE PLEASE.

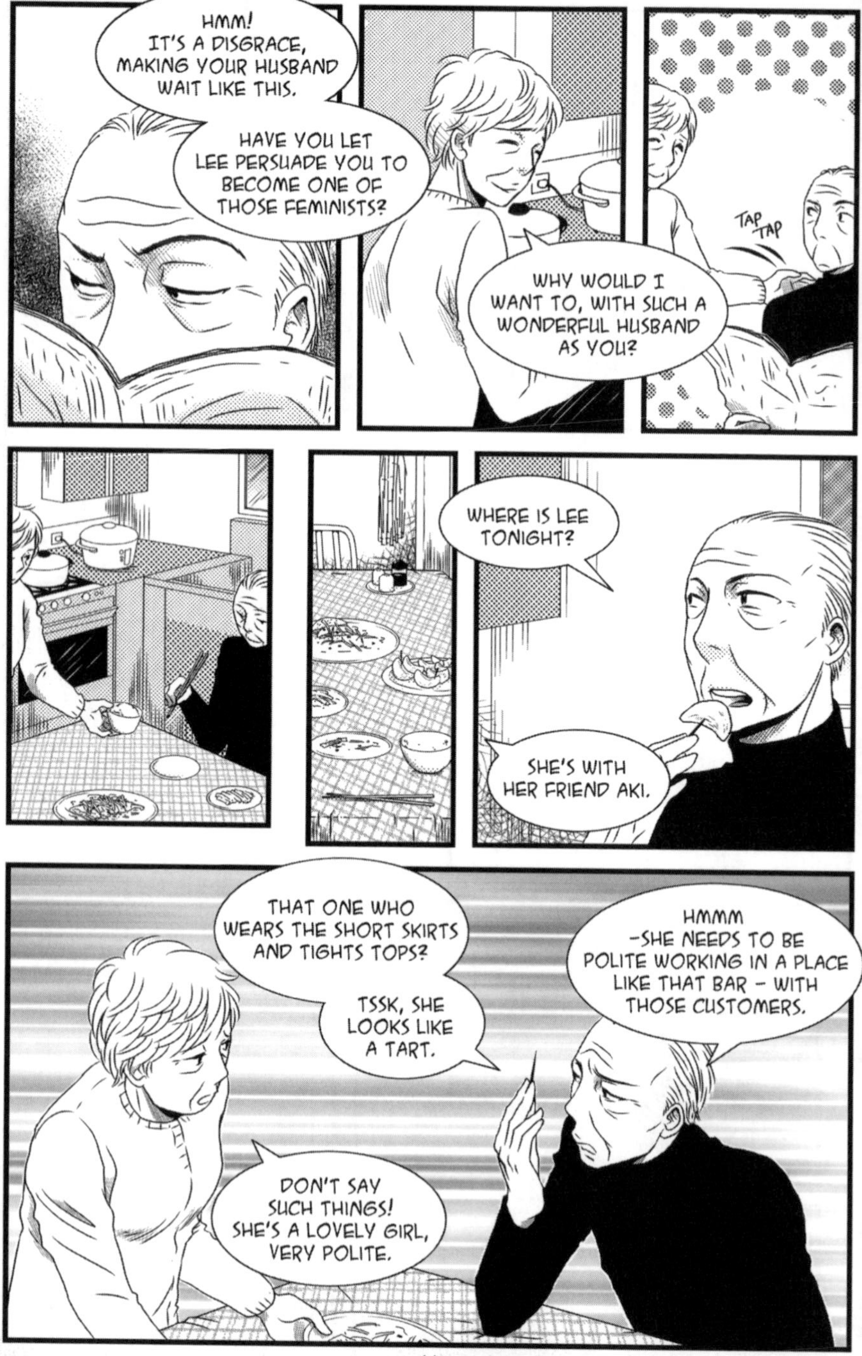
HMM! IT'S A DISGRACE, MAKING YOUR HUSBAND WAIT LIKE THIS.
HAVE YOU LET LEE PERSUADE YOU TO BECOME ONE OF THOSE FEMINISTS?
WHY WOULD I WANT TO, WITH SUCH A WONDERFUL HUSBAND AS YOU?
TAP TAP
WHERE IS LEE TONIGHT?
SHE'S WITH HER FRIEND AKI.
THAT ONE WHO WEARS THE SHORT SKIRTS AND TIGHTS TOPS?
TSSK, SHE LOOKS LIKE A TART.
DON'T SAY SUCH THINGS! SHE'S A LOVELY GIRL, VERY POLITE.
HMMM -SHE NEEDS TO BE POLITE WORKING IN A PLACE LIKE THAT BAR - WITH THOSE CUSTOMERS.

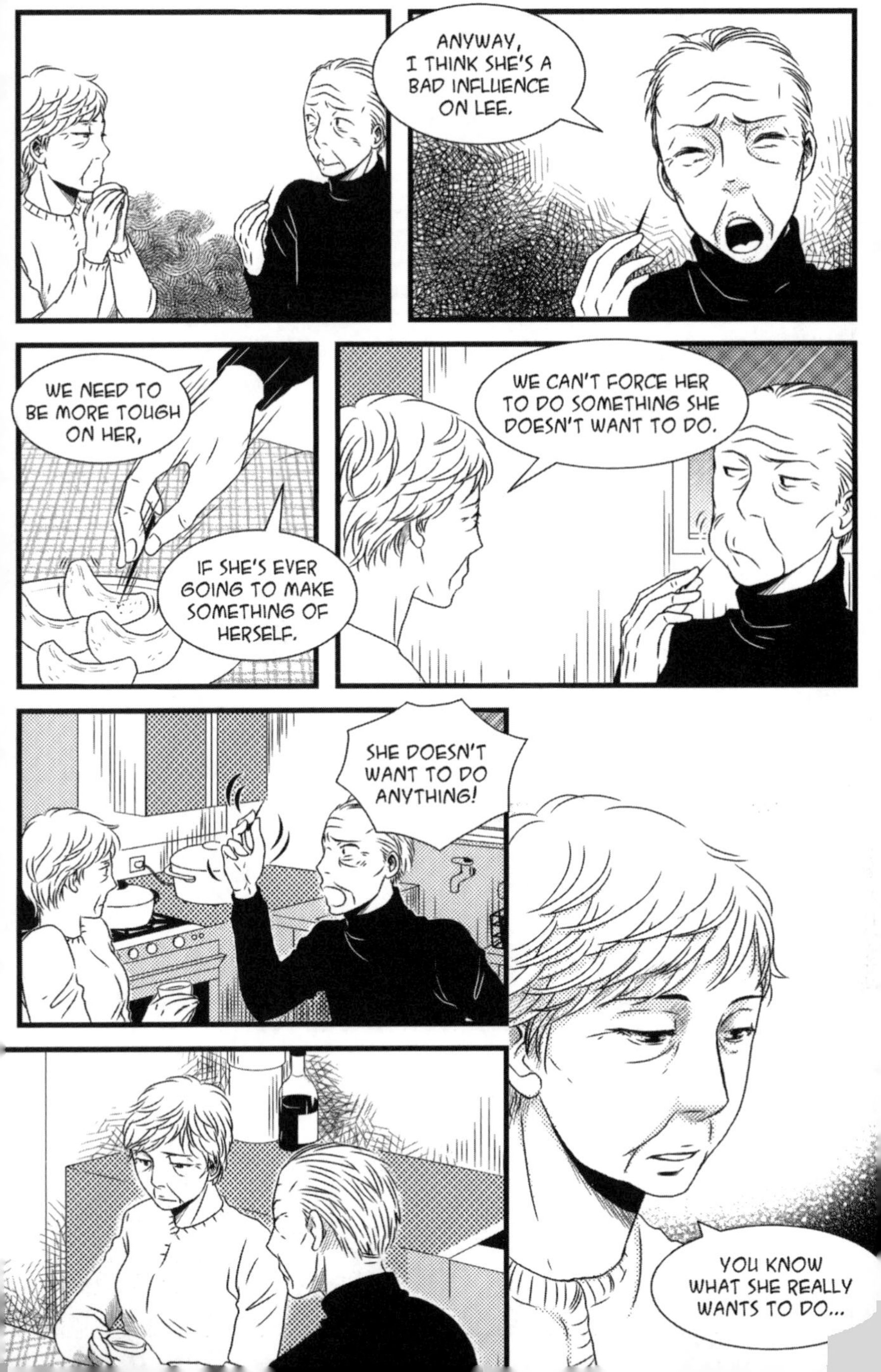
ANYWAY, I THINK SHE'S A BAD INFLUENCE ON LEE.
WE NEED TO BE MORE TOUGH ON HER,
IF SHE'S EVER GOING TO MAKE SOMETHING OF HERSELF.
WE CAN'T FORCE HER TO DO SOMETHING SHE DOESN'T WANT TO DO.
SHE DOESN'T WANT TO DO ANYTHING!
YOU KNOW WHAT SHE REALLY WANTS TO DO...

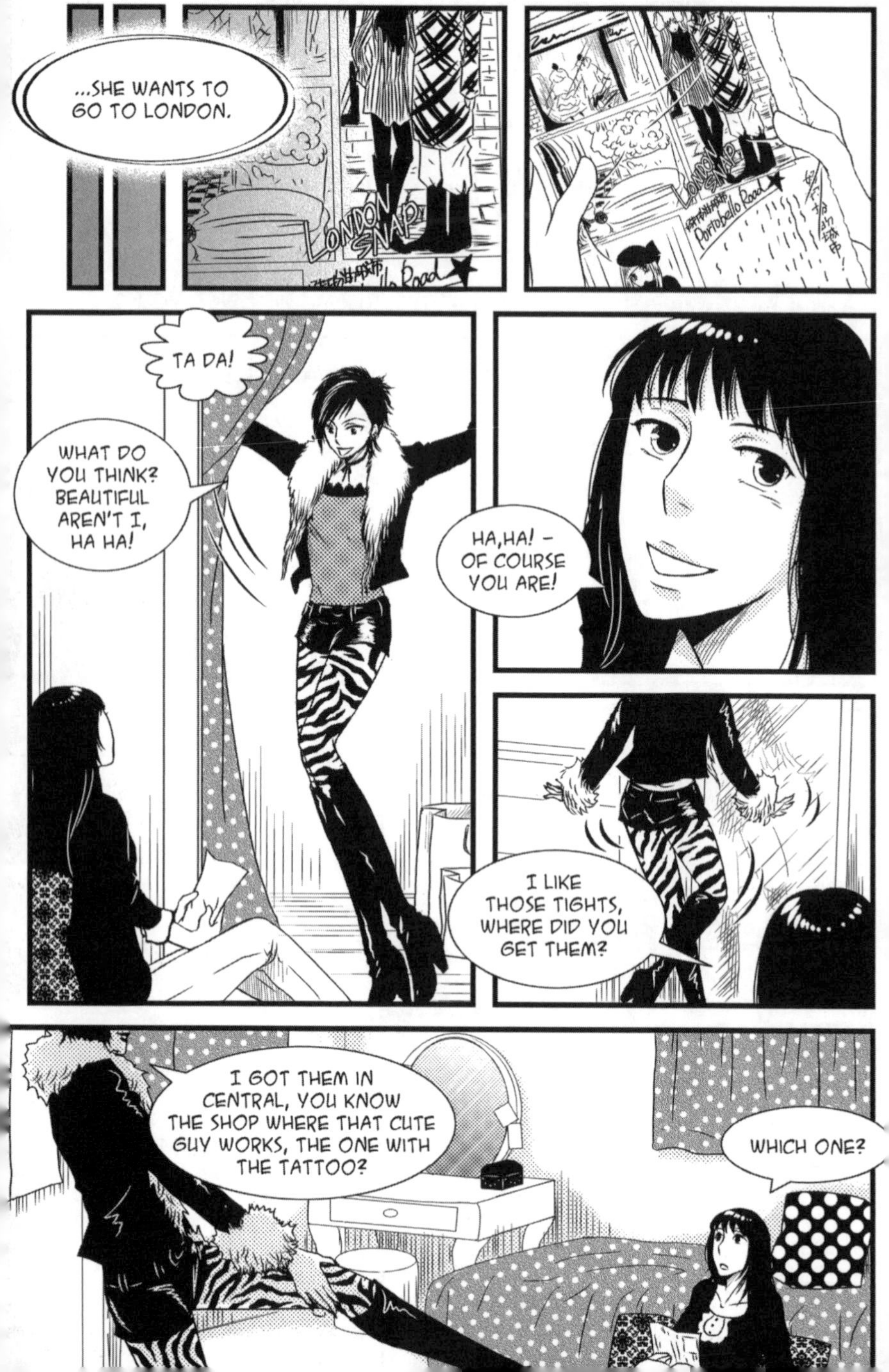
...SHE WANTS TO GO TO LONDON.
LONDON SNAP
LONDON SNAP
Portobello Road
TA DA!
WHAT DO YOU THINK? BEAUTIFUL AREN'T I, HA HA!
HA,HA! - OF COURSE YOU ARE!
I LIKE THOSE TIGHTS, WHERE DID YOU GET THEM?
I GOT THEM IN CENTRAL, YOU KNOW THE SHOP WHERE THAT CUTE GUY WORKS, THE ONE WITH THE TATTOO?
WHICH ONE?

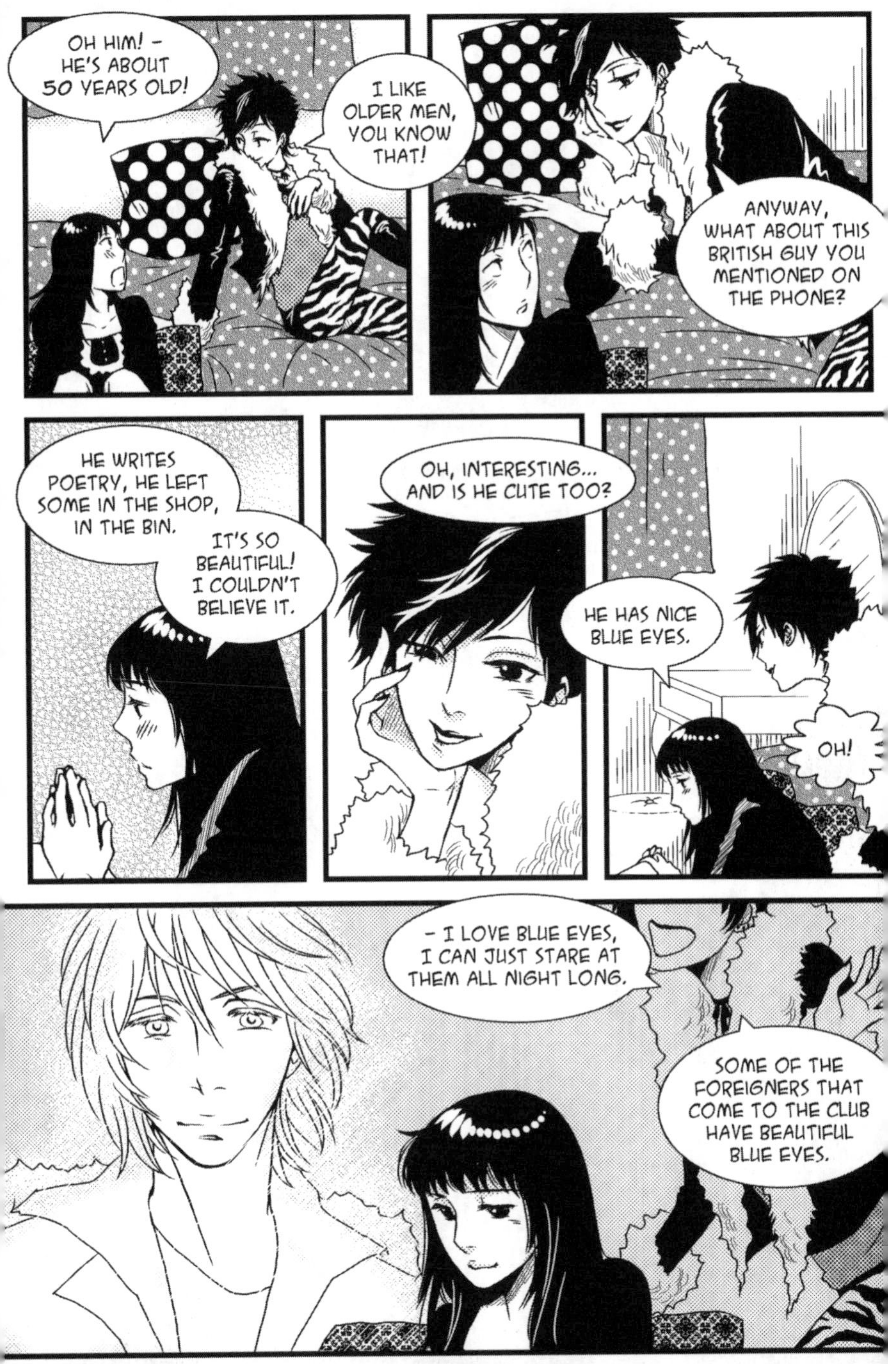
OH HIM! - HE'S ABOUT 50 YEARS OLD!
I LIKE OLDER MEN, YOU KNOW THAT!
ANYWAY, WHAT ABOUT THIS BRITISH GUY YOU MENTIONED ON THE PHONE?
HE WRITES POETRY, HE LEFT SOME IN THE SHOP, IN THE BIN.
IT'S SO BEAUTIFUL! I COULDN'T BELIEVE IT.
OH, INTERESTING... AND IS HE CUTE TOO?
HE HAS NICE BLUE EYES.
OH!
- I LOVE BLUE EYES, I CAN JUST STARE AT THEM ALL NIGHT LONG.
SOME OF THE FOREIGNERS THAT COME TO THE CLUB HAVE BEAUTIFUL BLUE EYES.

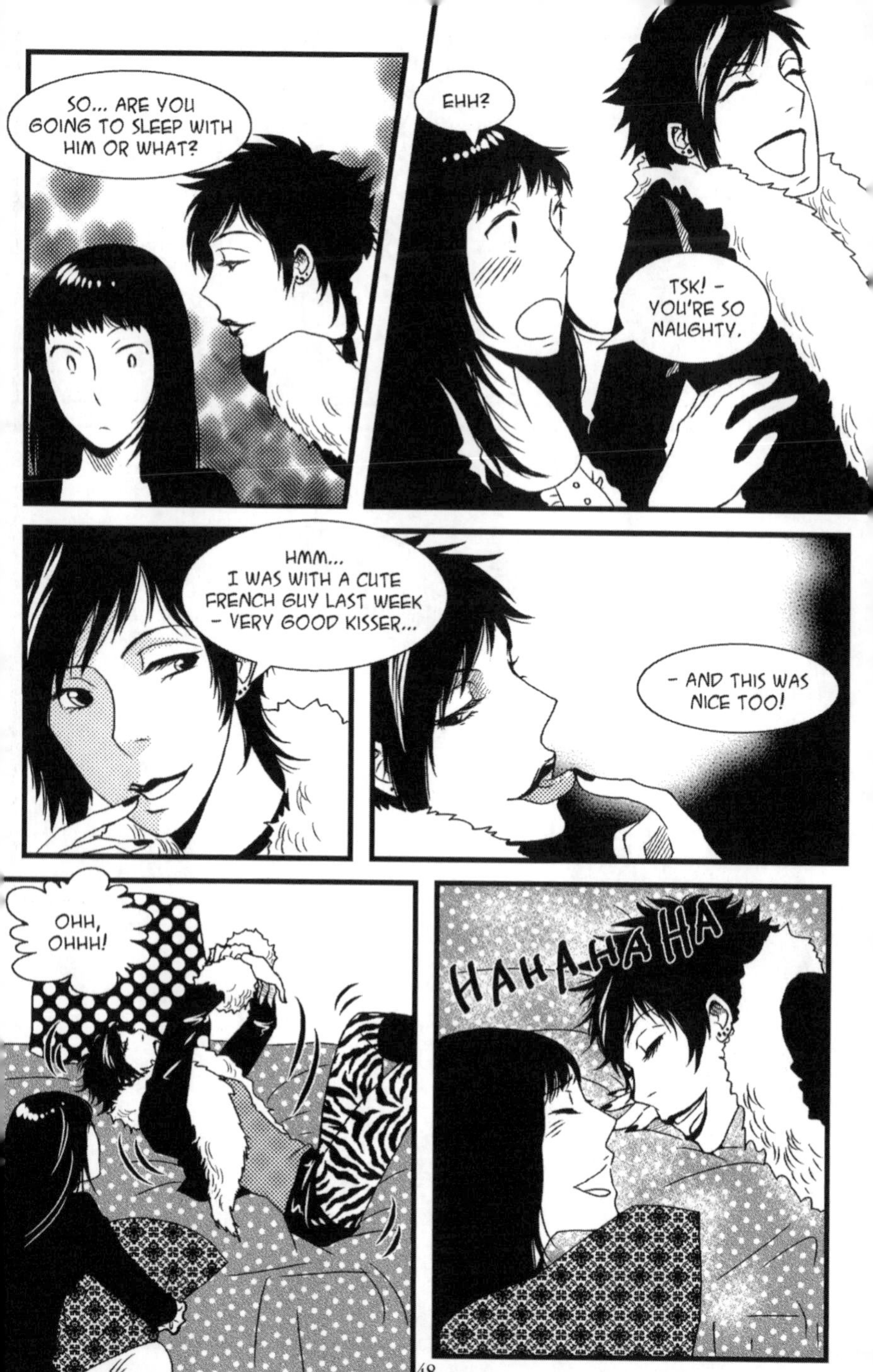
SO... ARE YOU GOING TO SLEEP WITH HIM OR WHAT?
EHH?
TSK! - YOU'RE SO NAUGHTY.
HMM... I WAS WITH A CUTE FRENCH GUY LAST WEEK - VERY GOOD KISSER...
- AND THIS WAS NICE TOO!
OHH, OHHH!
HAHAHAHAHA

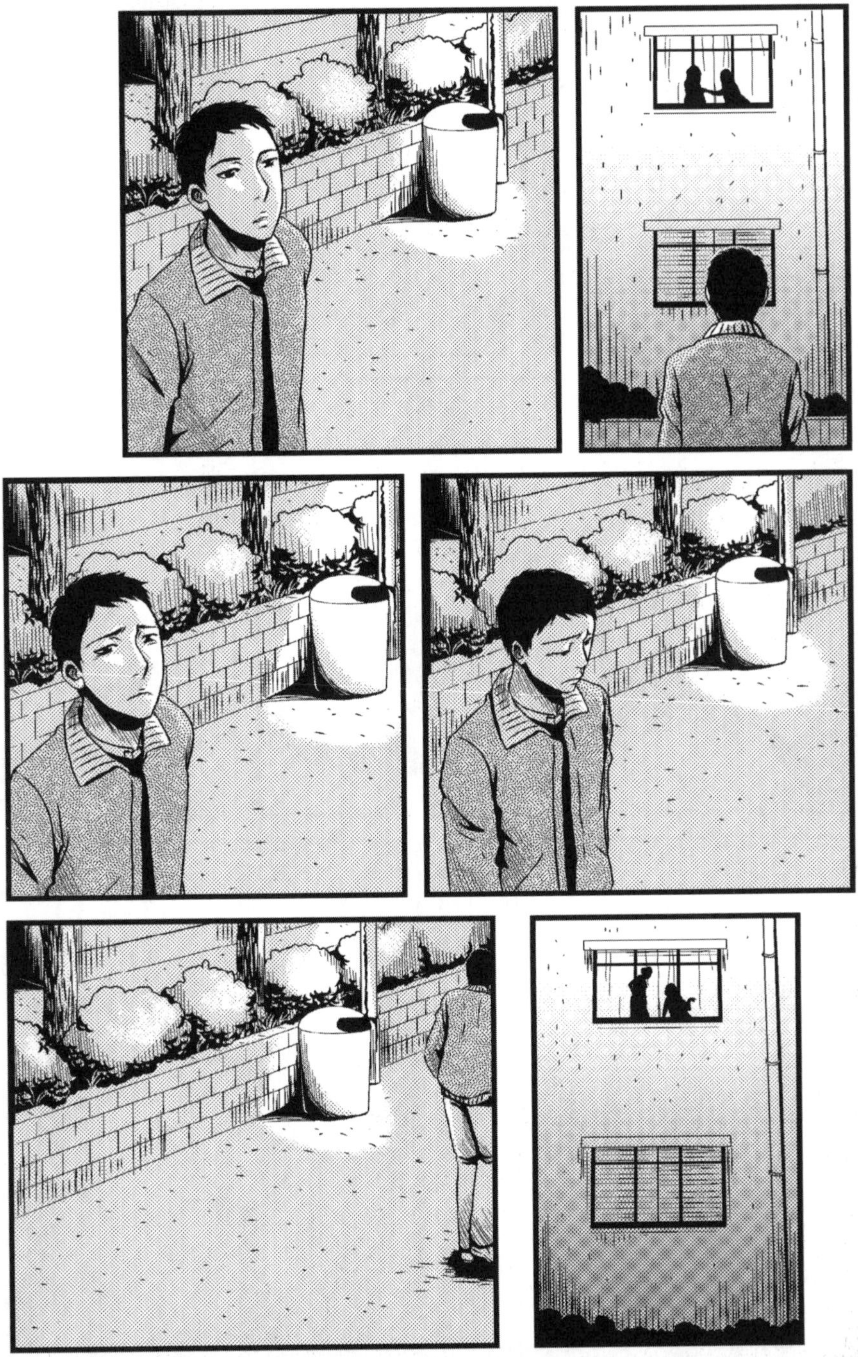

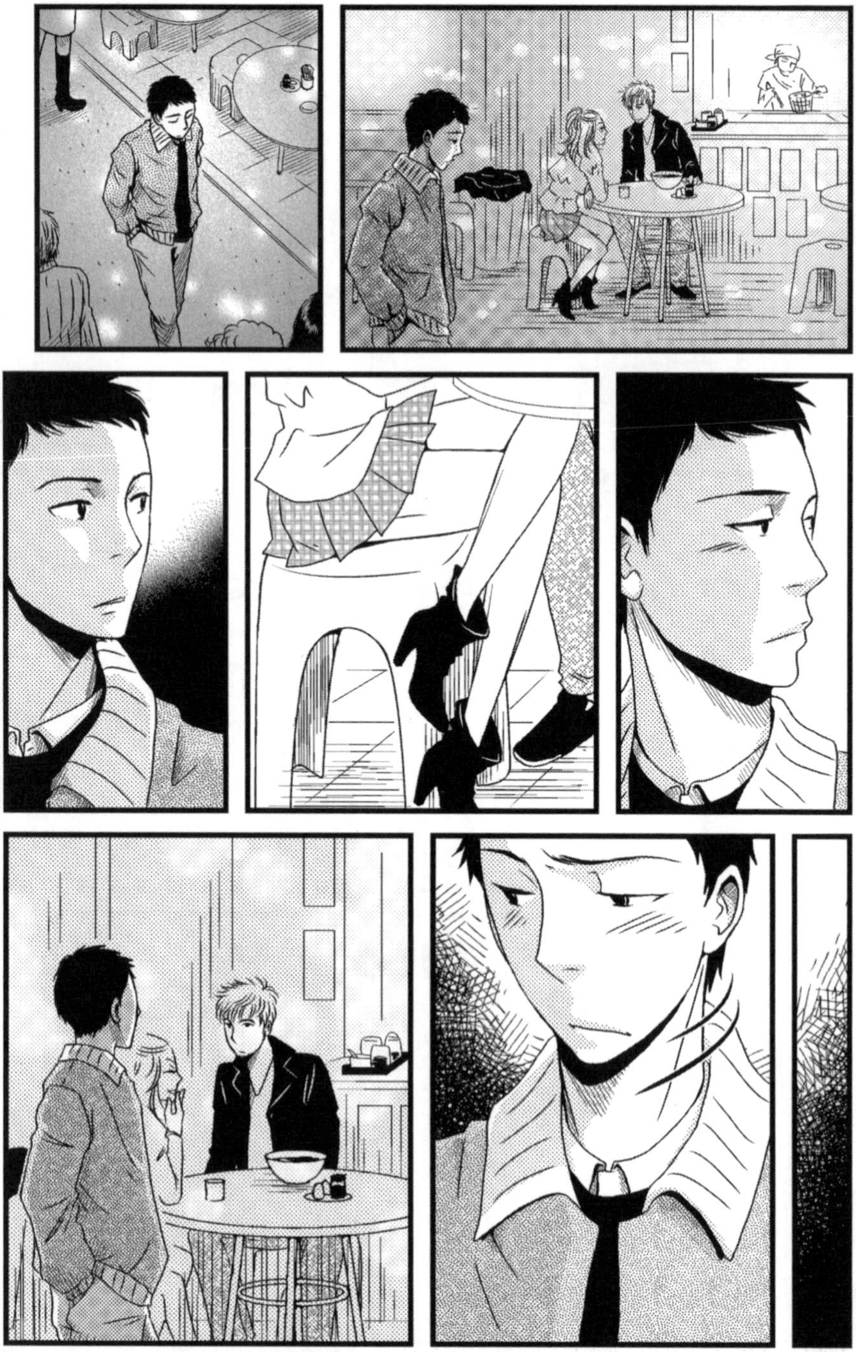

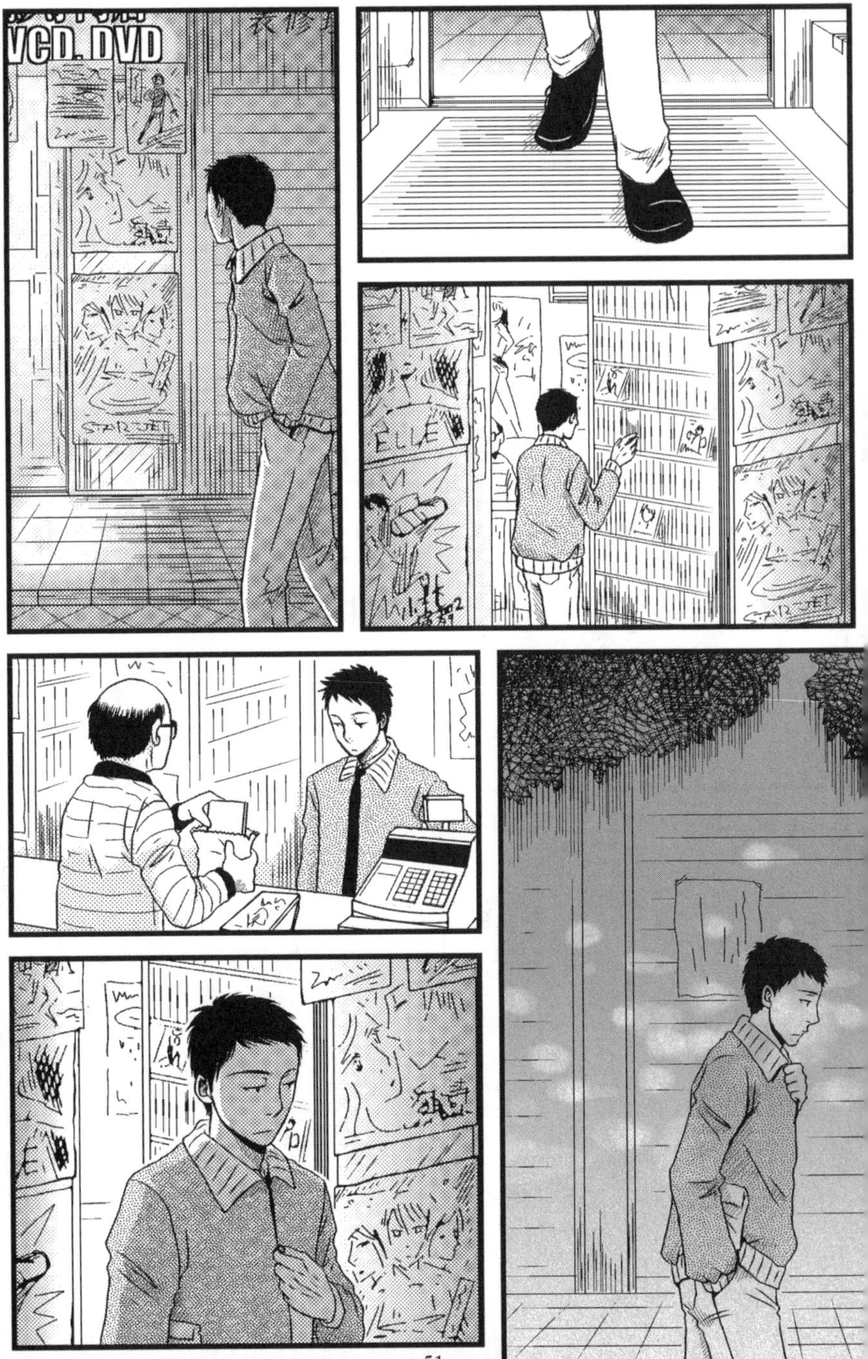
VCD. DVD
ELLE

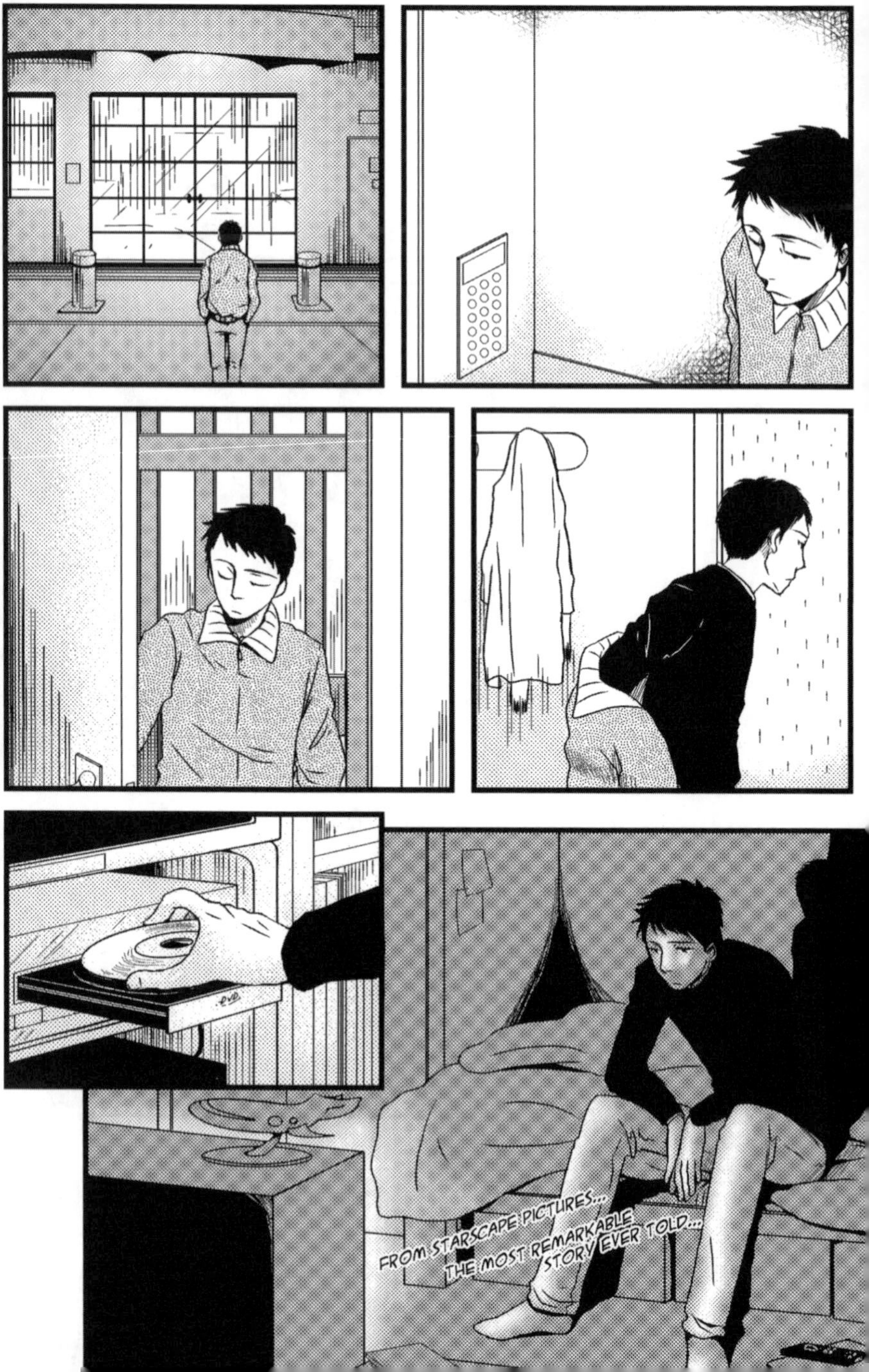
FROM STARSCAPE PICTURES...
THE MOST REMARKABLE
STORY EVER TOLD...

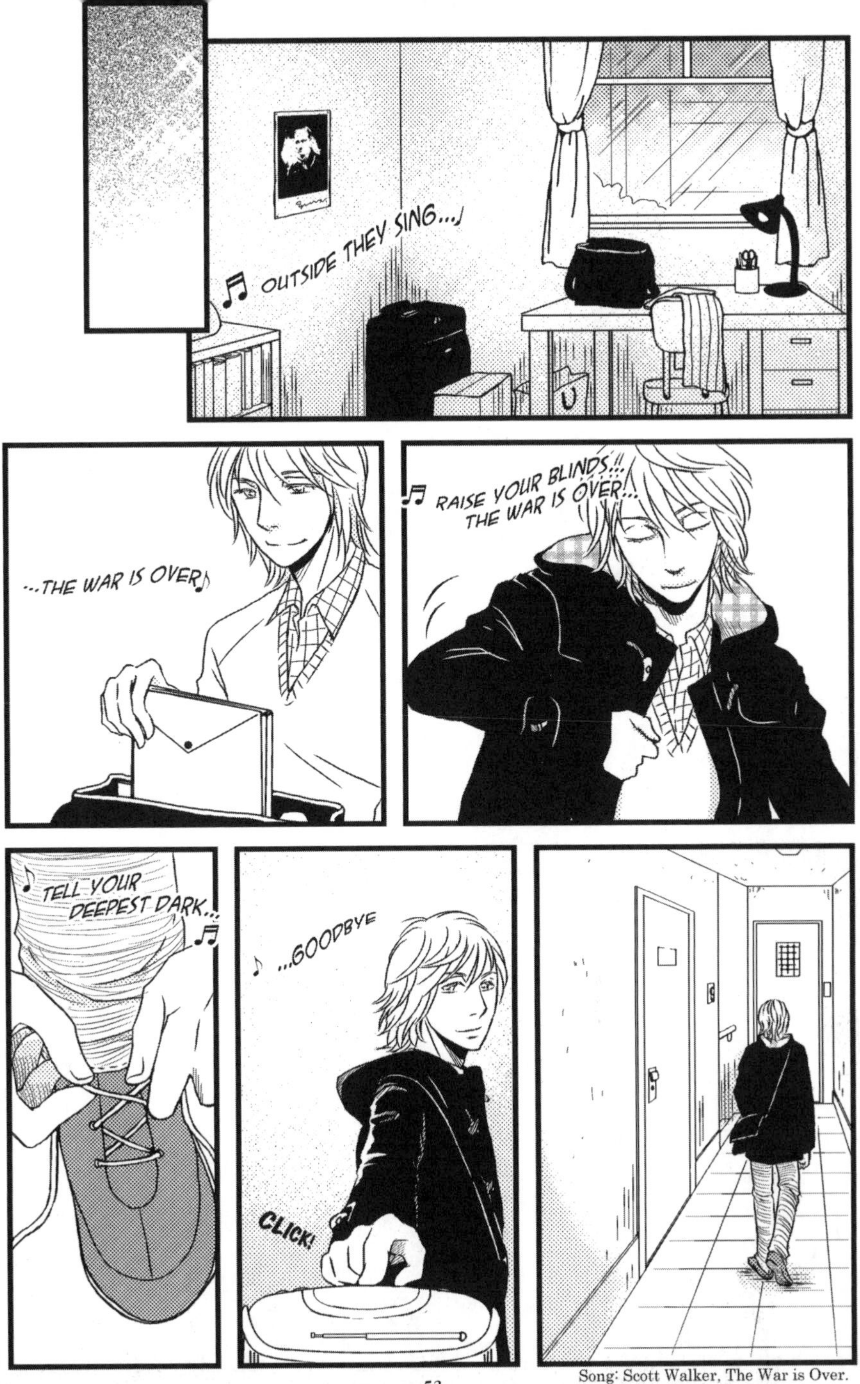

♬ OUTSIDE THEY SING...♩
...THE WAR IS OVER♪
♬ RAISE YOUR BLINDS... THE WAR IS OVER...
♪ TELL YOUR DEEPEST DARK... ♬
♪ ...GOODBYE
CLICK!

Song: Scott Walker, The War is Over.

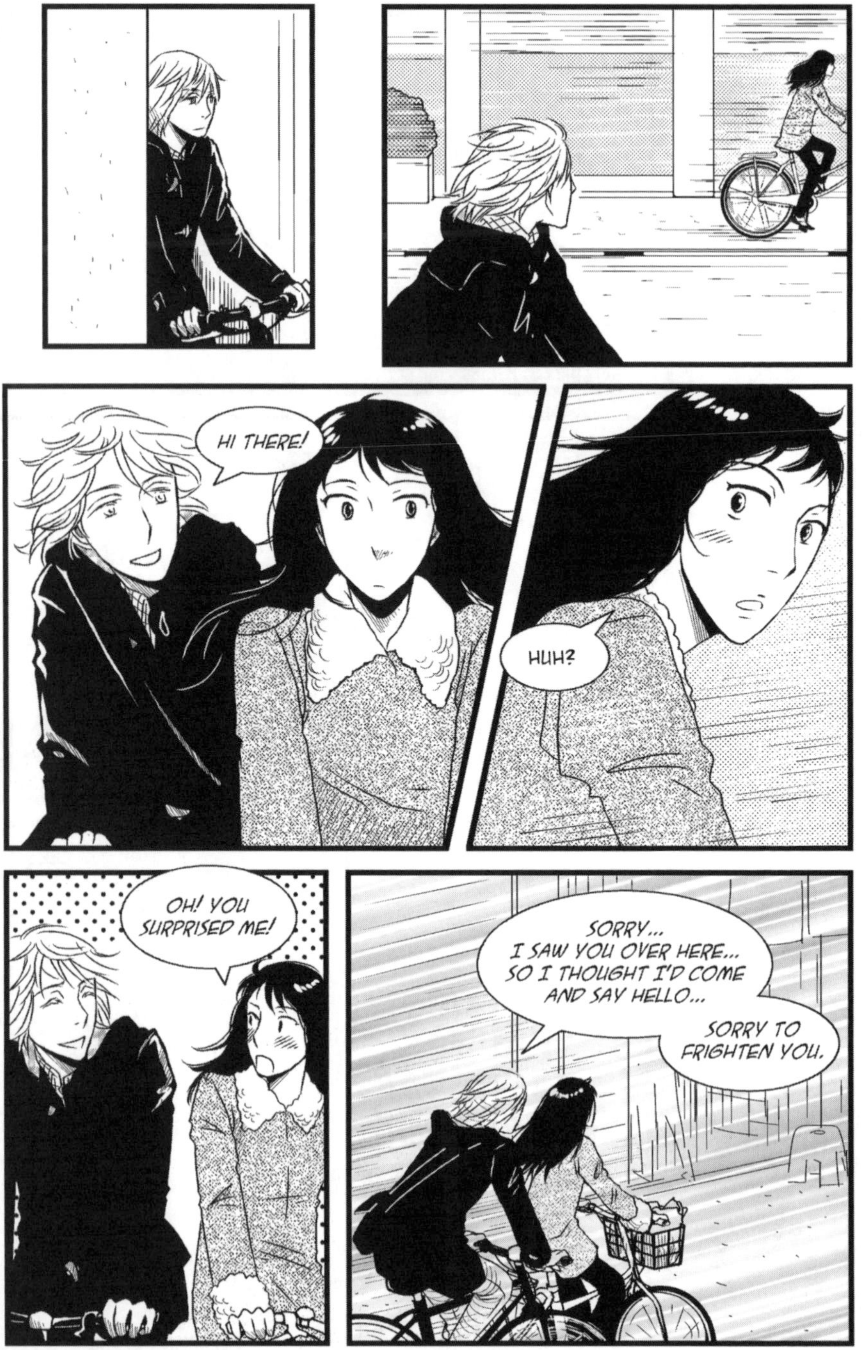
HI THERE!
HUH?
OH! YOU SURPRISED ME!
SORRY... I SAW YOU OVER HERE... SO I THOUGHT I'D COME AND SAY HELLO...
SORRY TO FRIGHTEN YOU.

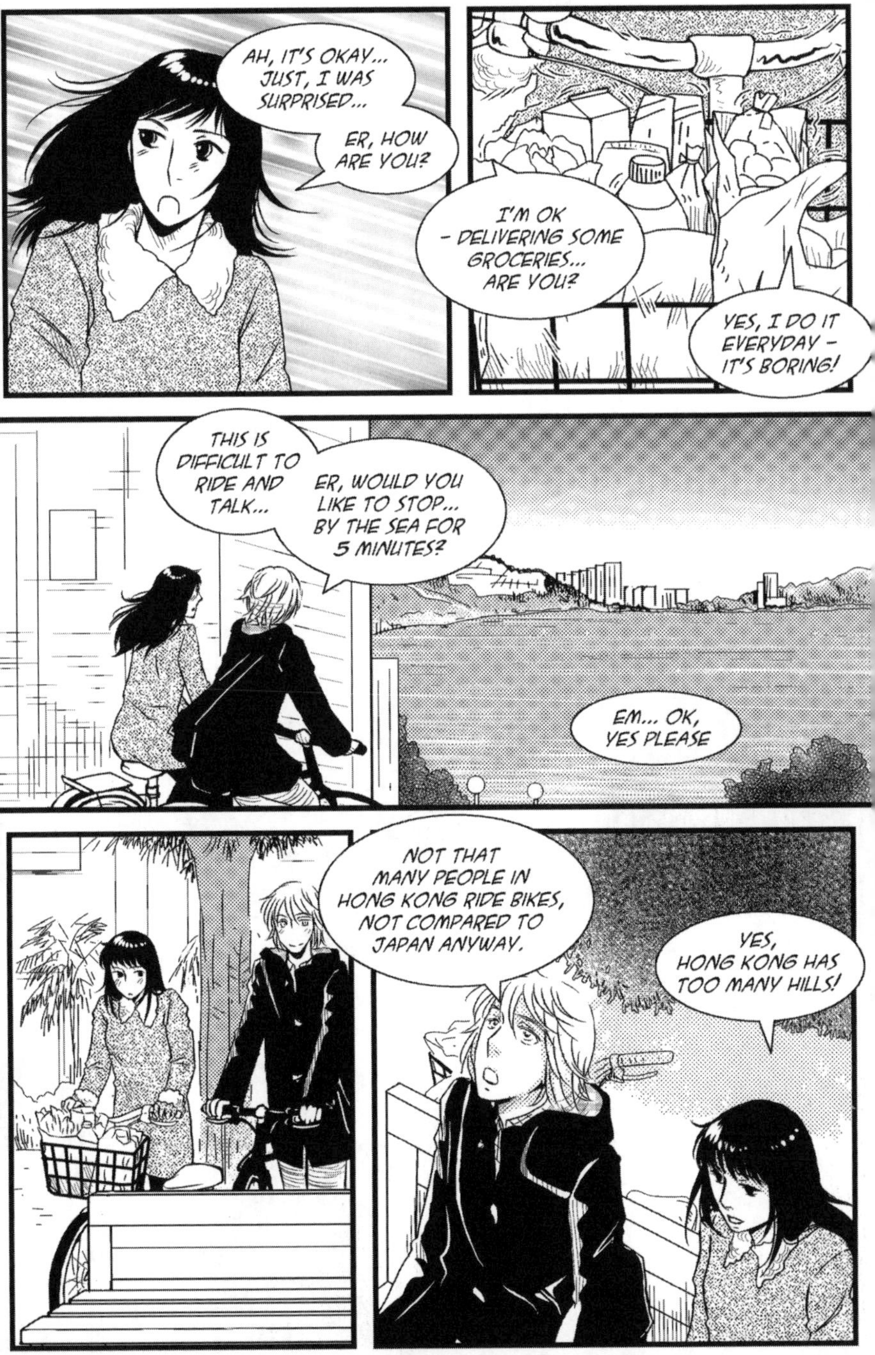
AH, IT'S OKAY... JUST, I WAS SURPRISED...
ER, HOW ARE YOU?
I'M OK - DELIVERING SOME GROCERIES... ARE YOU?
YES, I DO IT EVERYDAY - IT'S BORING!
THIS IS DIFFICULT TO RIDE AND TALK...
ER, WOULD YOU LIKE TO STOP... BY THE SEA FOR 5 MINUTES?
EM... OK, YES PLEASE
NOT THAT MANY PEOPLE IN HONG KONG RIDE BIKES, NOT COMPARED TO JAPAN ANYWAY.
YES, HONG KONG HAS TOO MANY HILLS!

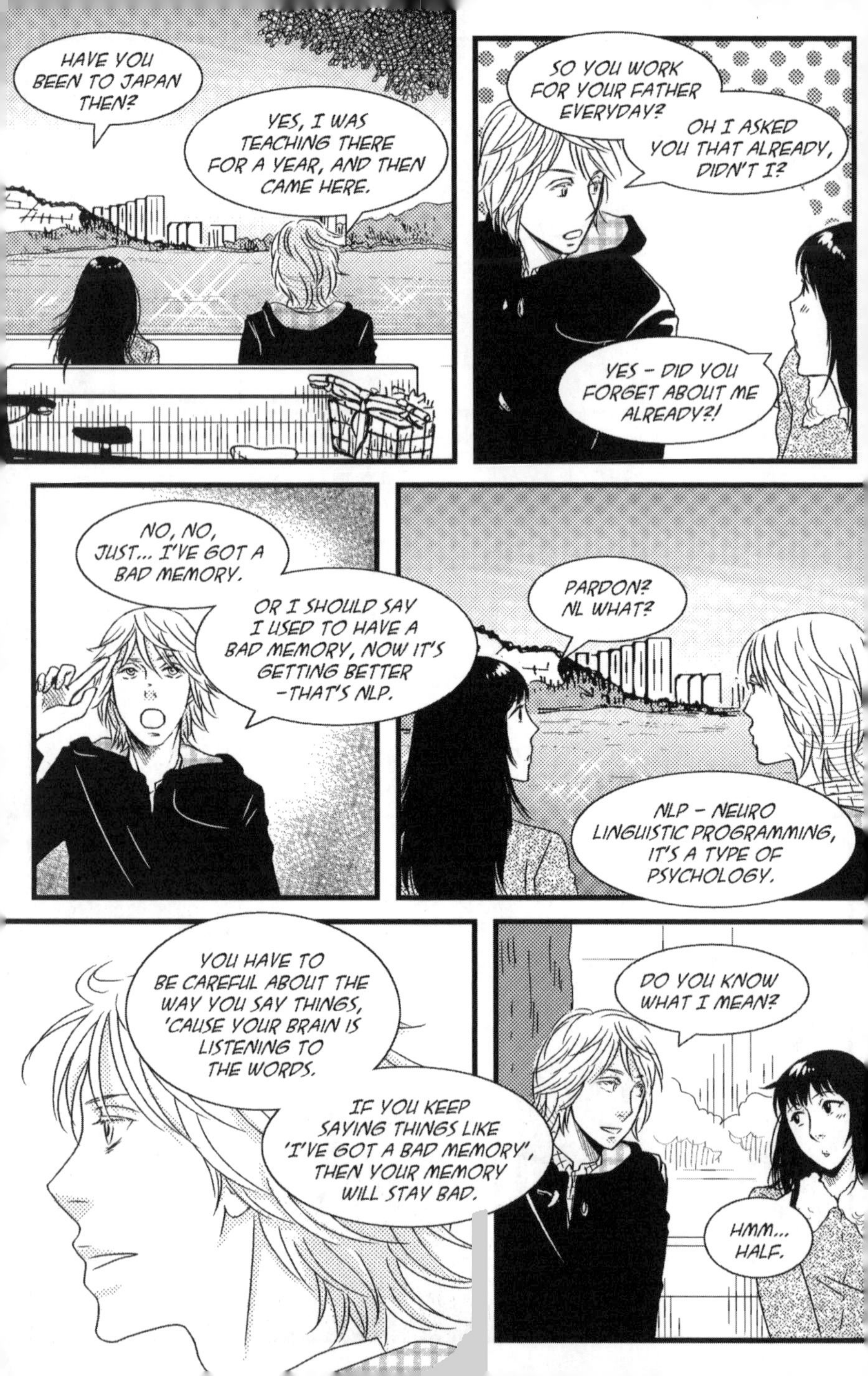
HAVE YOU BEEN TO JAPAN THEN?
YES, I WAS TEACHING THERE FOR A YEAR, AND THEN CAME HERE.
SO YOU WORK FOR YOUR FATHER EVERYDAY?
OH I ASKED YOU THAT ALREADY, DIDN'T I?
YES - DID YOU FORGET ABOUT ME ALREADY?!
NO, NO, JUST... I'VE GOT A BAD MEMORY.
OR I SHOULD SAY I USED TO HAVE A BAD MEMORY, NOW IT'S GETTING BETTER -THAT'S NLP.
PARDON? NL WHAT?
NLP - NEURO LINGUISTIC PROGRAMMING, IT'S A TYPE OF PSYCHOLOGY.
YOU HAVE TO BE CAREFUL ABOUT THE WAY YOU SAY THINGS, 'CAUSE YOUR BRAIN IS LISTENING TO THE WORDS.
IF YOU KEEP SAYING THINGS LIKE 'I'VE GOT A BAD MEMORY', THEN YOUR MEMORY WILL STAY BAD.
DO YOU KNOW WHAT I MEAN?
HMM... HALF.

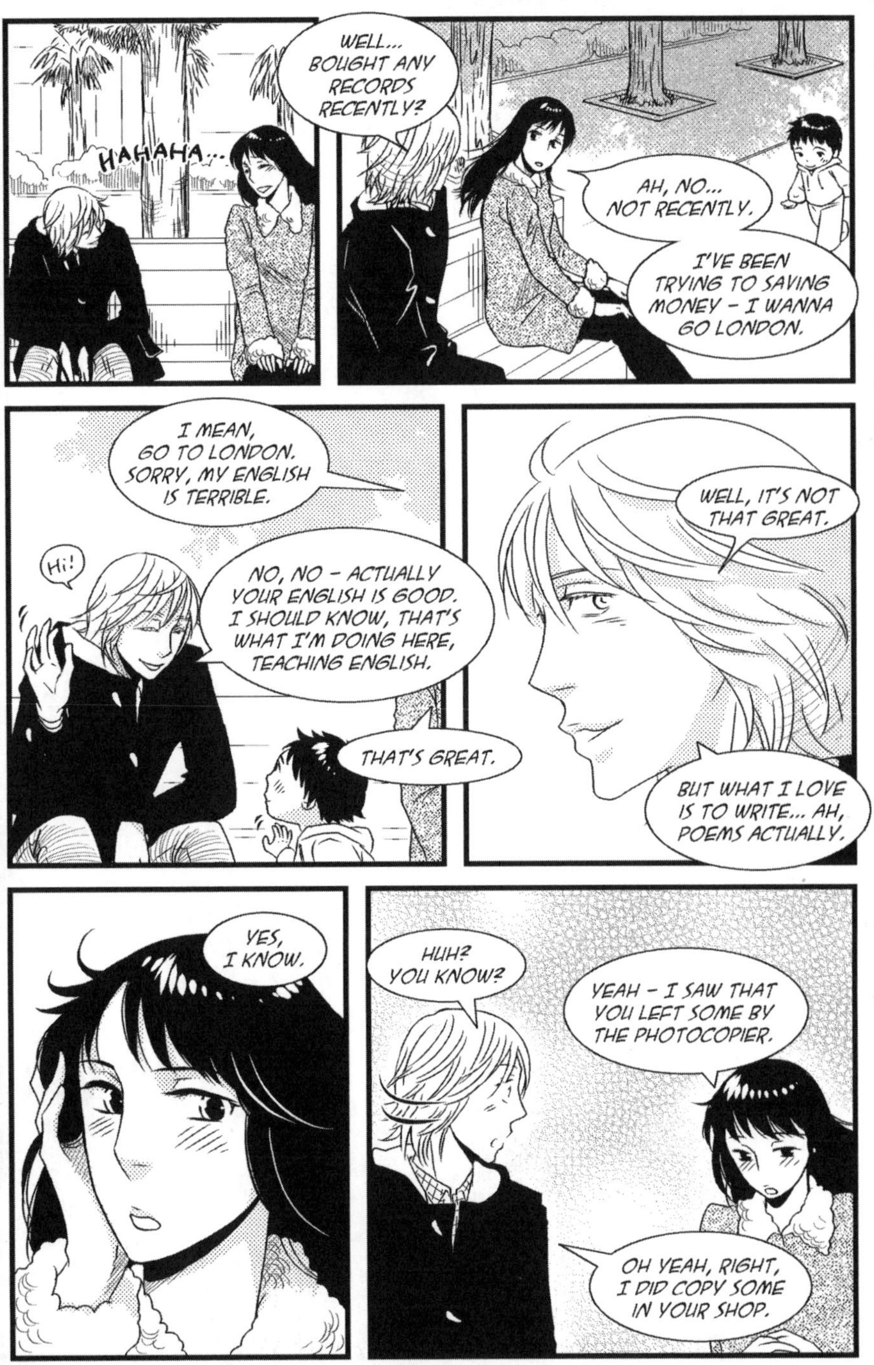
HAHAHA...
WELL... BOUGHT ANY RECORDS RECENTLY?
AH, NO... NOT RECENTLY.
I'VE BEEN TRYING TO SAVING MONEY - I WANNA GO LONDON.
I MEAN, GO TO LONDON. SORRY, MY ENGLISH IS TERRIBLE.
Hi!
NO, NO - ACTUALLY YOUR ENGLISH IS GOOD. I SHOULD KNOW, THAT'S WHAT I'M DOING HERE, TEACHING ENGLISH.
THAT'S GREAT.
WELL, IT'S NOT THAT GREAT.
BUT WHAT I LOVE IS TO WRITE... AH, POEMS ACTUALLY.
YES, I KNOW.
HUH? YOU KNOW?
YEAH - I SAW THAT YOU LEFT SOME BY THE PHOTOCOPIER.
OH YEAH, RIGHT, I DID COPY SOME IN YOUR SHOP.

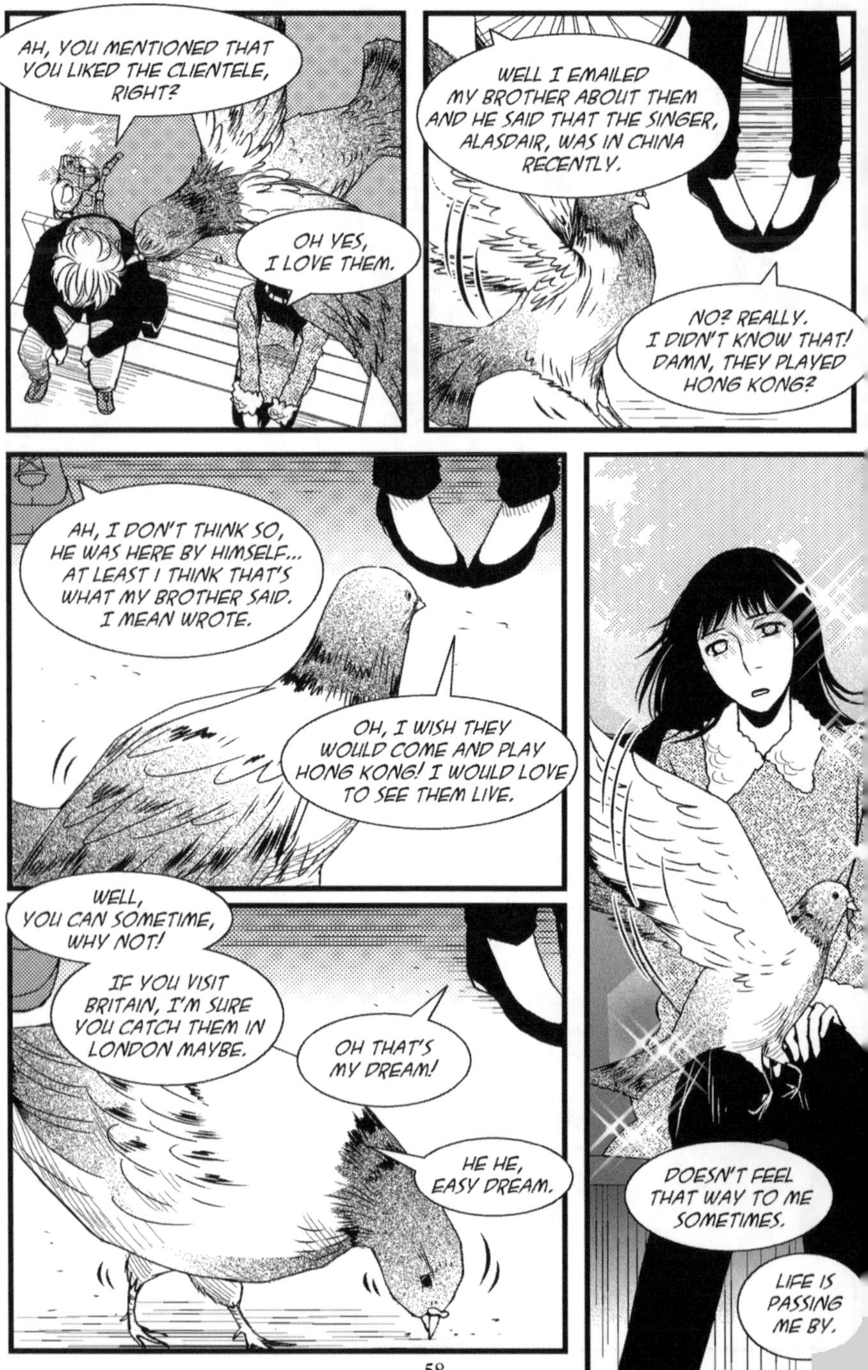
AH, YOU MENTIONED THAT YOU LIKED THE CLIENTELE, RIGHT?
OH YES, I LOVE THEM.
WELL I EMAILED MY BROTHER ABOUT THEM AND HE SAID THAT THE SINGER, ALASDAIR, WAS IN CHINA RECENTLY.
NO? REALLY. I DIDN'T KNOW THAT! DAMN, THEY PLAYED HONG KONG?
AH, I DON'T THINK SO, HE WAS HERE BY HIMSELF... AT LEAST I THINK THAT'S WHAT MY BROTHER SAID. I MEAN WROTE.
OH, I WISH THEY WOULD COME AND PLAY HONG KONG! I WOULD LOVE TO SEE THEM LIVE.
WELL, YOU CAN SOMETIME, WHY NOT!
IF YOU VISIT BRITAIN, I'M SURE YOU CATCH THEM IN LONDON MAYBE.
OH THAT'S MY DREAM!
HE HE, EASY DREAM.
DOESN'T FEEL THAT WAY TO ME SOMETIMES.
LIFE IS PASSING ME BY.

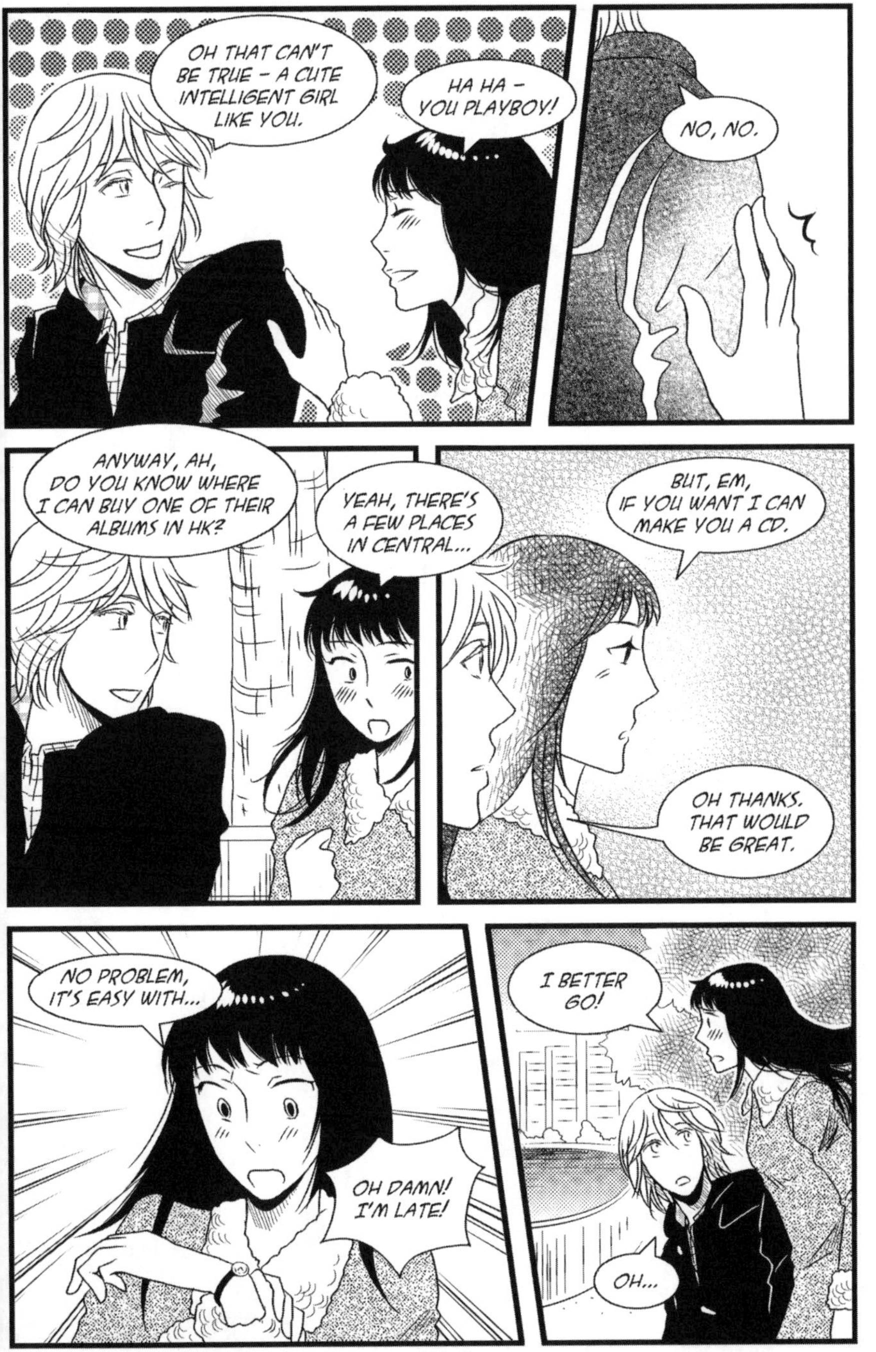
OH THAT CAN'T BE TRUE - A CUTE INTELLIGENT GIRL LIKE YOU.
HA HA - YOU PLAYBOY!
NO, NO.
ANYWAY, AH, DO YOU KNOW WHERE I CAN BUY ONE OF THEIR ALBUMS IN HK?
YEAH, THERE'S A FEW PLACES IN CENTRAL...
BUT, EM, IF YOU WANT I CAN MAKE YOU A CD.
OH THANKS. THAT WOULD BE GREAT.
NO PROBLEM, IT'S EASY WITH...
OH DAMN! I'M LATE!
I BETTER GO!
OH...

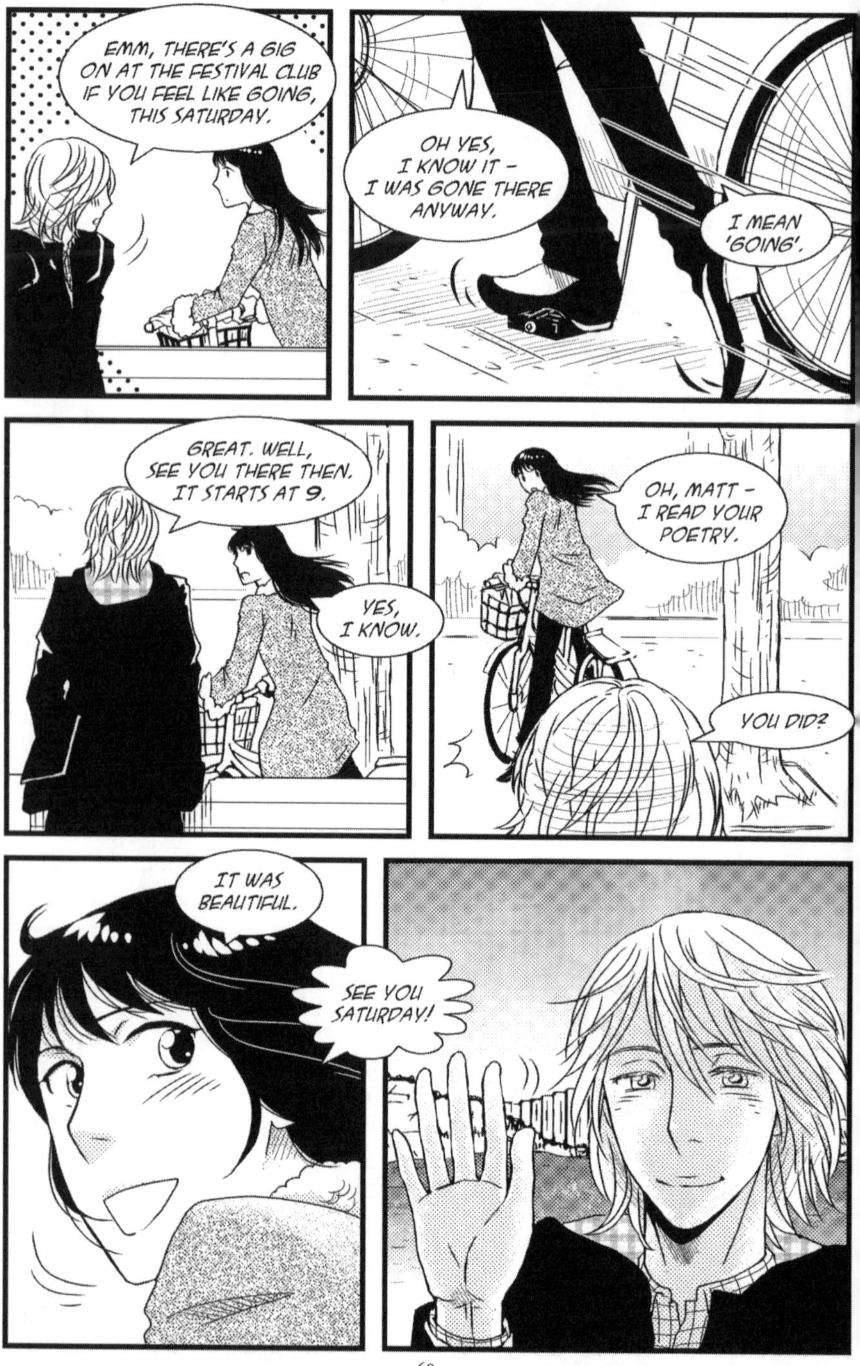
EMM, THERE'S A GIG ON AT THE FESTIVAL CLUB IF YOU FEEL LIKE GOING, THIS SATURDAY.
OH YES, I KNOW IT - I WAS GONE THERE ANYWAY.
I MEAN 'GOING'.
GREAT. WELL, SEE YOU THERE THEN. IT STARTS AT 9.
YES, I KNOW.
OH, MATT - I READ YOUR POETRY.
YOU DID?
IT WAS BEAUTIFUL.
SEE YOU SATURDAY!

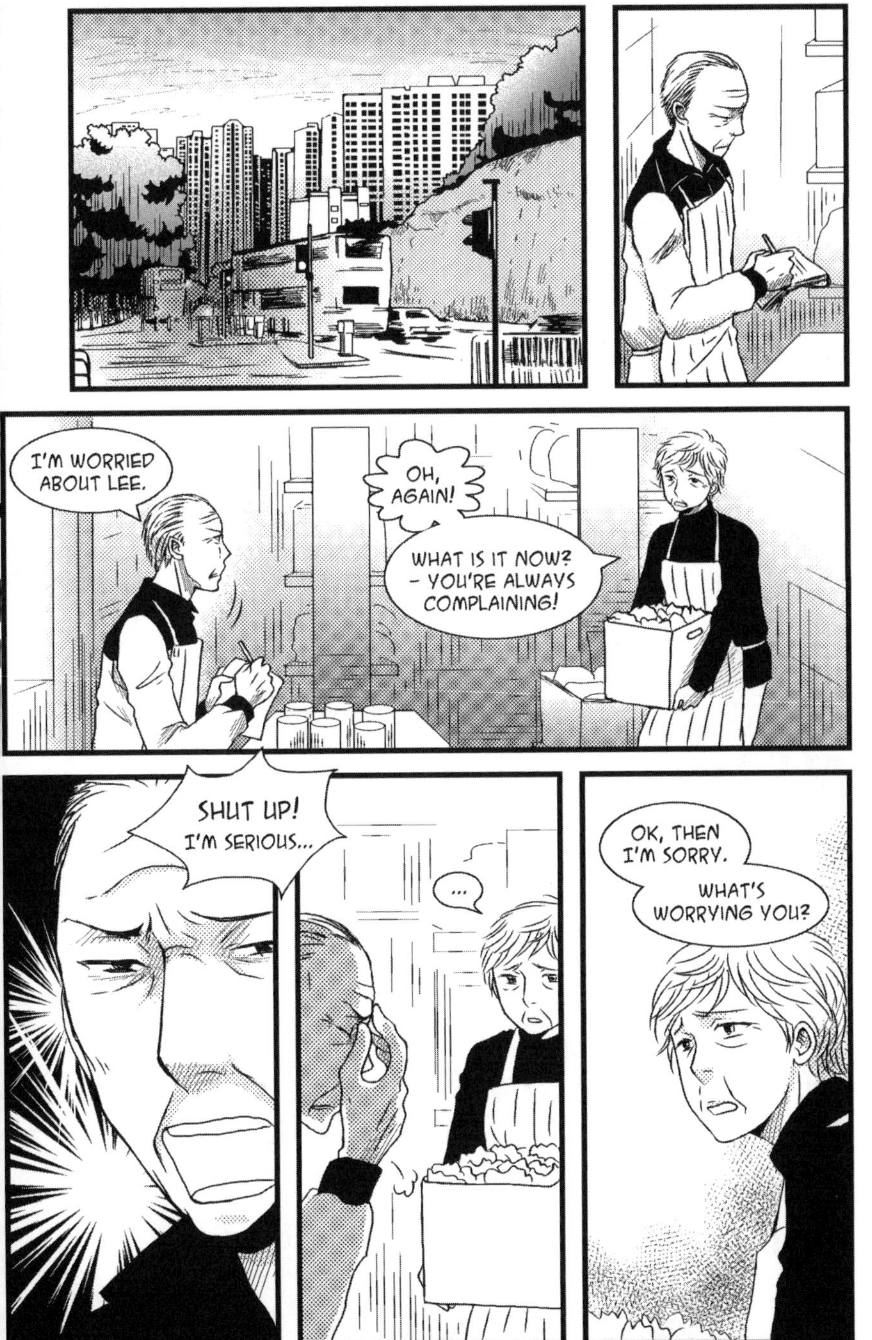
I'M WORRIED ABOUT LEE.
OH, AGAIN!
WHAT IS IT NOW? - YOU'RE ALWAYS COMPLAINING!
SHUT UP! I'M SERIOUS...
...
OK, THEN I'M SORRY.
WHAT'S WORRYING YOU?

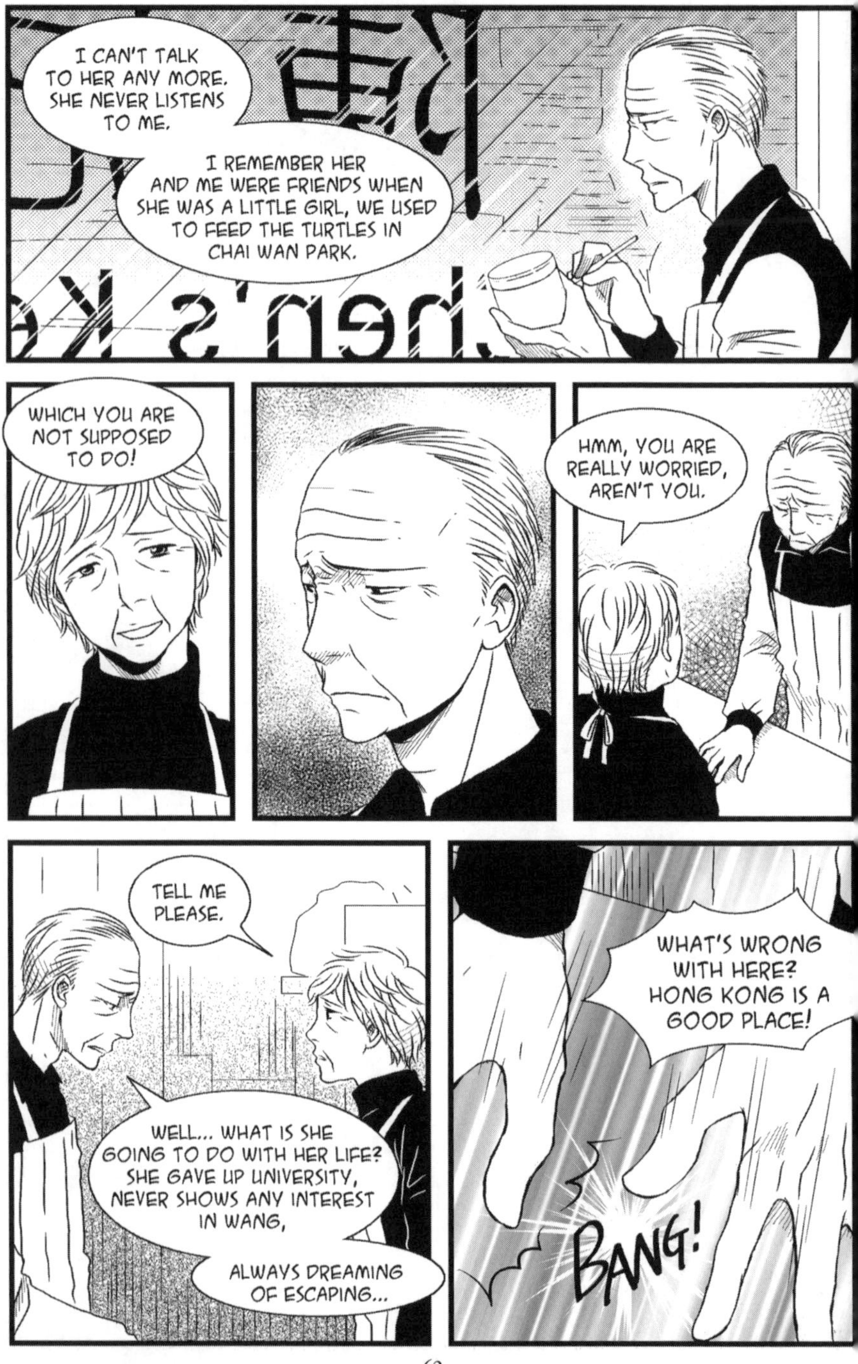

I CAN'T TALK TO HER ANY MORE. SHE NEVER LISTENS TO ME.
I REMEMBER HER AND ME WERE FRIENDS WHEN SHE WAS A LITTLE GIRL, WE USED TO FEED THE TURTLES IN CHAI WAN PARK.
WHICH YOU ARE NOT SUPPOSED TO DO!
HMM, YOU ARE REALLY WORRIED, AREN'T YOU.
TELL ME PLEASE.
WELL... WHAT IS SHE GOING TO DO WITH HER LIFE? SHE GAVE UP UNIVERSITY, NEVER SHOWS ANY INTEREST IN WANG,
ALWAYS DREAMING OF ESCAPING...
WHAT'S WRONG WITH HERE? HONG KONG IS A GOOD PLACE!
BANG!

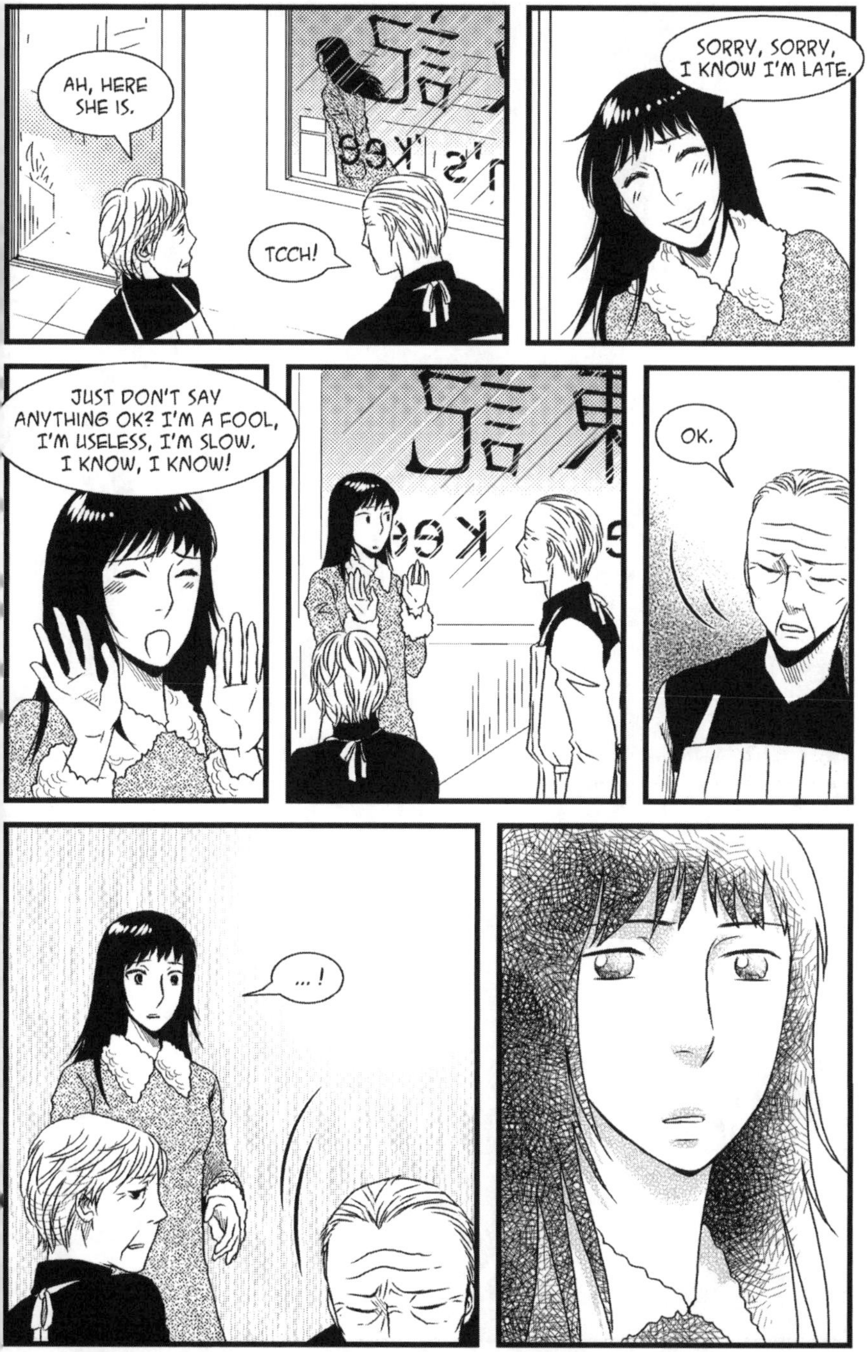
AH, HERE SHE IS.
TCCH!
SORRY, SORRY, I KNOW I'M LATE.
JUST DON'T SAY ANYTHING OK? I'M A FOOL, I'M USELESS, I'M SLOW. I KNOW, I KNOW!
OK.
...!

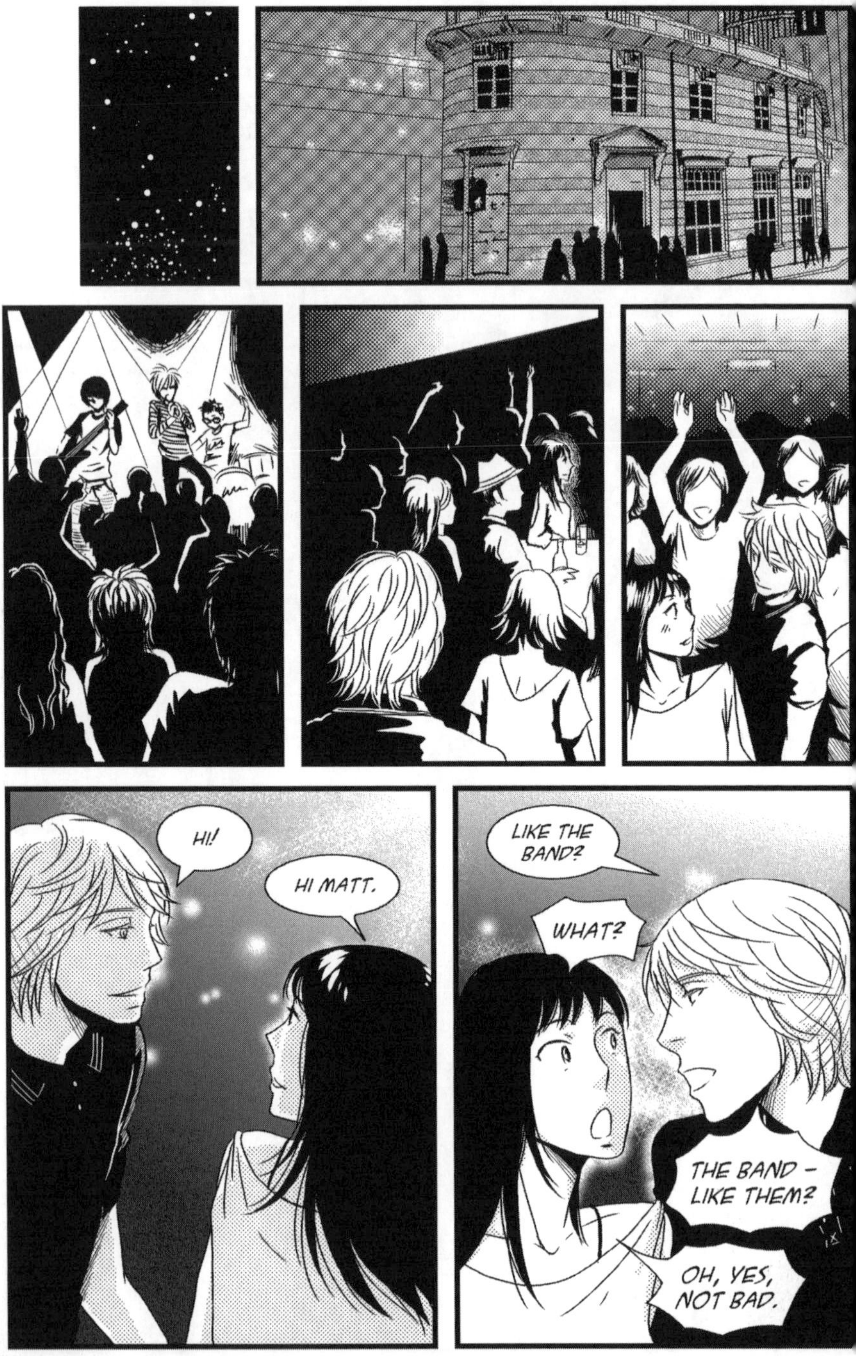
HI!
HI MATT.
LIKE THE BAND?
WHAT?
THE BAND - LIKE THEM?
OH, YES, NOT BAD.

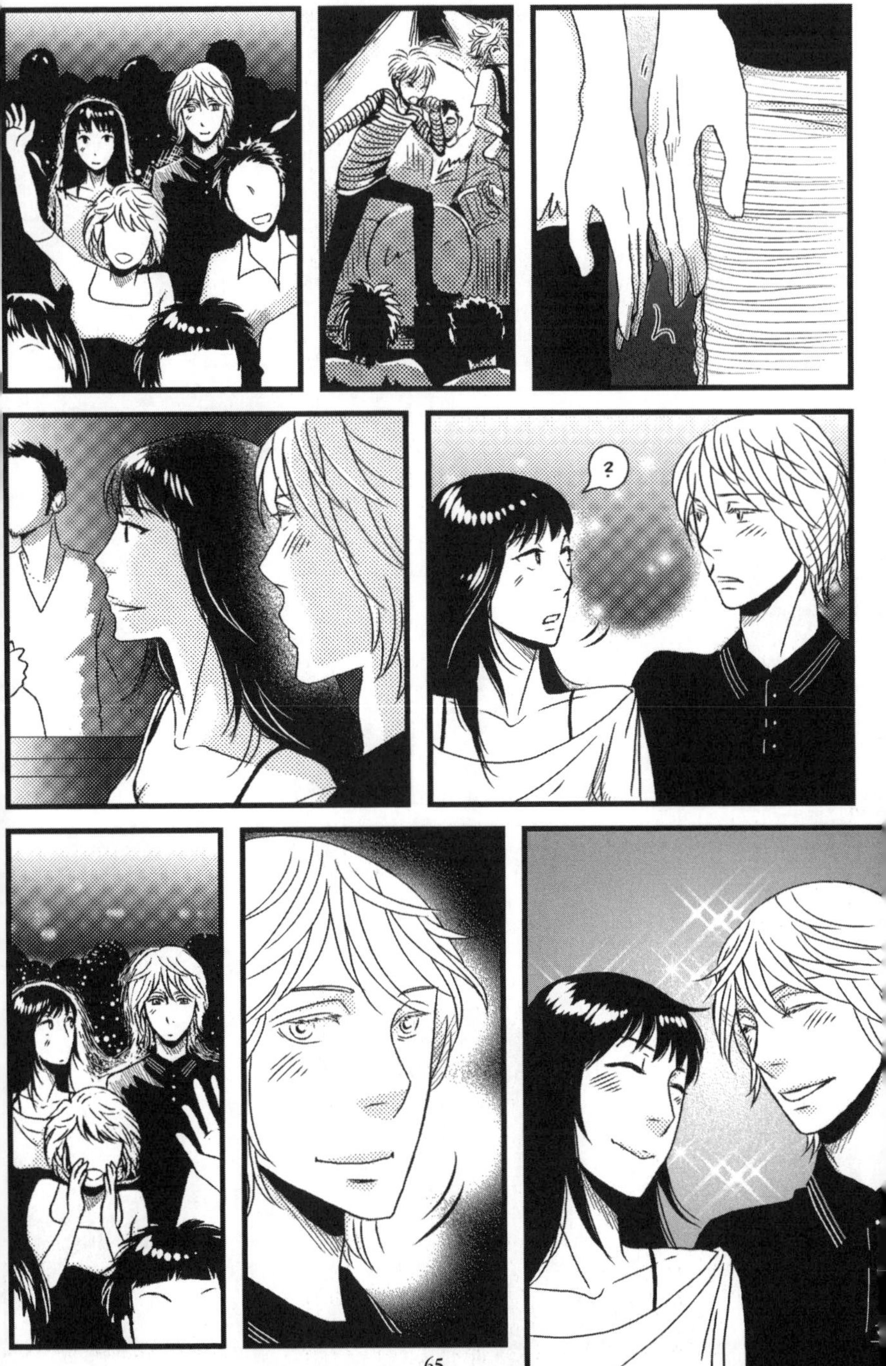
?

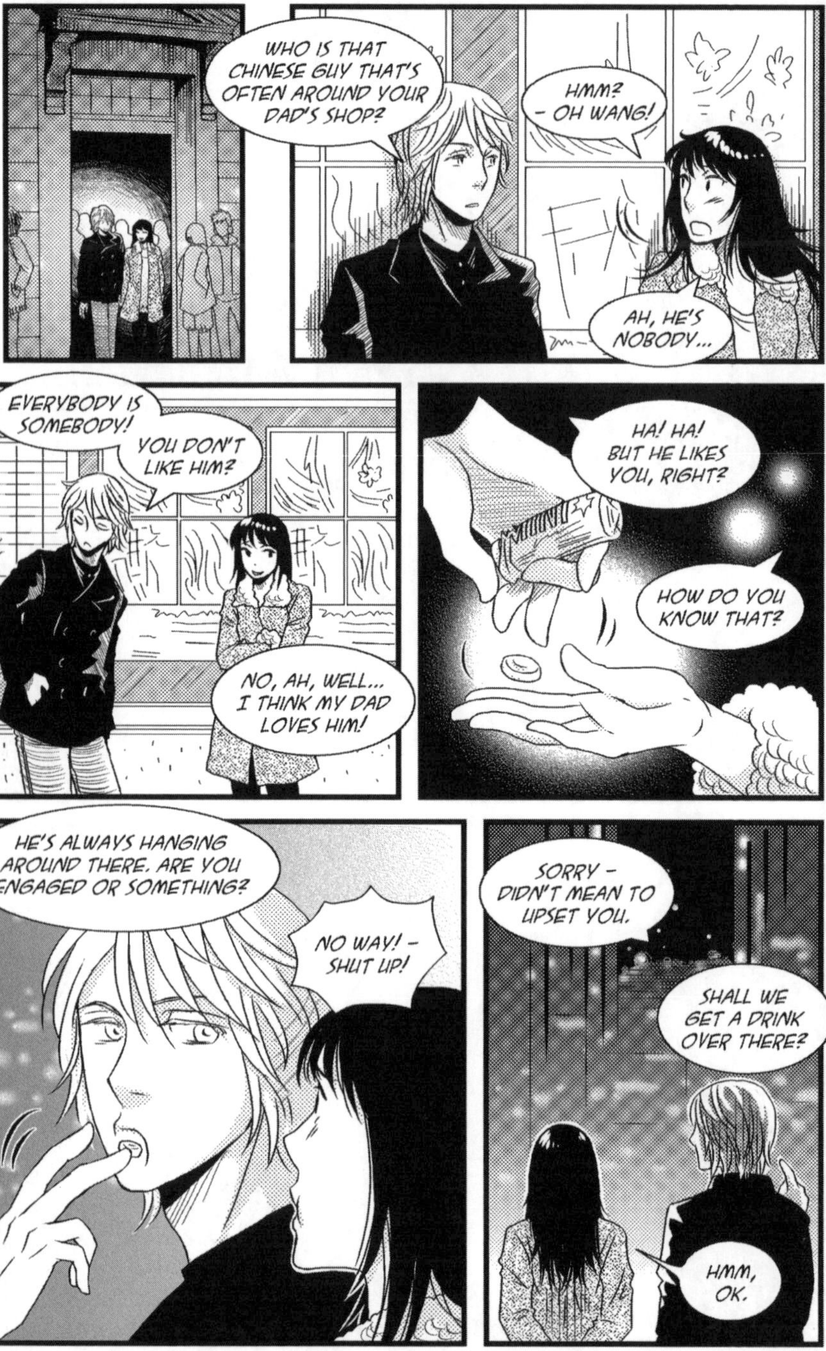
WHO IS THAT CHINESE GUY THAT'S OFTEN AROUND YOUR DAD'S SHOP?
HMM? - OH WANG!
AH, HE'S NOBODY...
EVERYBODY IS SOMEBODY!
YOU DON'T LIKE HIM?
NO, AH, WELL... I THINK MY DAD LOVES HIM!
HA! HA! BUT HE LIKES YOU, RIGHT?
HOW DO YOU KNOW THAT?
HE'S ALWAYS HANGING AROUND THERE. ARE YOU ENGAGED OR SOMETHING?
NO WAY! - SHUT UP!
SORRY - DIDN'T MEAN TO UPSET YOU.
SHALL WE GET A DRINK OVER THERE?
HMM, OK.

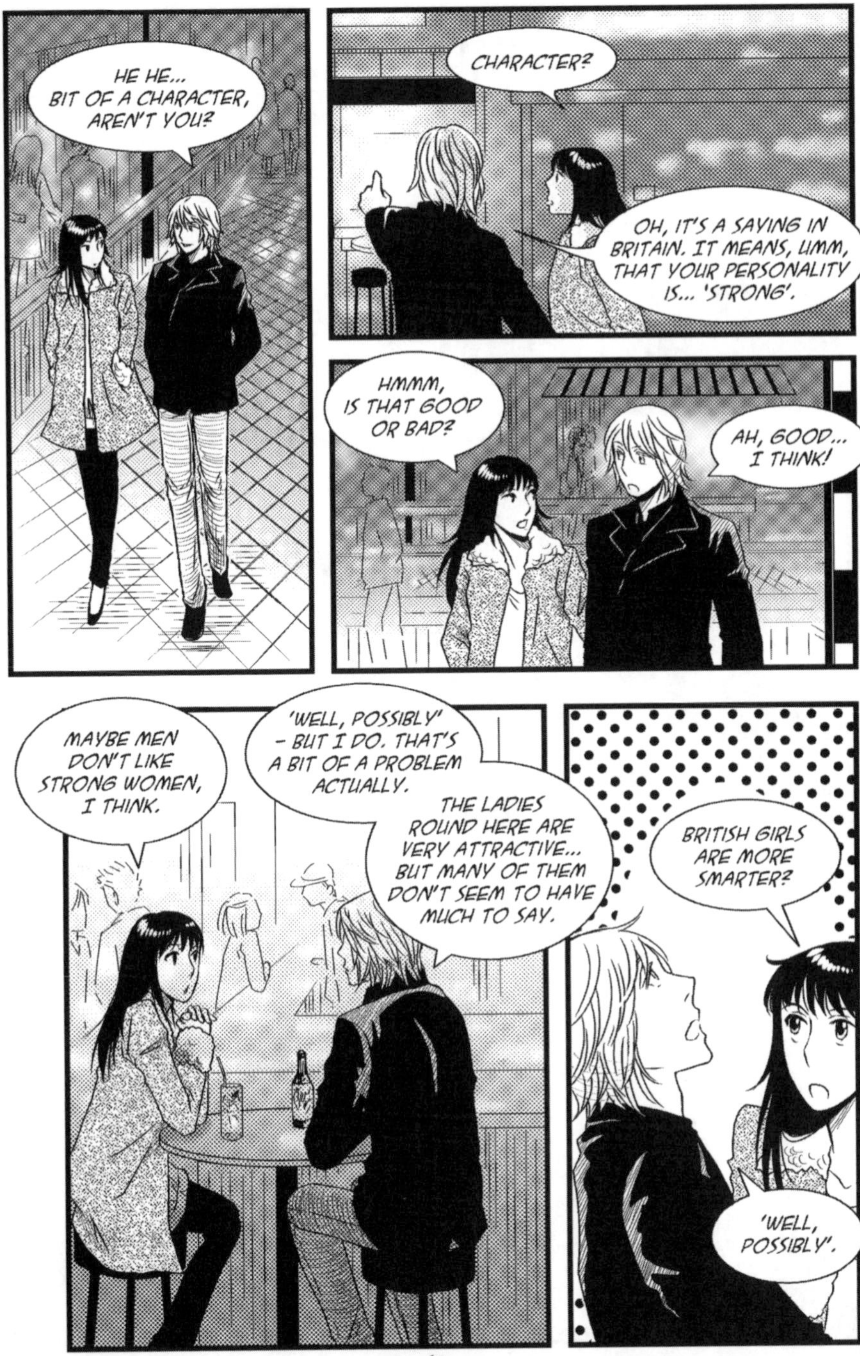
HE HE... BIT OF A CHARACTER, AREN'T YOU?
CHARACTER?
OH, IT'S A SAYING IN BRITAIN. IT MEANS, UMM, THAT YOUR PERSONALITY IS... 'STRONG'.
HMMM, IS THAT GOOD OR BAD?
AH, GOOD... I THINK!
MAYBE MEN DON'T LIKE STRONG WOMEN, I THINK.
'WELL, POSSIBLY' - BUT I DO. THAT'S A BIT OF A PROBLEM ACTUALLY.
THE LADIES ROUND HERE ARE VERY ATTRACTIVE... BUT MANY OF THEM DON'T SEEM TO HAVE MUCH TO SAY.
BRITISH GIRLS ARE MORE SMARTER?
'WELL, POSSIBLY'.

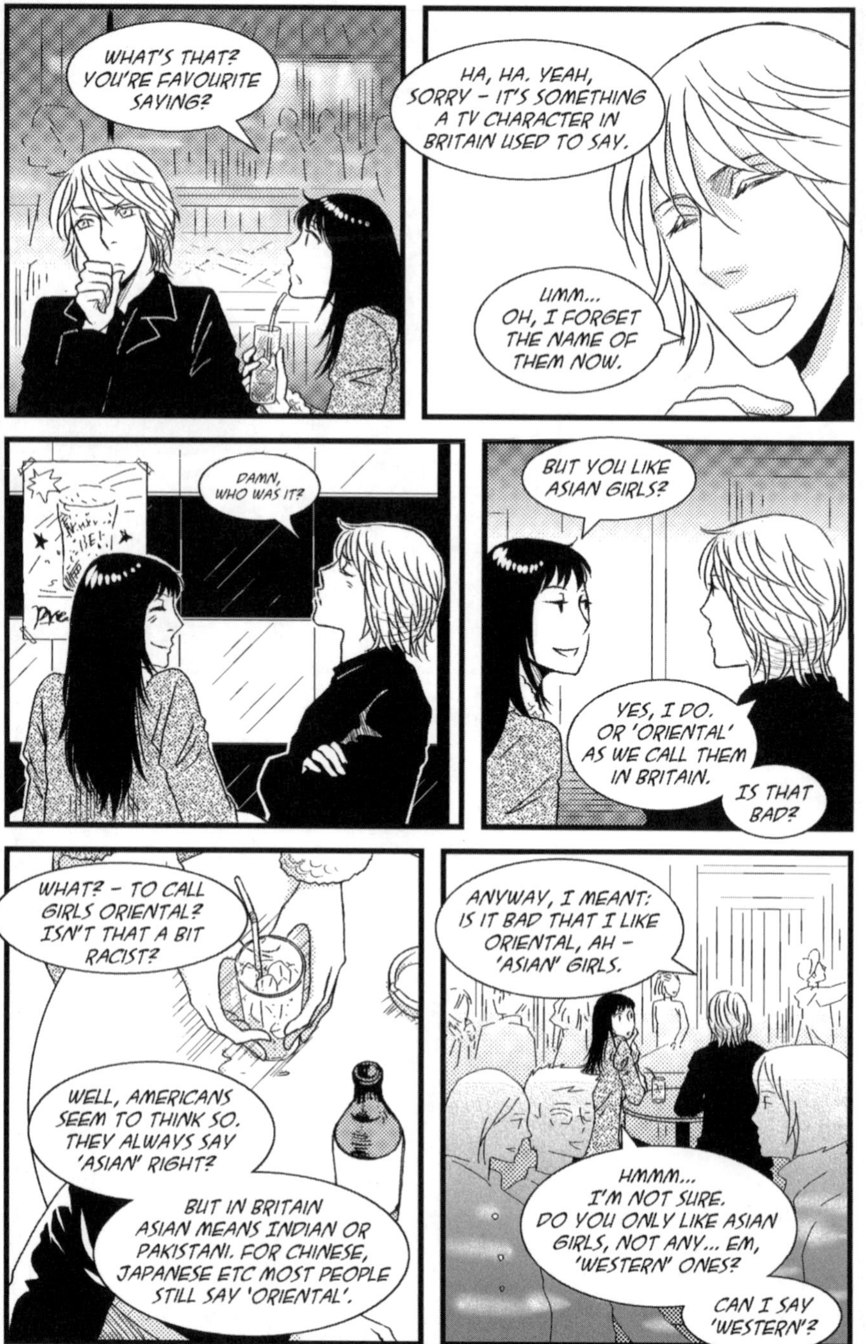
WHAT'S THAT? YOU'RE FAVOURITE SAYING?
HA, HA. YEAH, SORRY – IT'S SOMETHING A TV CHARACTER IN BRITAIN USED TO SAY.
UMM... OH, I FORGET THE NAME OF THEM NOW.
DAMN, WHO WAS IT?
BUT YOU LIKE ASIAN GIRLS?
YES, I DO. OR 'ORIENTAL' AS WE CALL THEM IN BRITAIN.
IS THAT BAD?
WHAT? – TO CALL GIRLS ORIENTAL? ISN'T THAT A BIT RACIST?
WELL, AMERICANS SEEM TO THINK SO. THEY ALWAYS SAY 'ASIAN' RIGHT?
BUT IN BRITAIN ASIAN MEANS INDIAN OR PAKISTANI. FOR CHINESE, JAPANESE ETC MOST PEOPLE STILL SAY 'ORIENTAL'.
ANYWAY, I MEANT: IS IT BAD THAT I LIKE ORIENTAL, AH – 'ASIAN' GIRLS.
HMMM... I'M NOT SURE. DO YOU ONLY LIKE ASIAN GIRLS, NOT ANY... EM, 'WESTERN' ONES?
CAN I SAY 'WESTERN'?

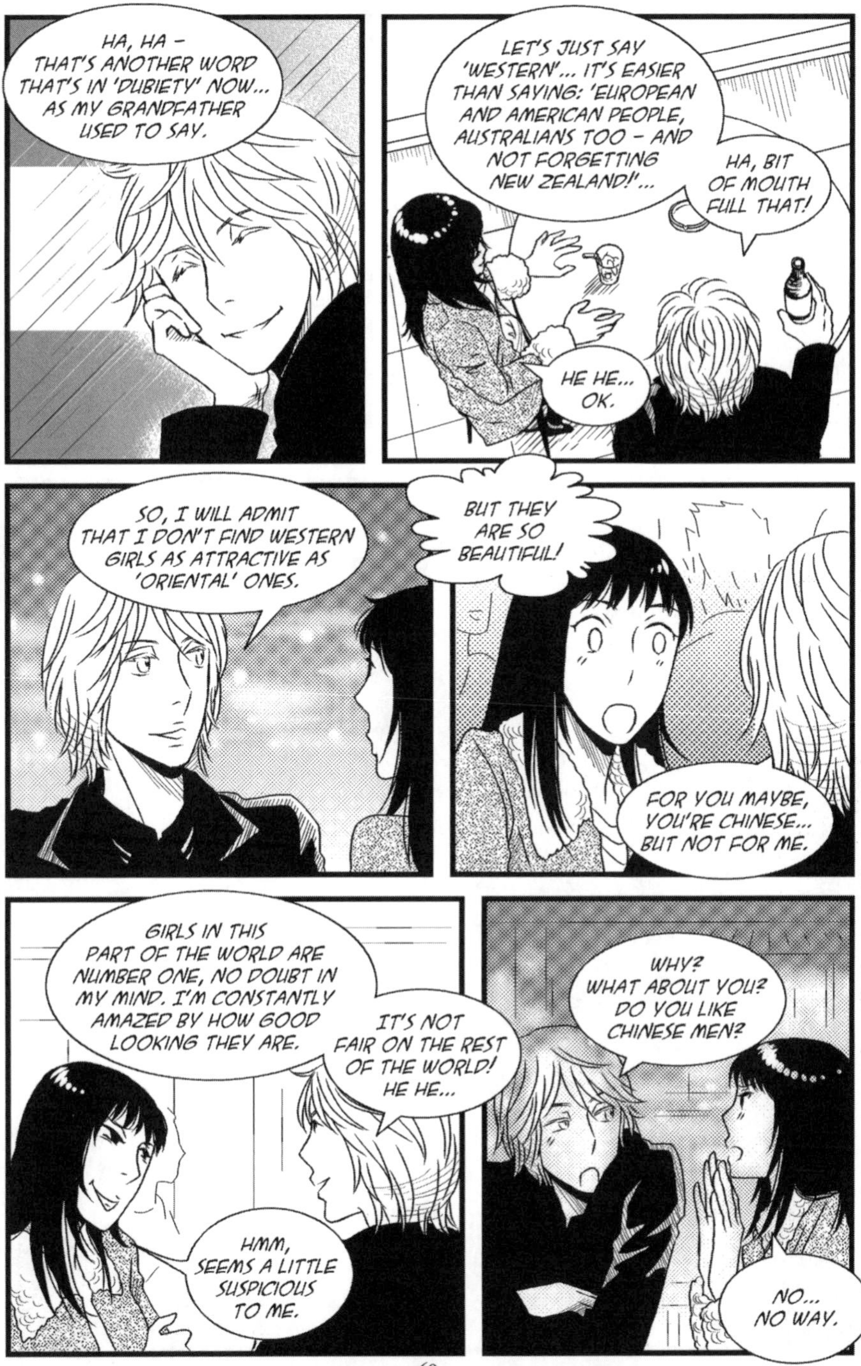
HA, HA - THAT'S ANOTHER WORD THAT'S IN 'DUBIETY' NOW... AS MY GRANDFATHER USED TO SAY.
LET'S JUST SAY 'WESTERN'... IT'S EASIER THAN SAYING: 'EUROPEAN AND AMERICAN PEOPLE, AUSTRALIANS TOO - AND NOT FORGETTING NEW ZEALAND!'...
HA, BIT OF MOUTH FULL THAT!
HE HE... OK.
SO, I WILL ADMIT THAT I DON'T FIND WESTERN GIRLS AS ATTRACTIVE AS 'ORIENTAL' ONES.
BUT THEY ARE SO BEAUTIFUL!
FOR YOU MAYBE, YOU'RE CHINESE... BUT NOT FOR ME.
GIRLS IN THIS PART OF THE WORLD ARE NUMBER ONE, NO DOUBT IN MY MIND. I'M CONSTANTLY AMAZED BY HOW GOOD LOOKING THEY ARE.
IT'S NOT FAIR ON THE REST OF THE WORLD! HE HE...
HMM, SEEMS A LITTLE SUSPICIOUS TO ME.
WHY? WHAT ABOUT YOU? DO YOU LIKE CHINESE MEN?
NO... NO WAY.

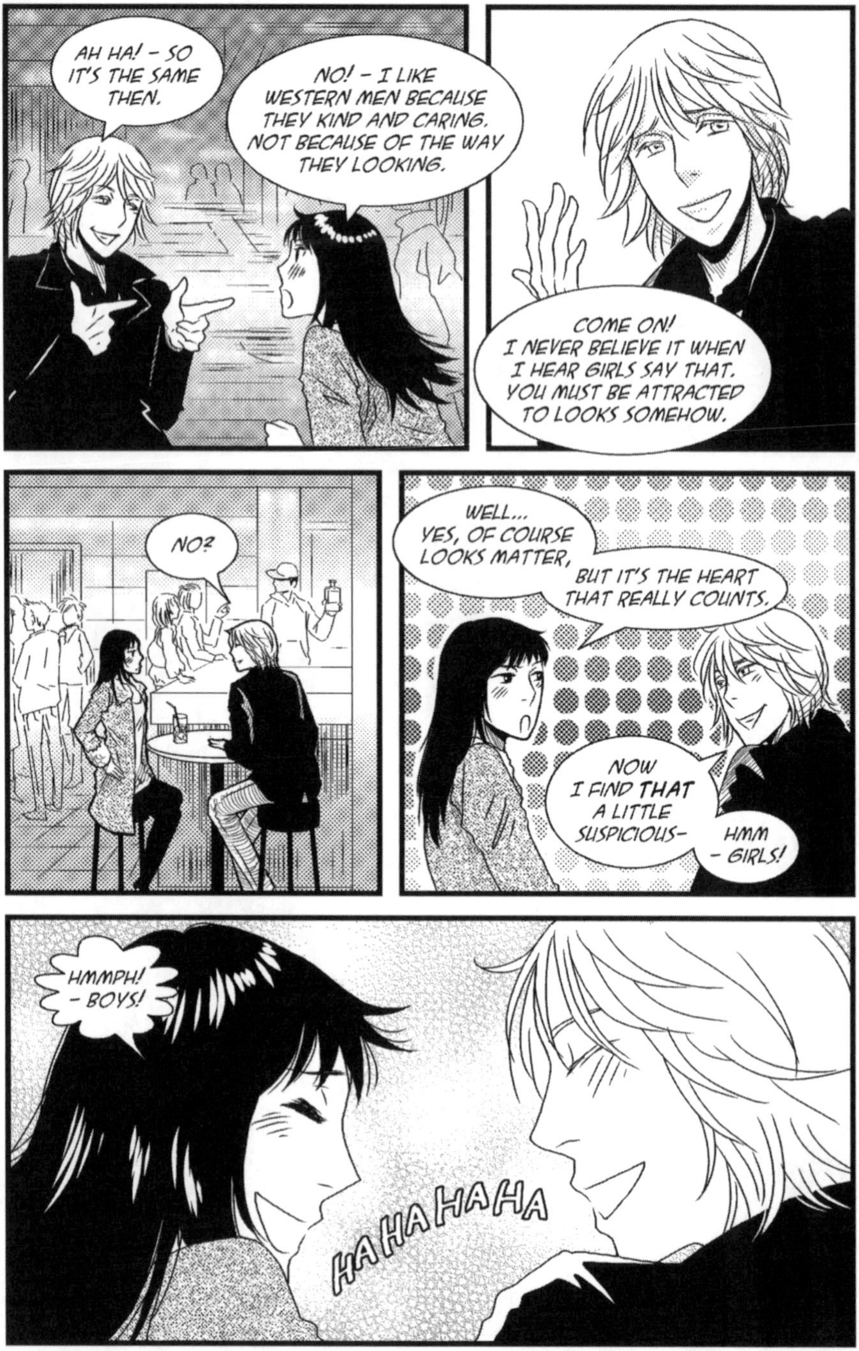
AH HA! - SO IT'S THE SAME THEN.
NO! - I LIKE WESTERN MEN BECAUSE THEY KIND AND CARING. NOT BECAUSE OF THE WAY THEY LOOKING.
COME ON! I NEVER BELIEVE IT WHEN I HEAR GIRLS SAY THAT. YOU MUST BE ATTRACTED TO LOOKS SOMEHOW.
NO?
WELL... YES, OF COURSE LOOKS MATTER,
BUT IT'S THE HEART THAT REALLY COUNTS.
NOW I FIND THAT A LITTLE SUSPICIOUS-
HMM - GIRLS!
HMMPH! - BOYS!
HA HA HA HA HA HA

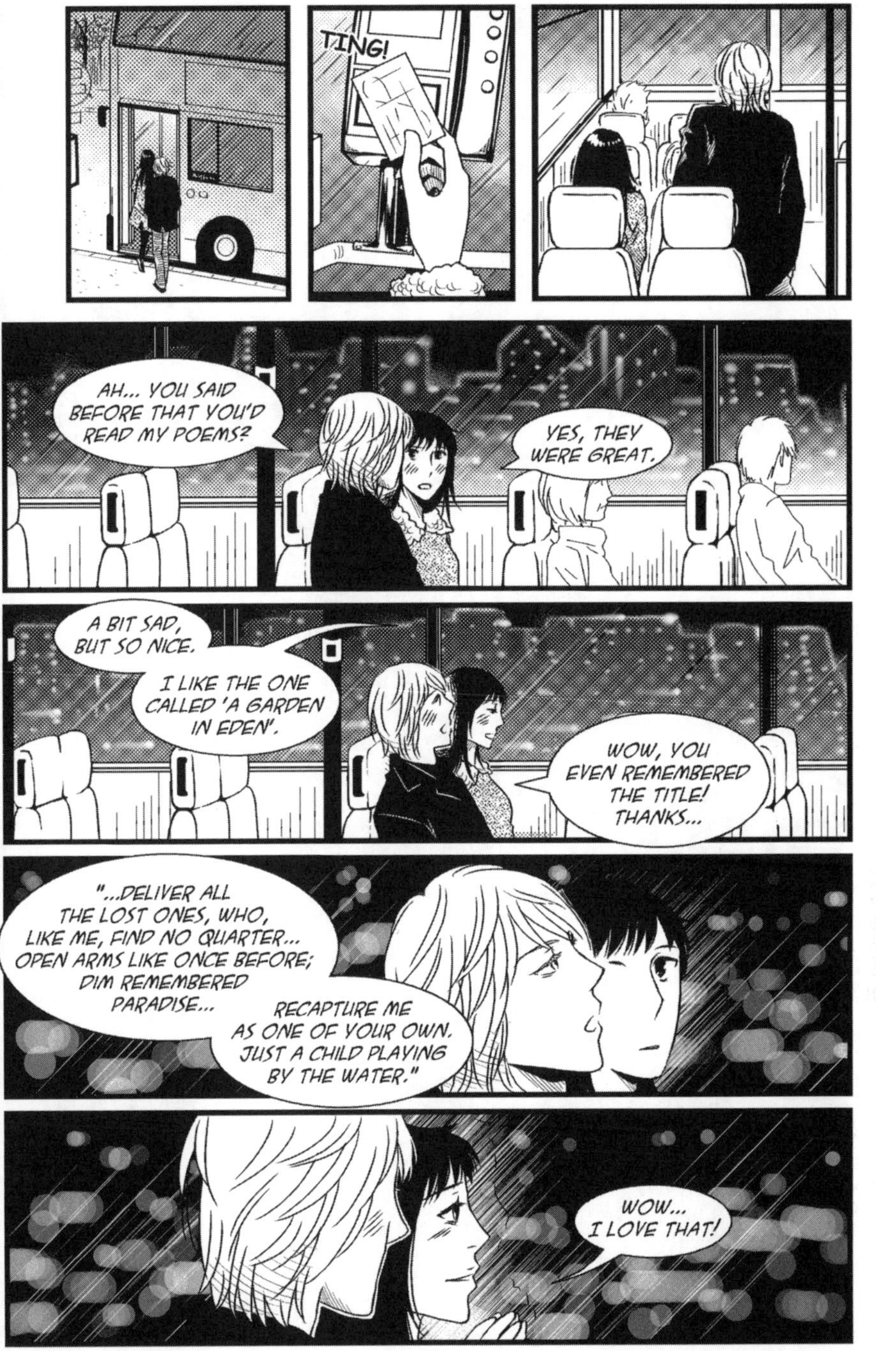
TING!
AH... YOU SAID BEFORE THAT YOU'D READ MY POEMS?
YES, THEY WERE GREAT.
A BIT SAD, BUT SO NICE.
I LIKE THE ONE CALLED 'A GARDEN IN EDEN'.
WOW, YOU EVEN REMEMBERED THE TITLE! THANKS...
"...DELIVER ALL THE LOST ONES, WHO, LIKE ME, FIND NO QUARTER... OPEN ARMS LIKE ONCE BEFORE; DIM REMEMBERED PARADISE...
RECAPTURE ME AS ONE OF YOUR OWN. JUST A CHILD PLAYING BY THE WATER."
WOW... I LOVE THAT!

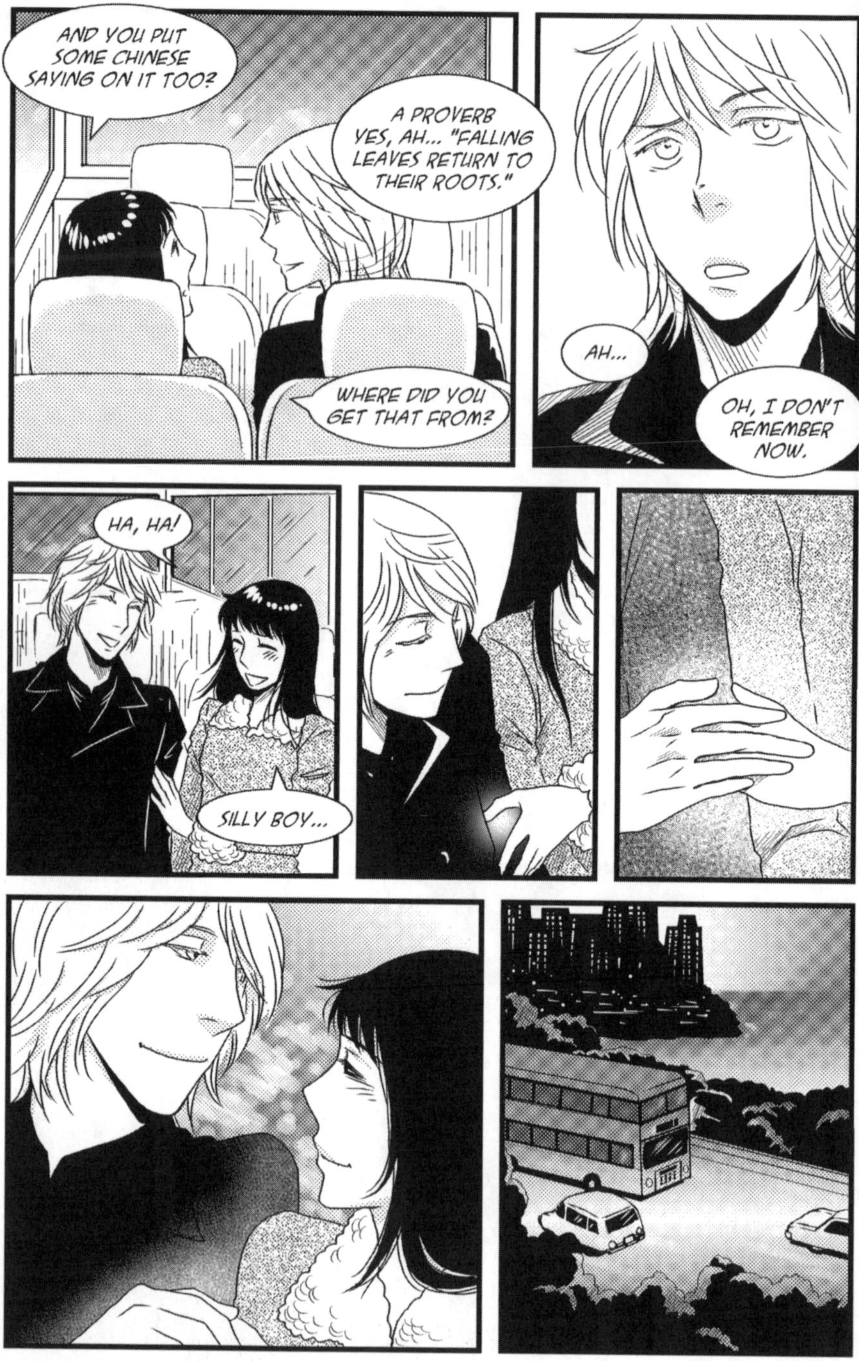
AND YOU PUT SOME CHINESE SAYING ON IT TOO?
A PROVERB YES, AH... "FALLING LEAVES RETURN TO THEIR ROOTS."
WHERE DID YOU GET THAT FROM?
AH...
OH, I DON'T REMEMBER NOW.
HA, HA!
SILLY BOY...

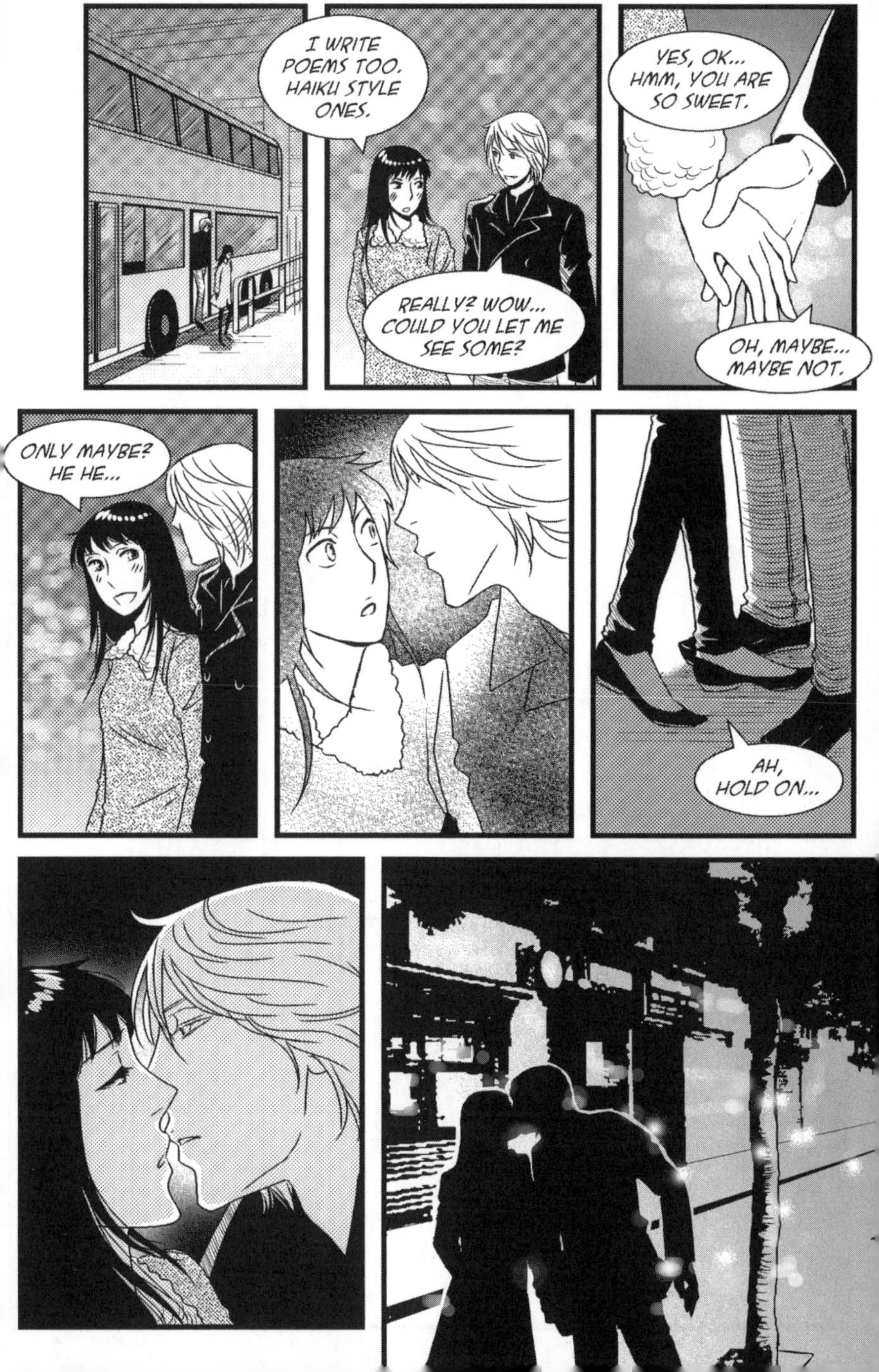
I WRITE POEMS TOO. HAIKU STYLE ONES.
REALLY? WOW... COULD YOU LET ME SEE SOME?
YES, OK... HMM, YOU ARE SO SWEET.
OH, MAYBE... MAYBE NOT.
ONLY MAYBE? HE HE...
AH, HOLD ON...

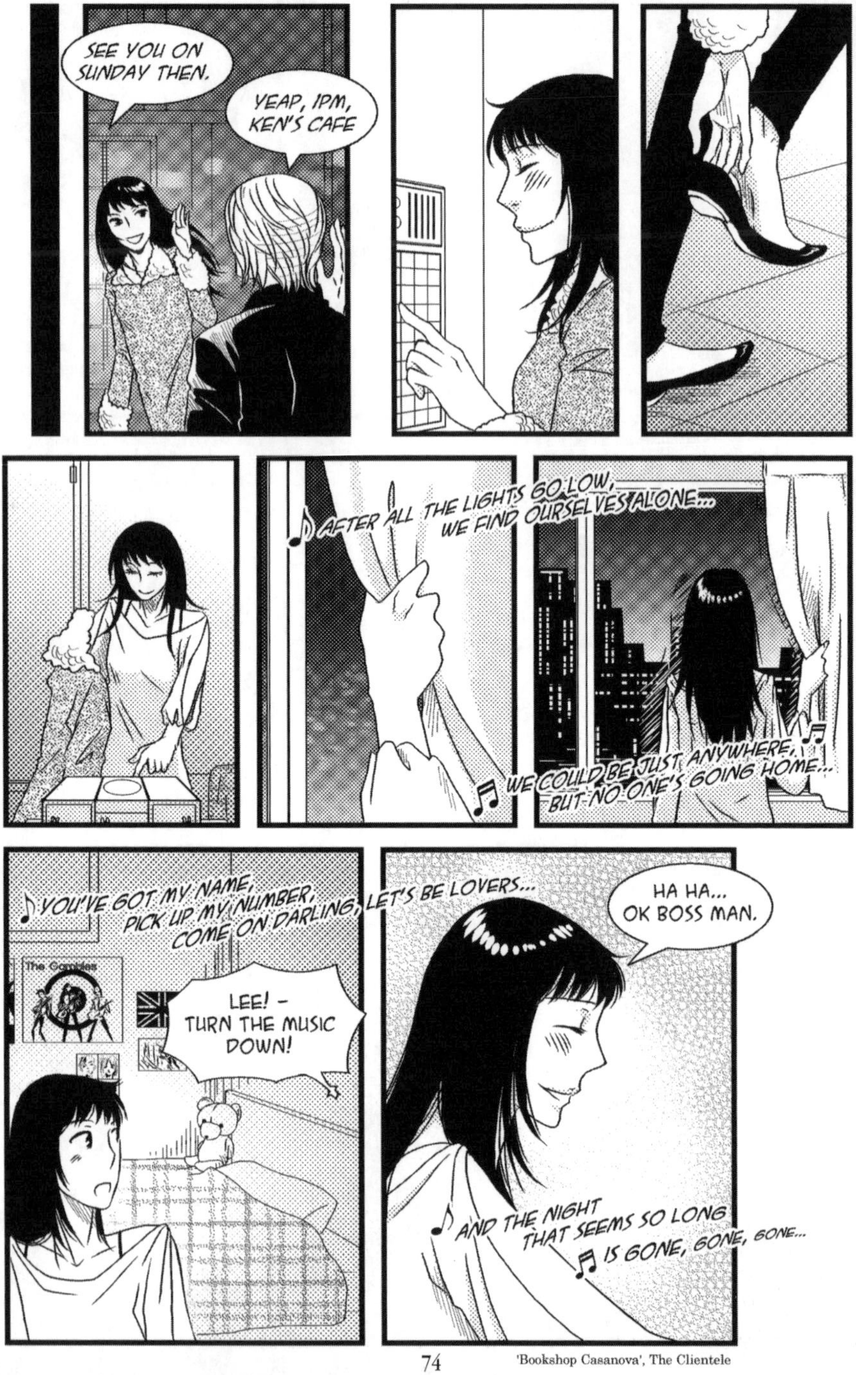
SEE YOU ON SUNDAY THEN.
YEAP, 1PM, KEN'S CAFE
AFTER ALL THE LIGHTS GO LOW, WE FIND OURSELVES ALONE...
WE COULD BE JUST ANYWHERE, BUT NO ONE'S GOING HOME...
YOU'VE GOT MY NAME, PICK UP MY NUMBER, COME ON DARLING, LET'S BE LOVERS...
LEE! - TURN THE MUSIC DOWN!
HA HA... OK BOSS MAN.
AND THE NIGHT THAT SEEMS SO LONG
IS GONE, GONE, GONE...

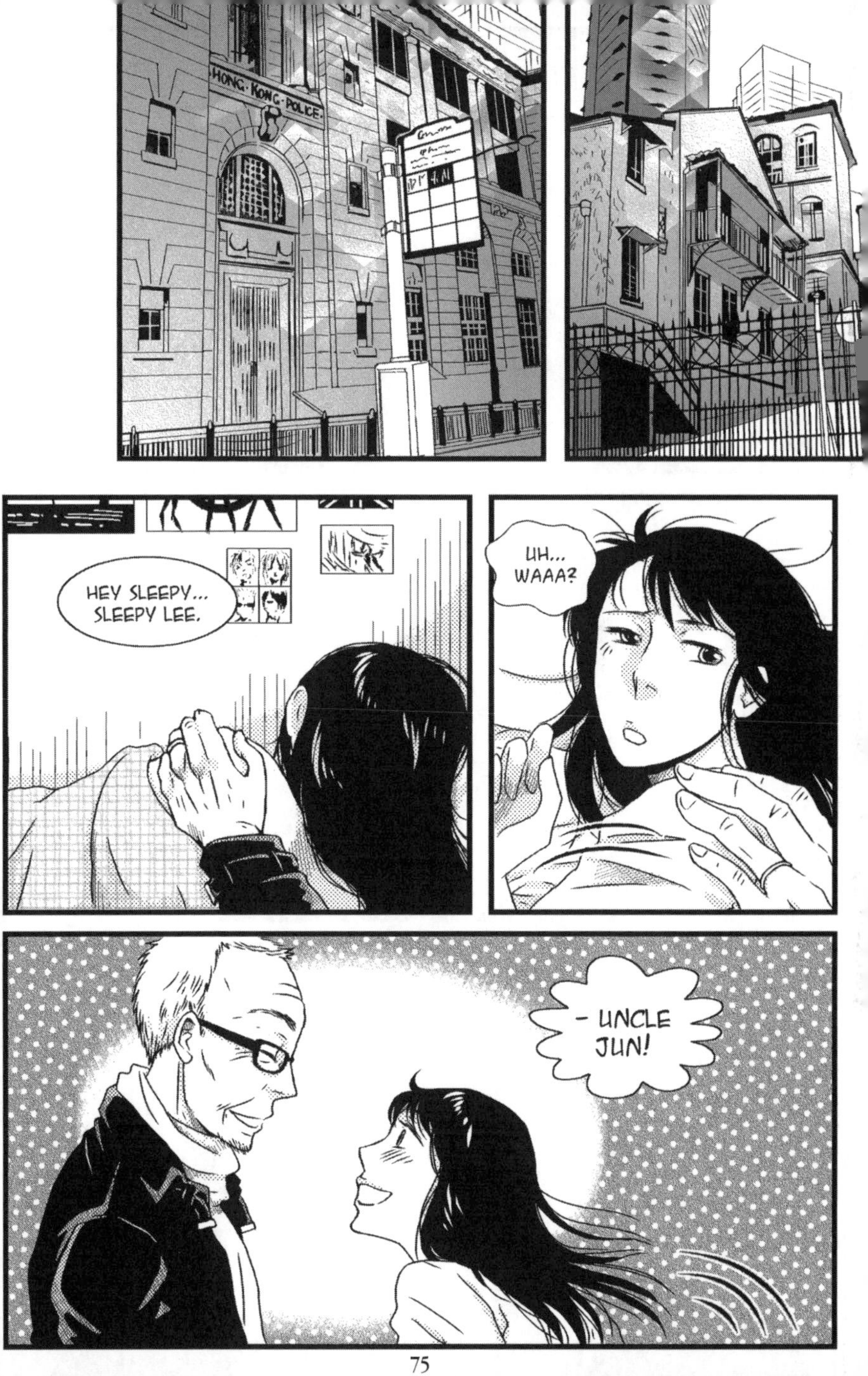
HONG·KONG·POLICE
HEY SLEEPY... SLEEPY LEE.
UH... WAAA?
- UNCLE JUN!

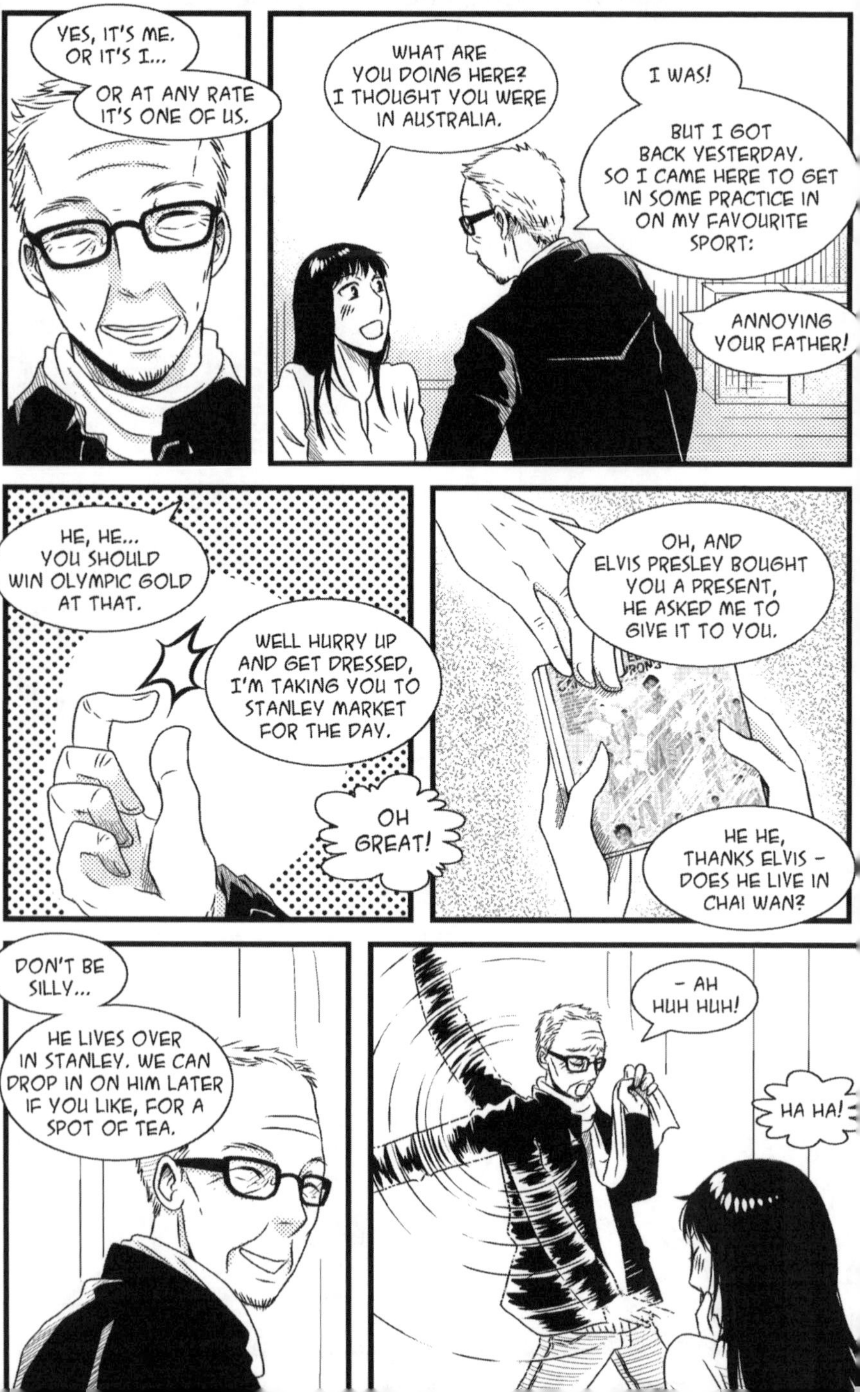

YES, IT'S ME. OR IT'S I...
OR AT ANY RATE IT'S ONE OF US.
WHAT ARE YOU DOING HERE? I THOUGHT YOU WERE IN AUSTRALIA.
I WAS!
BUT I GOT BACK YESTERDAY. SO I CAME HERE TO GET IN SOME PRACTICE IN ON MY FAVOURITE SPORT:
ANNOYING YOUR FATHER!
HE, HE... YOU SHOULD WIN OLYMPIC GOLD AT THAT.
WELL HURRY UP AND GET DRESSED, I'M TAKING YOU TO STANLEY MARKET FOR THE DAY.
OH GREAT!
OH, AND ELVIS PRESLEY BOUGHT YOU A PRESENT, HE ASKED ME TO GIVE IT TO YOU.
HE HE, THANKS ELVIS - DOES HE LIVE IN CHAI WAN?
DON'T BE SILLY...
HE LIVES OVER IN STANLEY. WE CAN DROP IN ON HIM LATER IF YOU LIKE, FOR A SPOT OF TEA.
- AH HUH HUH!
HA HA!

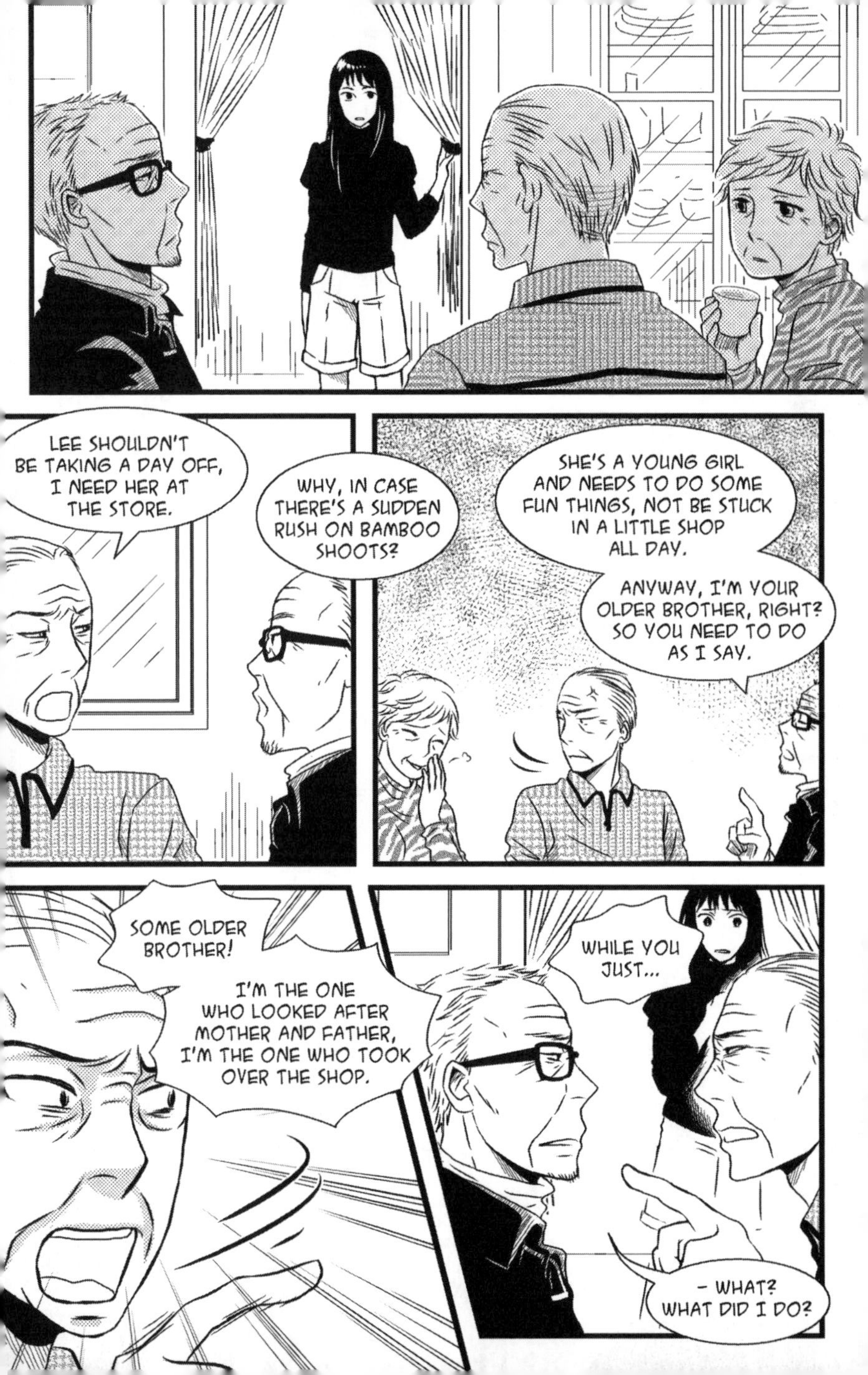
LEE SHOULDN'T BE TAKING A DAY OFF, I NEED HER AT THE STORE.
WHY, IN CASE THERE'S A SUDDEN RUSH ON BAMBOO SHOOTS?
SHE'S A YOUNG GIRL AND NEEDS TO DO SOME FUN THINGS, NOT BE STUCK IN A LITTLE SHOP ALL DAY.
ANYWAY, I'M YOUR OLDER BROTHER, RIGHT? SO YOU NEED TO DO AS I SAY.
SOME OLDER BROTHER!
I'M THE ONE WHO LOOKED AFTER MOTHER AND FATHER, I'M THE ONE WHO TOOK OVER THE SHOP.
WHILE YOU JUST...
- WHAT? WHAT DID I DO?

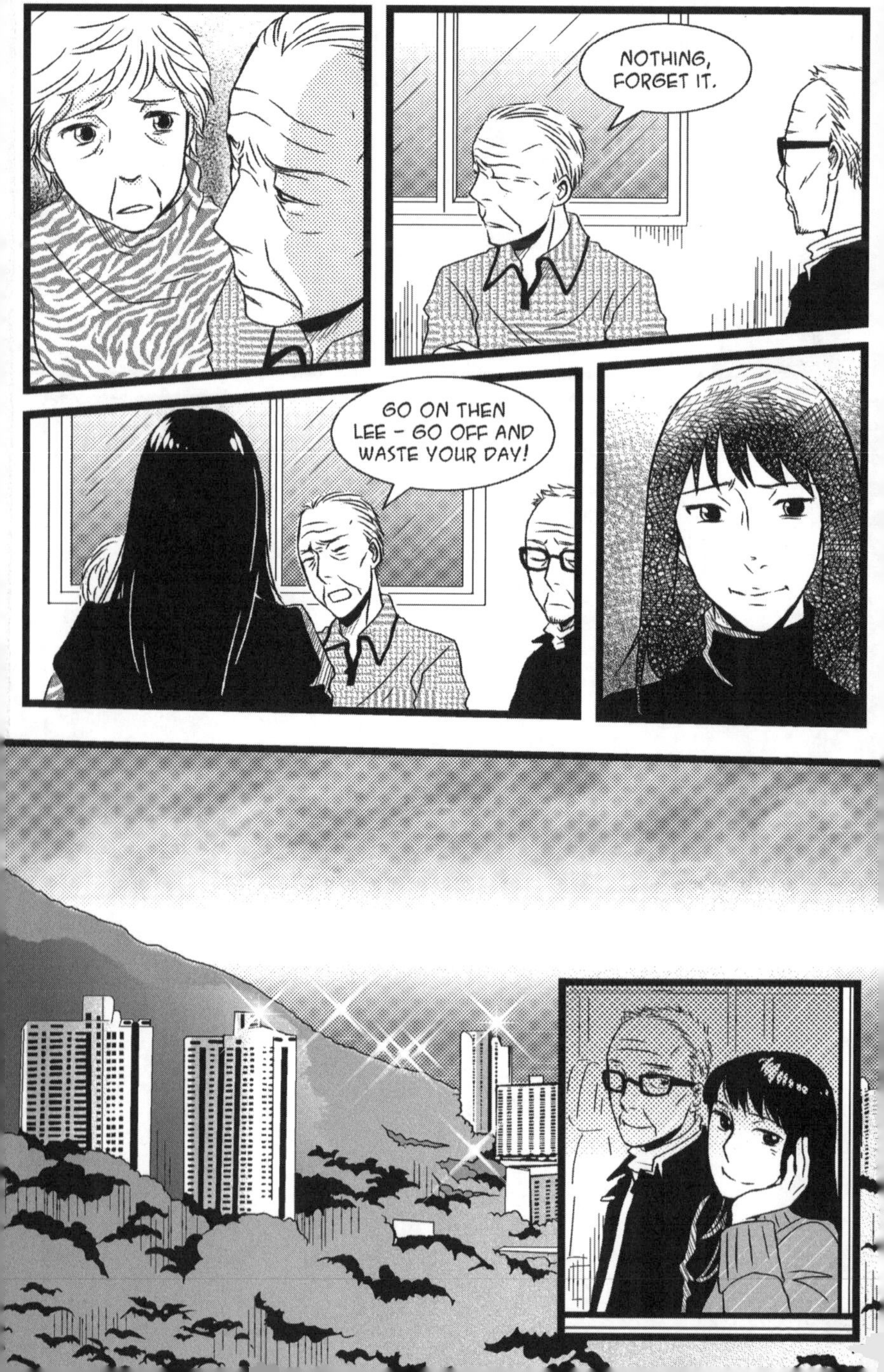
NOTHING, FORGET IT.
GO ON THEN LEE - GO OFF AND WASTE YOUR DAY!

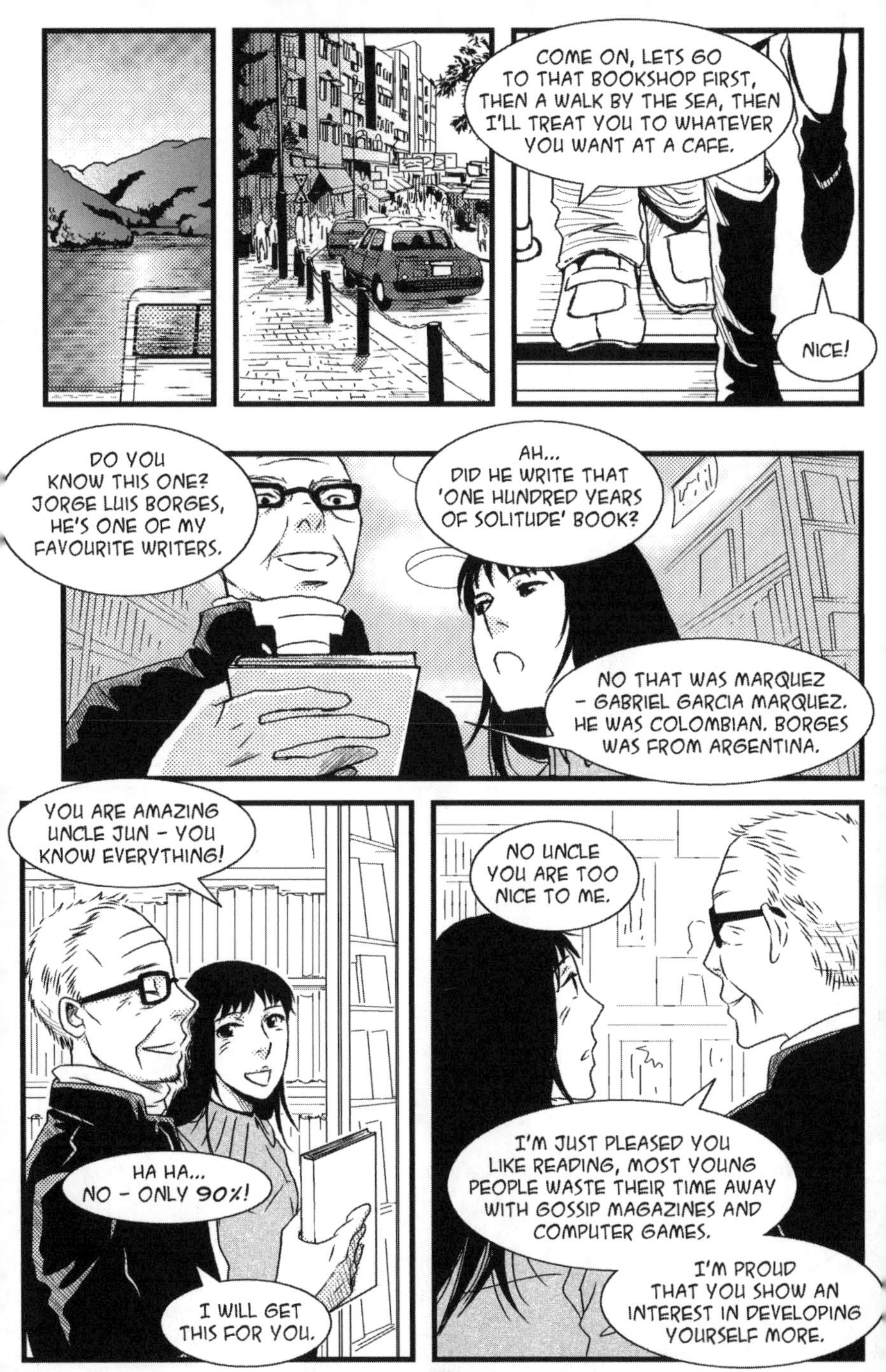
COME ON, LETS GO TO THAT BOOKSHOP FIRST, THEN A WALK BY THE SEA, THEN I'LL TREAT YOU TO WHATEVER YOU WANT AT A CAFE.
NICE!
DO YOU KNOW THIS ONE? JORGE LUIS BORGES, HE'S ONE OF MY FAVOURITE WRITERS.
AH... DID HE WRITE THAT 'ONE HUNDRED YEARS OF SOLITUDE' BOOK?
NO THAT WAS MARQUEZ - GABRIEL GARCIA MARQUEZ. HE WAS COLOMBIAN. BORGES WAS FROM ARGENTINA.
YOU ARE AMAZING UNCLE JUN - YOU KNOW EVERYTHING!
HA HA... NO - ONLY 90%!
I WILL GET THIS FOR YOU.
NO UNCLE YOU ARE TOO NICE TO ME.
I'M JUST PLEASED YOU LIKE READING, MOST YOUNG PEOPLE WASTE THEIR TIME AWAY WITH GOSSIP MAGAZINES AND COMPUTER GAMES.
I'M PROUD THAT YOU SHOW AN INTEREST IN DEVELOPING YOURSELF MORE.

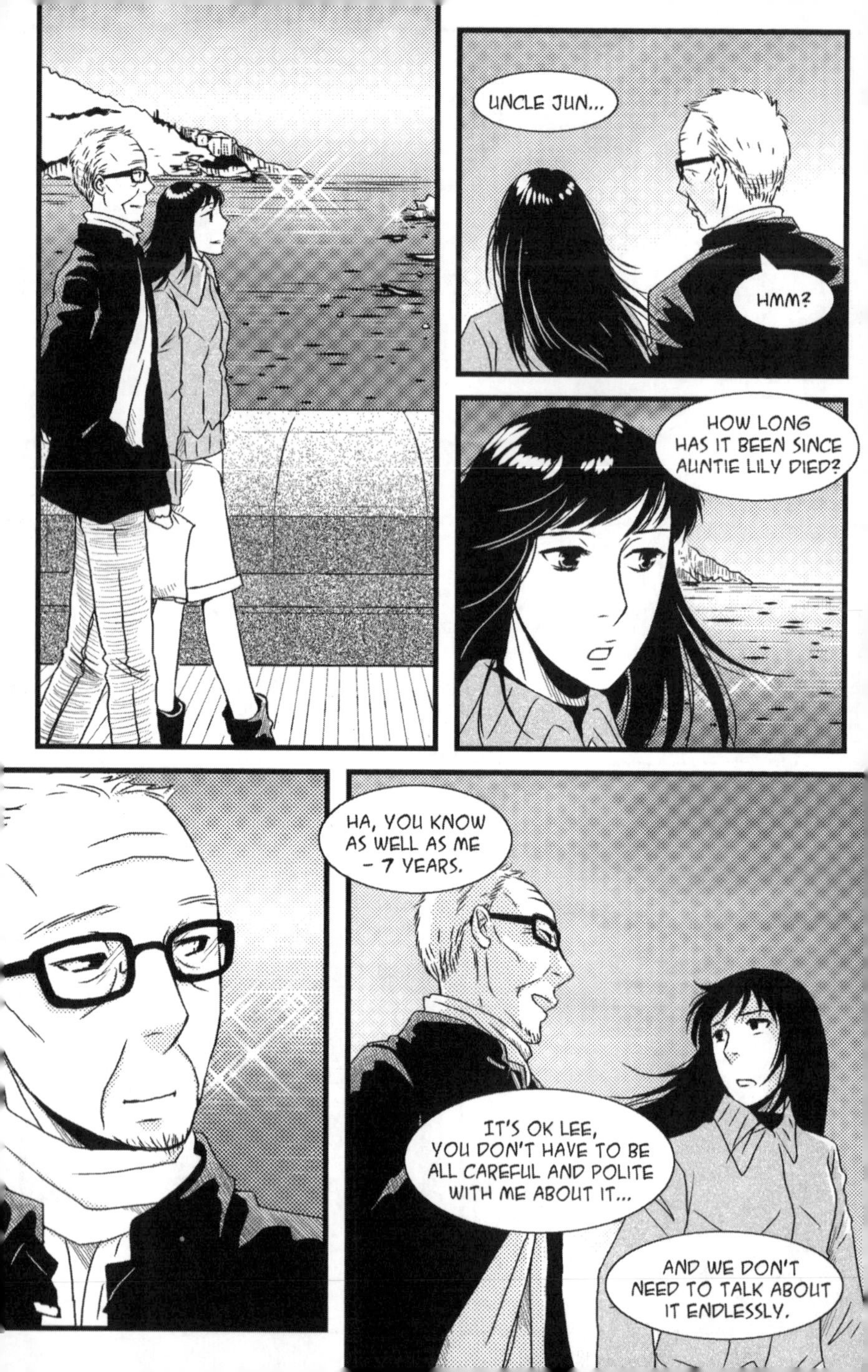
UNCLE JUN...
HMM?
HOW LONG HAS IT BEEN SINCE AUNTIE LILY DIED?
HA, YOU KNOW AS WELL AS ME - 7 YEARS.
IT'S OK LEE, YOU DON'T HAVE TO BE ALL CAREFUL AND POLITE WITH ME ABOUT IT...
AND WE DON'T NEED TO TALK ABOUT IT ENDLESSLY.

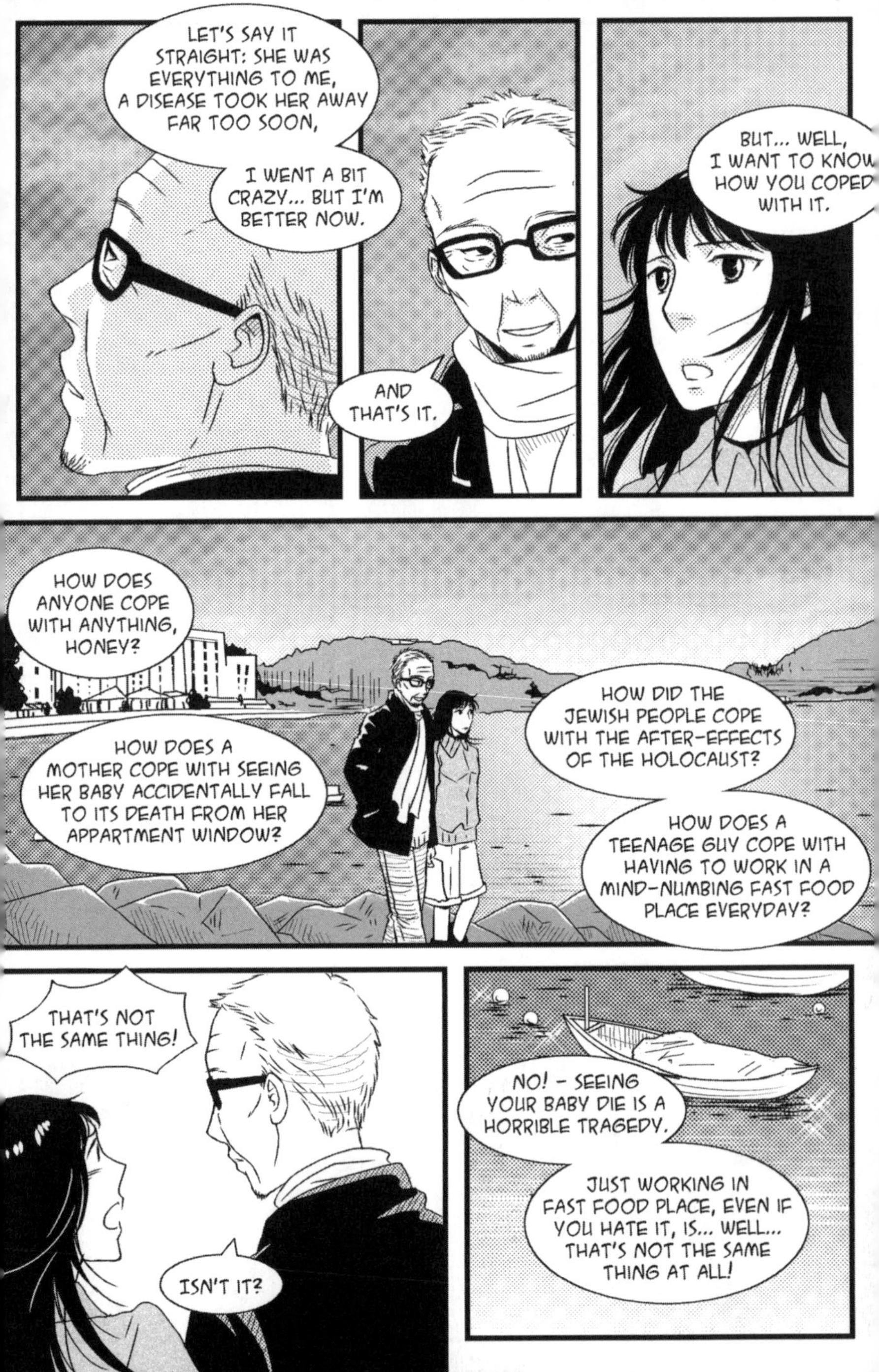
LET'S SAY IT STRAIGHT: SHE WAS EVERYTHING TO ME, A DISEASE TOOK HER AWAY FAR TOO SOON,
I WENT A BIT CRAZY... BUT I'M BETTER NOW.
AND THAT'S IT.
BUT... WELL, I WANT TO KNOW HOW YOU COPED WITH IT.
HOW DOES ANYONE COPE WITH ANYTHING, HONEY?
HOW DOES A MOTHER COPE WITH SEEING HER BABY ACCIDENTALLY FALL TO ITS DEATH FROM HER APPARTMENT WINDOW?
HOW DID THE JEWISH PEOPLE COPE WITH THE AFTER-EFFECTS OF THE HOLOCAUST?
HOW DOES A TEENAGE GUY COPE WITH HAVING TO WORK IN A MIND-NUMBING FAST FOOD PLACE EVERYDAY?
THAT'S NOT THE SAME THING!
ISN'T IT?
NO! - SEEING YOUR BABY DIE IS A HORRIBLE TRAGEDY.
JUST WORKING IN FAST FOOD PLACE, EVEN IF YOU HATE IT, IS... WELL... THAT'S NOT THE SAME THING AT ALL!

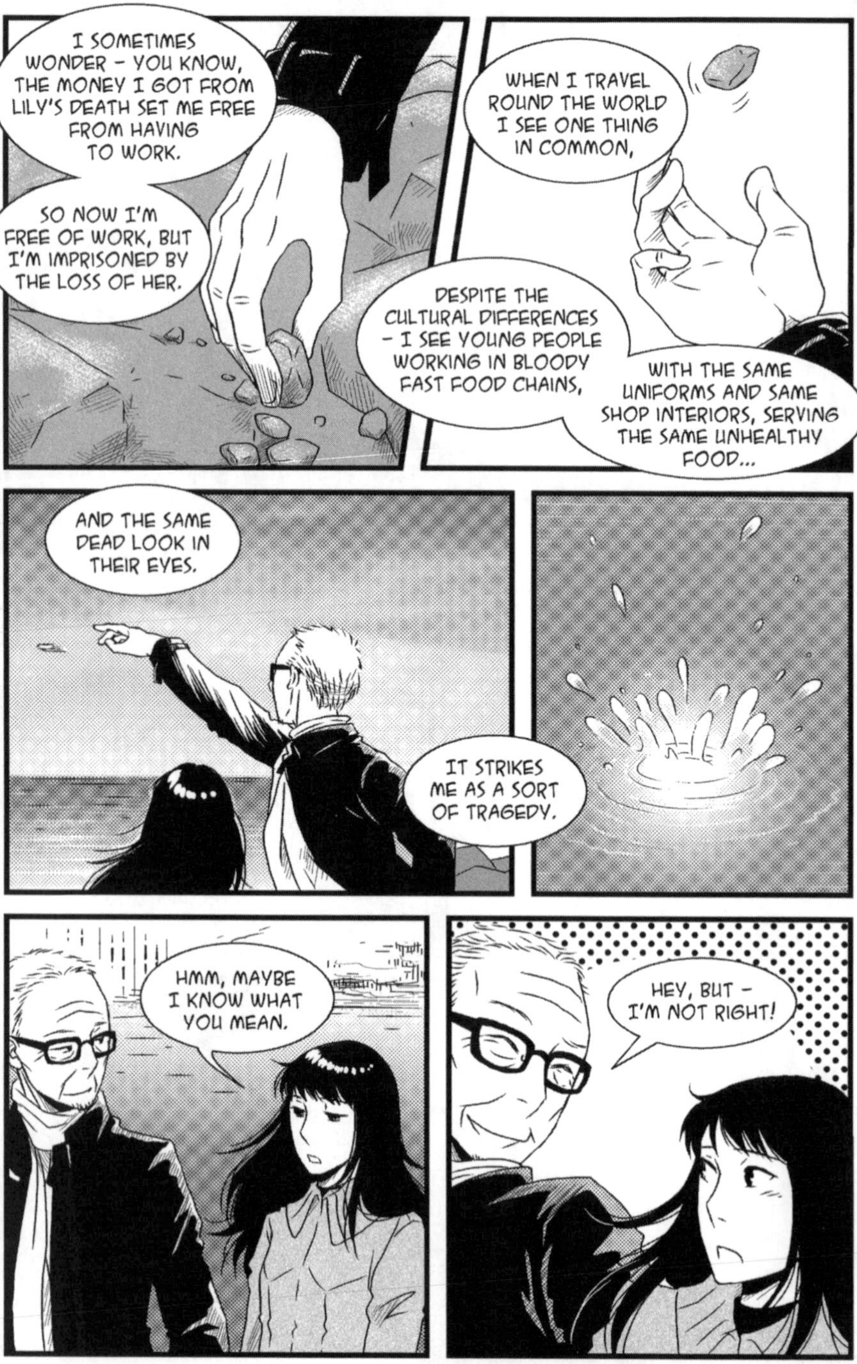
I SOMETIMES WONDER - YOU KNOW, THE MONEY I GOT FROM LILY'S DEATH SET ME FREE FROM HAVING TO WORK.
SO NOW I'M FREE OF WORK, BUT I'M IMPRISONED BY THE LOSS OF HER.
WHEN I TRAVEL ROUND THE WORLD I SEE ONE THING IN COMMON,
DESPITE THE CULTURAL DIFFERENCES - I SEE YOUNG PEOPLE WORKING IN BLOODY FAST FOOD CHAINS,
WITH THE SAME UNIFORMS AND SAME SHOP INTERIORS, SERVING THE SAME UNHEALTHY FOOD...
AND THE SAME DEAD LOOK IN THEIR EYES.
IT STRIKES ME AS A SORT OF TRAGEDY.
HMM, MAYBE I KNOW WHAT YOU MEAN.
HEY, BUT - I'M NOT RIGHT!

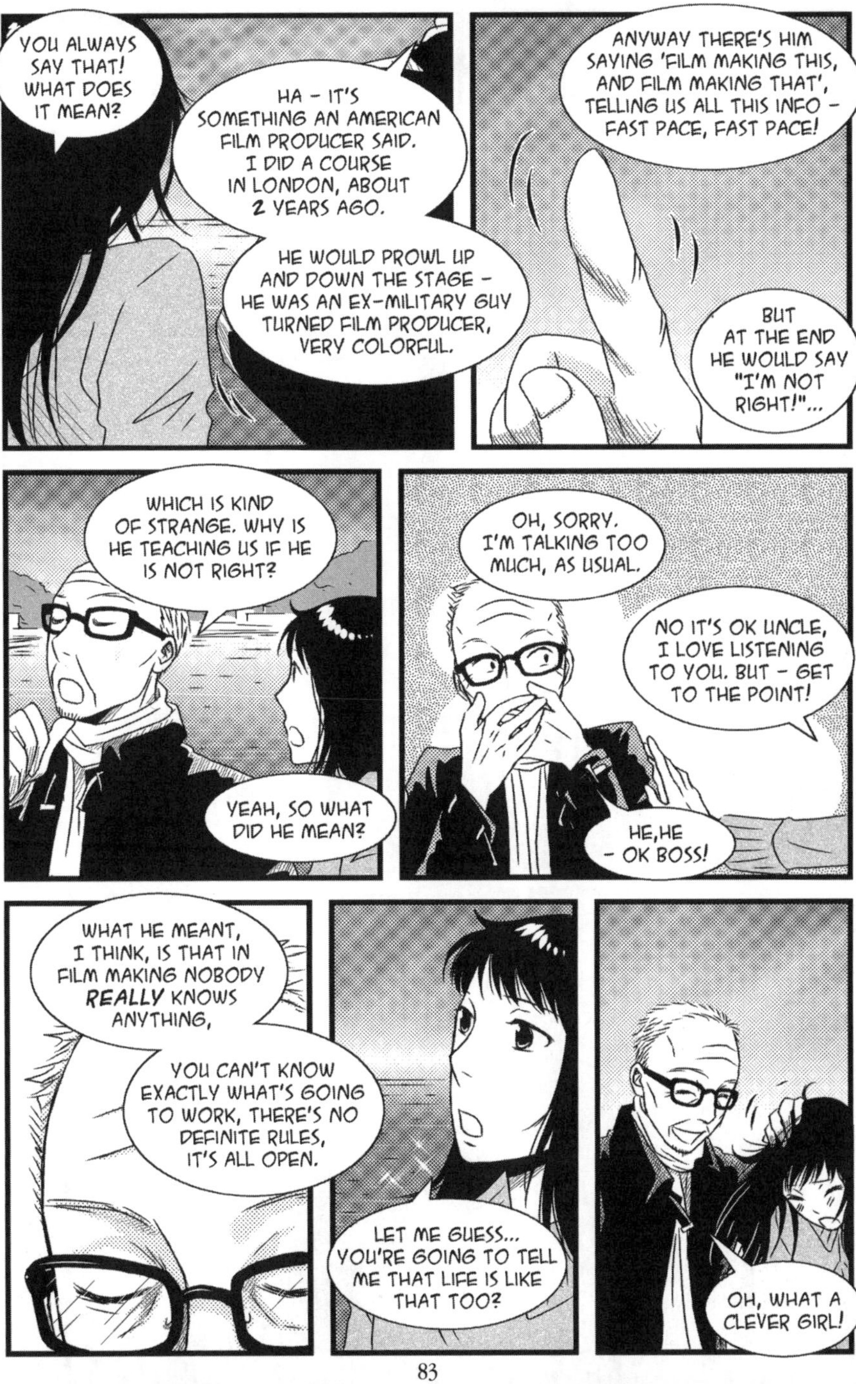
YOU ALWAYS SAY THAT! WHAT DOES IT MEAN?
HA - IT'S SOMETHING AN AMERICAN FILM PRODUCER SAID. I DID A COURSE IN LONDON, ABOUT 2 YEARS AGO.
HE WOULD PROWL UP AND DOWN THE STAGE - HE WAS AN EX-MILITARY GUY TURNED FILM PRODUCER, VERY COLORFUL.
ANYWAY THERE'S HIM SAYING 'FILM MAKING THIS, AND FILM MAKING THAT', TELLING US ALL THIS INFO - FAST PACE, FAST PACE!
BUT AT THE END HE WOULD SAY "I'M NOT RIGHT!"...
WHICH IS KIND OF STRANGE. WHY IS HE TEACHING US IF HE IS NOT RIGHT?
YEAH, SO WHAT DID HE MEAN?
OH, SORRY. I'M TALKING TOO MUCH, AS USUAL.
NO IT'S OK UNCLE, I LOVE LISTENING TO YOU. BUT - GET TO THE POINT!
HE,HE - OK BOSS!
WHAT HE MEANT, I THINK, IS THAT IN FILM MAKING NOBODY REALLY KNOWS ANYTHING,
YOU CAN'T KNOW EXACTLY WHAT'S GOING TO WORK, THERE'S NO DEFINITE RULES, IT'S ALL OPEN.
LET ME GUESS... YOU'RE GOING TO TELL ME THAT LIFE IS LIKE THAT TOO?
OH, WHAT A CLEVER GIRL!

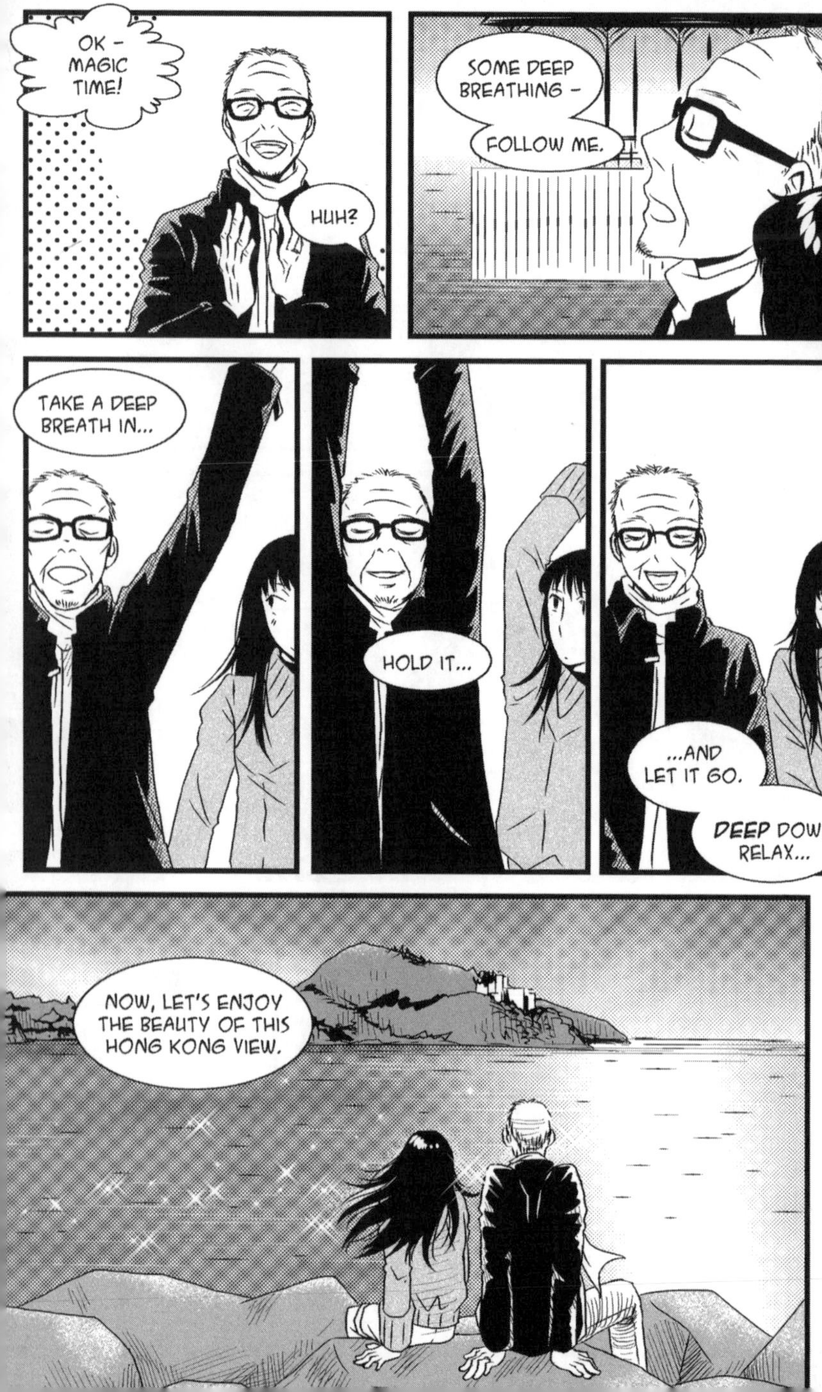
OK - MAGIC TIME!
HUH?
SOME DEEP BREATHING -
FOLLOW ME.
TAKE A DEEP BREATH IN...
HOLD IT...
...AND LET IT GO.
DEEP DOWN RELAX...
NOW, LET'S ENJOY THE BEAUTY OF THIS HONG KONG VIEW.

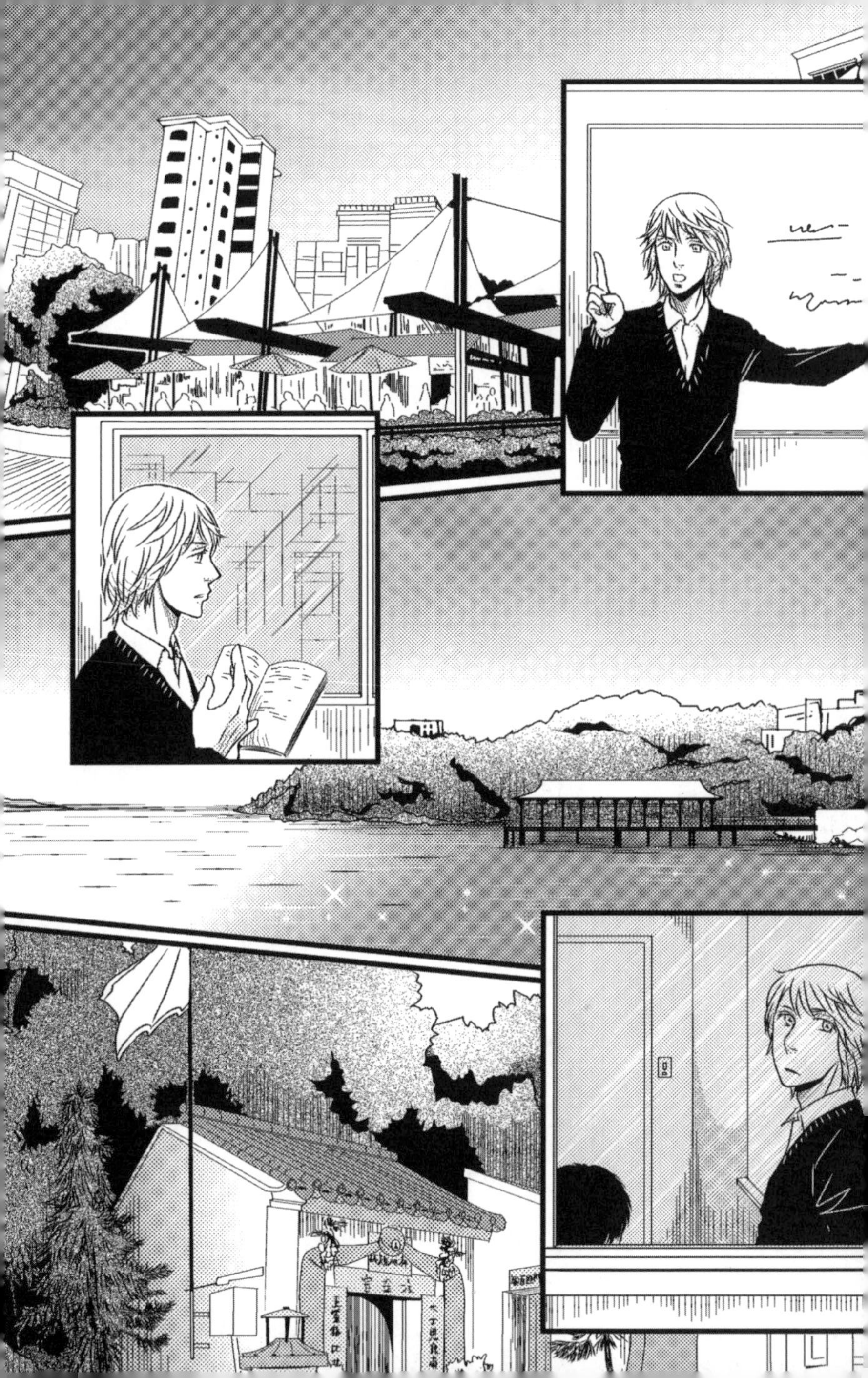

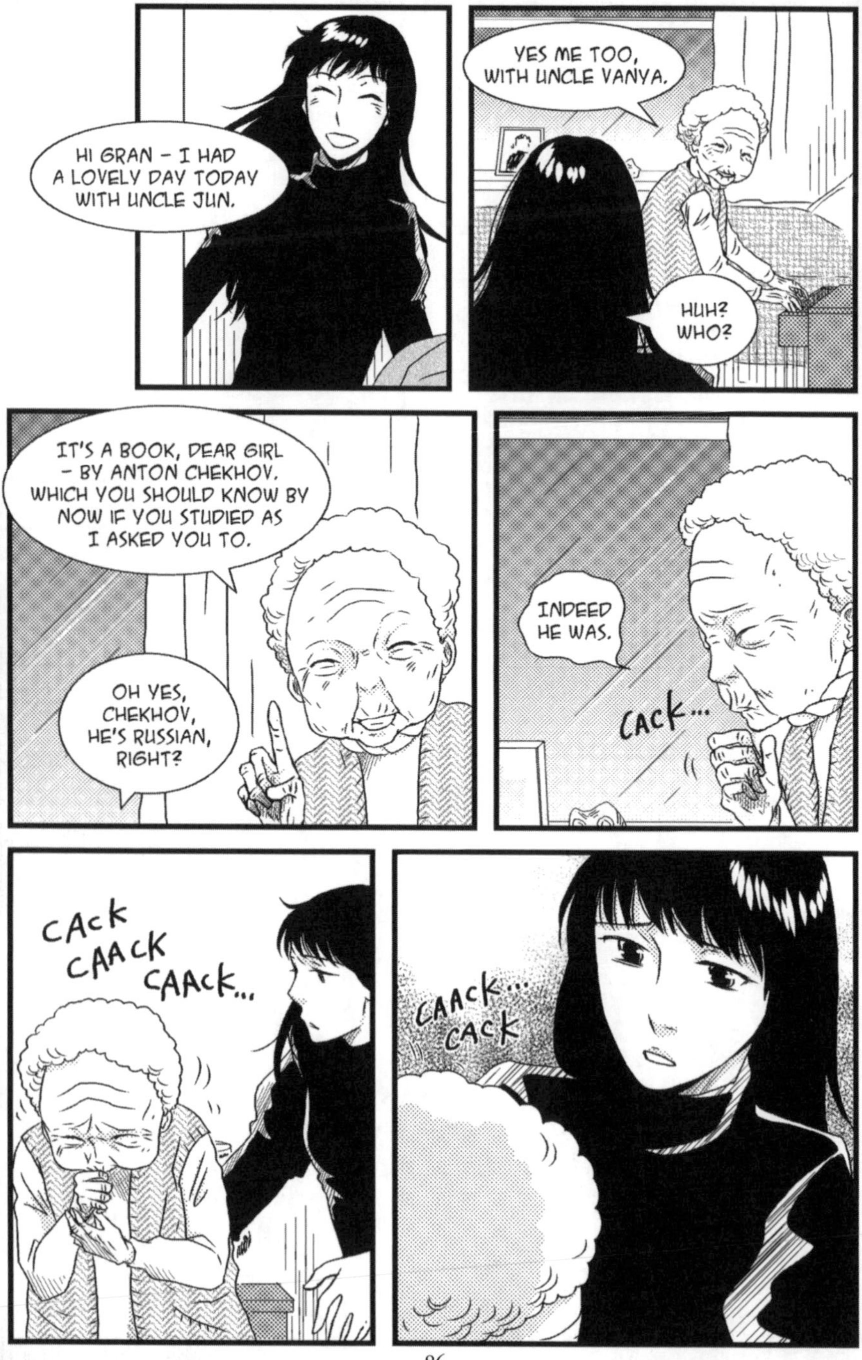
HI GRAN – I HAD A LOVELY DAY TODAY WITH UNCLE JUN.
YES ME TOO, WITH UNCLE VANYA.
HUH? WHO?
IT'S A BOOK, DEAR GIRL – BY ANTON CHEKHOV. WHICH YOU SHOULD KNOW BY NOW IF YOU STUDIED AS I ASKED YOU TO.
OH YES, CHEKHOV, HE'S RUSSIAN, RIGHT?
INDEED HE WAS.
CACK...
CACK CAACK CAACK...
CAACK... CACK

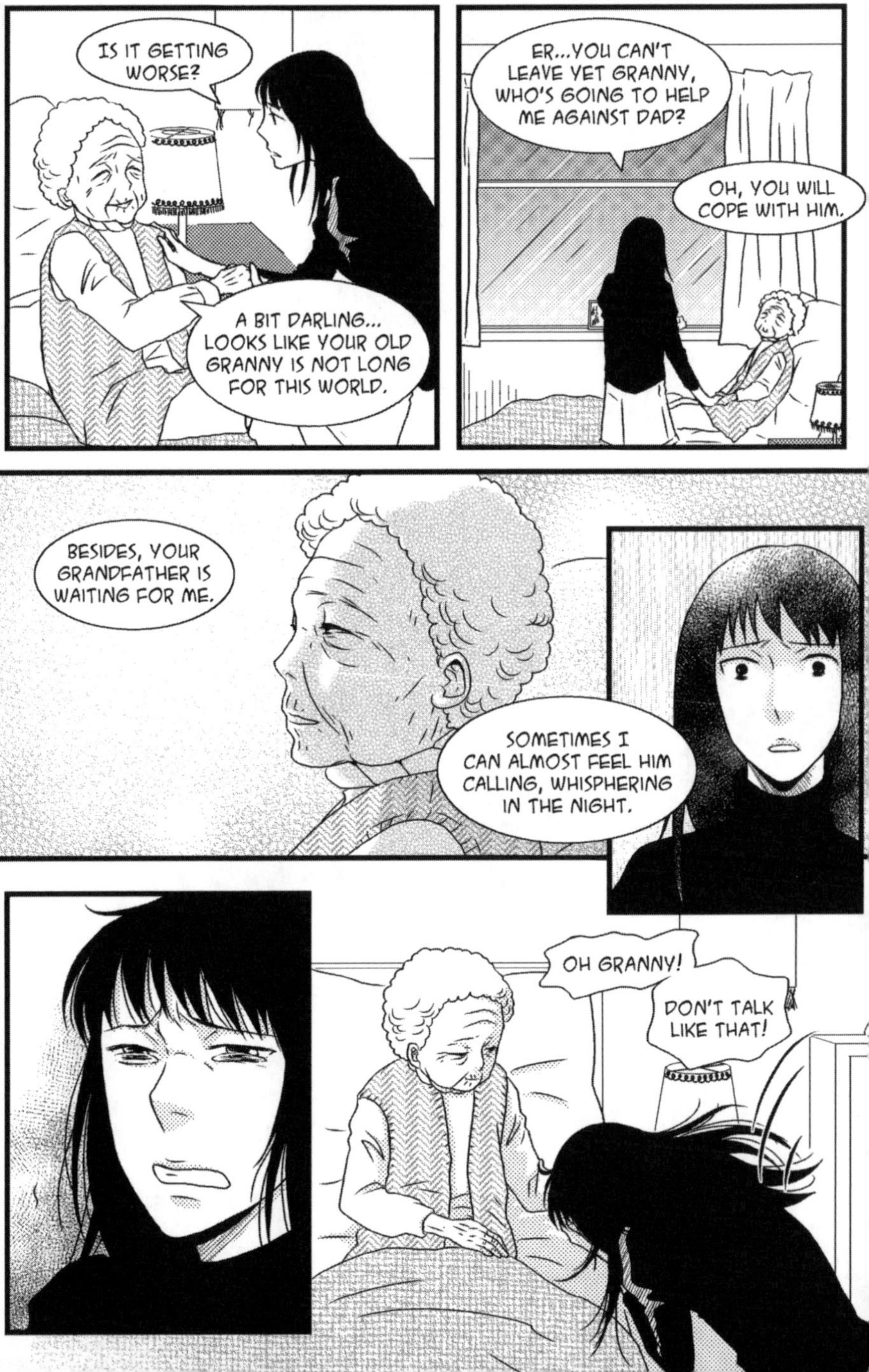
IS IT GETTING WORSE?
A BIT DARLING... LOOKS LIKE YOUR OLD GRANNY IS NOT LONG FOR THIS WORLD.
ER...YOU CAN'T LEAVE YET GRANNY, WHO'S GOING TO HELP ME AGAINST DAD?
OH, YOU WILL COPE WITH HIM.
BESIDES, YOUR GRANDFATHER IS WAITING FOR ME.
SOMETIMES I CAN ALMOST FEEL HIM CALLING, WHISPHERING IN THE NIGHT.
OH GRANNY!
DON'T TALK LIKE THAT!

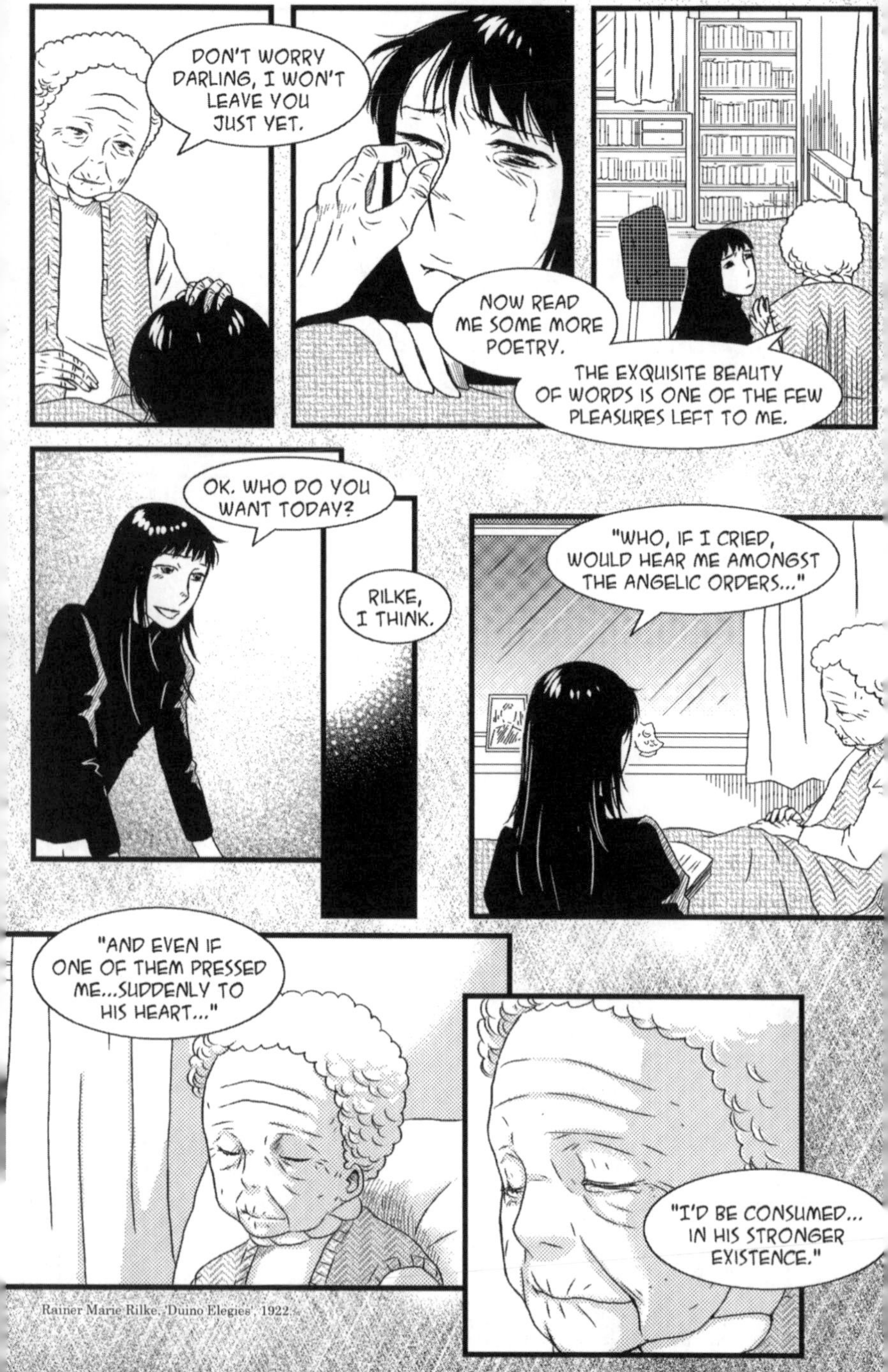
DON'T WORRY DARLING, I WON'T LEAVE YOU JUST YET.
NOW READ ME SOME MORE POETRY.
THE EXQUISITE BEAUTY OF WORDS IS ONE OF THE FEW PLEASURES LEFT TO ME.
OK. WHO DO YOU WANT TODAY?
RILKE, I THINK.
"WHO, IF I CRIED, WOULD HEAR ME AMONGST THE ANGELIC ORDERS..."
"AND EVEN IF ONE OF THEM PRESSED ME...SUDDENLY TO HIS HEART..."
"I'D BE CONSUMED... IN HIS STRONGER EXISTENCE."
Rainer Marie Rilke, 'Duino Elegies', 1922

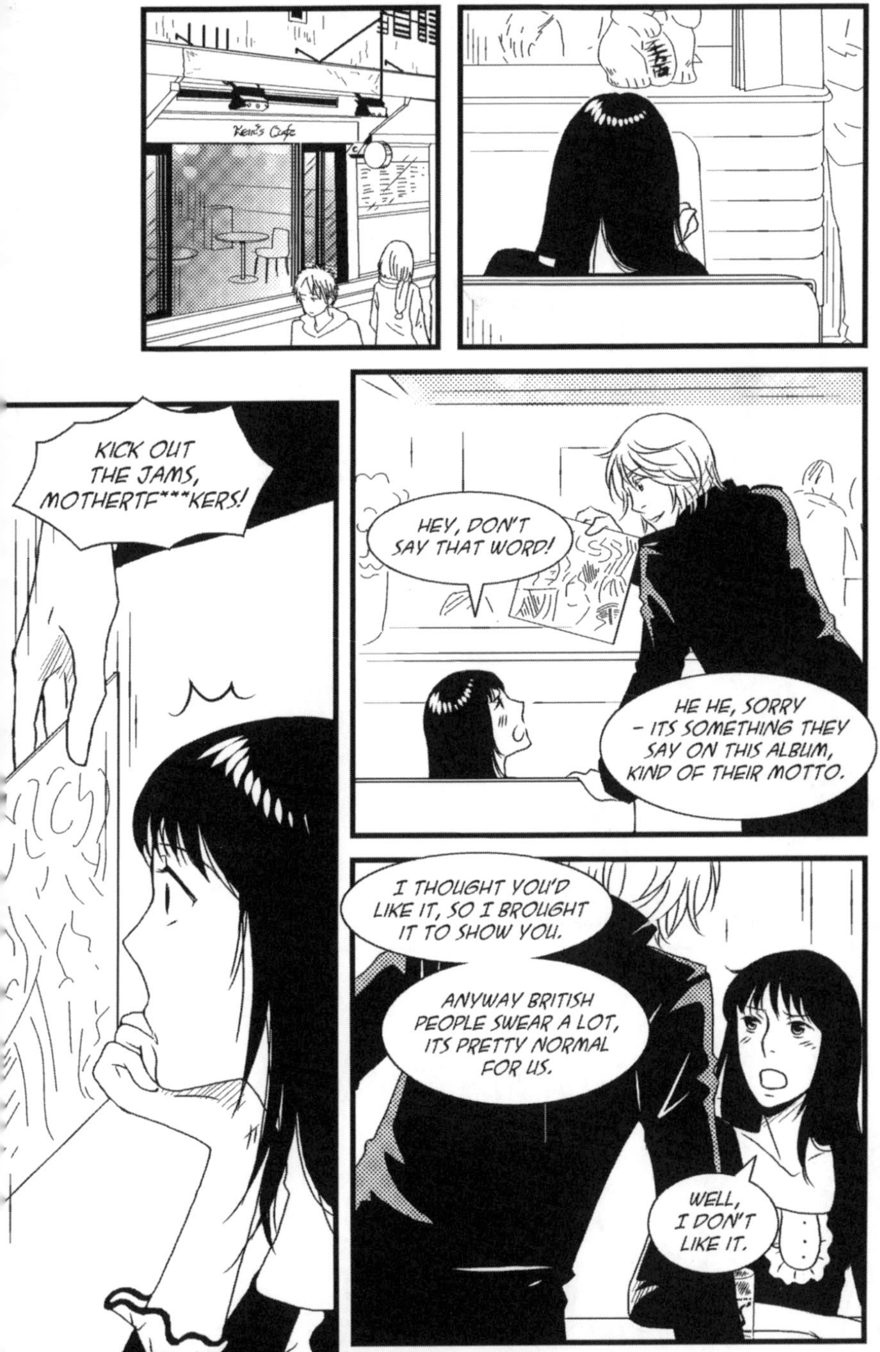
KICK OUT THE JAMS, MOTHERTF***KERS!
HEY, DON'T SAY THAT WORD!
HE HE, SORRY - ITS SOMETHING THEY SAY ON THIS ALBUM, KIND OF THEIR MOTTO.
I THOUGHT YOU'D LIKE IT, SO I BROUGHT IT TO SHOW YOU.
ANYWAY BRITISH PEOPLE SWEAR A LOT, ITS PRETTY NORMAL FOR US.
WELL, I DON'T LIKE IT.

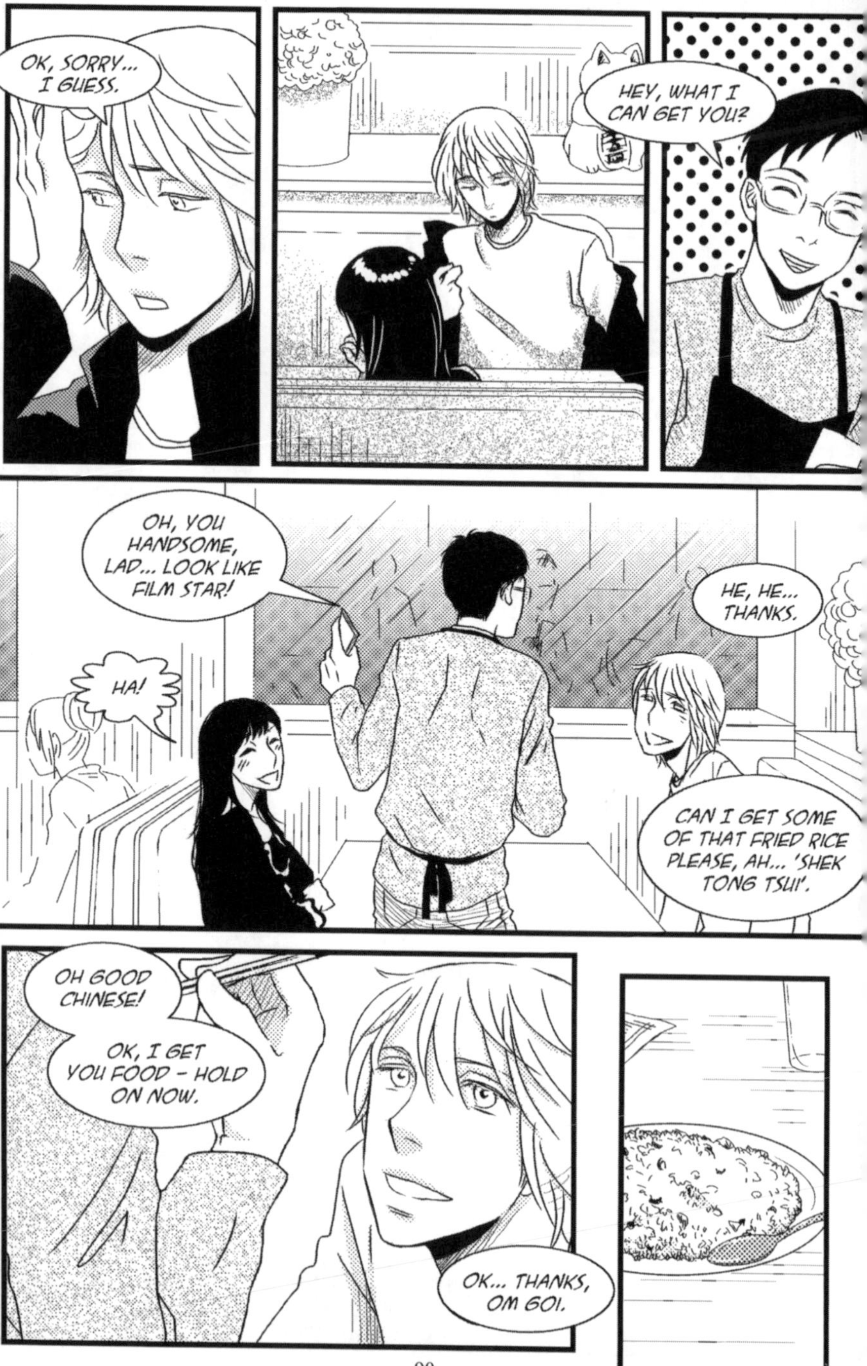
OK, SORRY... I GUESS.
HEY, WHAT I CAN GET YOU?
OH, YOU HANDSOME, LAD... LOOK LIKE FILM STAR!
HE, HE... THANKS.
HA!
CAN I GET SOME OF THAT FRIED RICE PLEASE, AH... 'SHEK TONG TSUI'.
OH GOOD CHINESE!
OK, I GET YOU FOOD - HOLD ON NOW.
OK... THANKS, OM GOI.

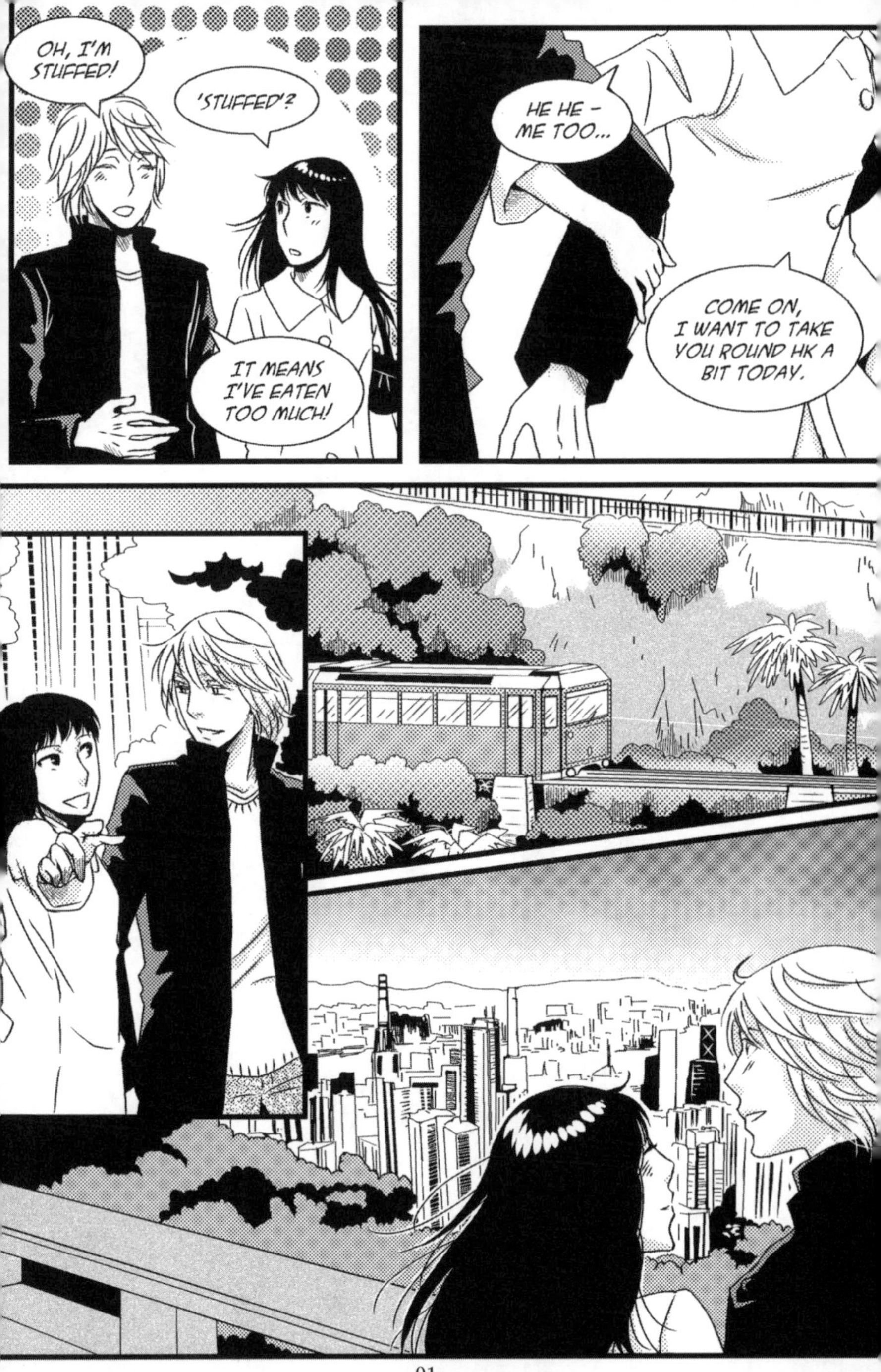
OH, I'M STUFFED!
'STUFFED'?
IT MEANS I'VE EATEN TOO MUCH!
HE HE - ME TOO...
COME ON, I WANT TO TAKE YOU ROUND HK A BIT TODAY.

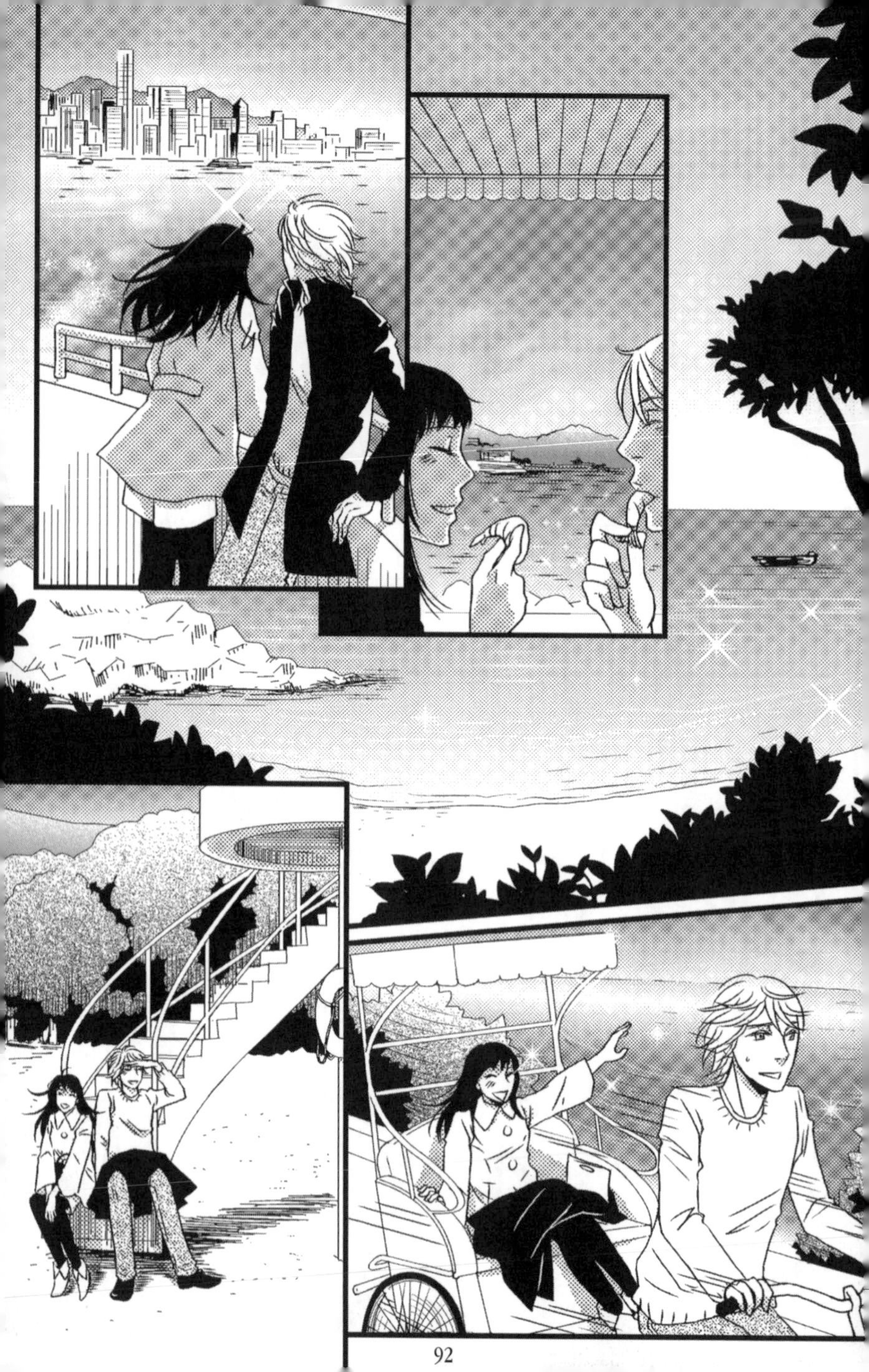

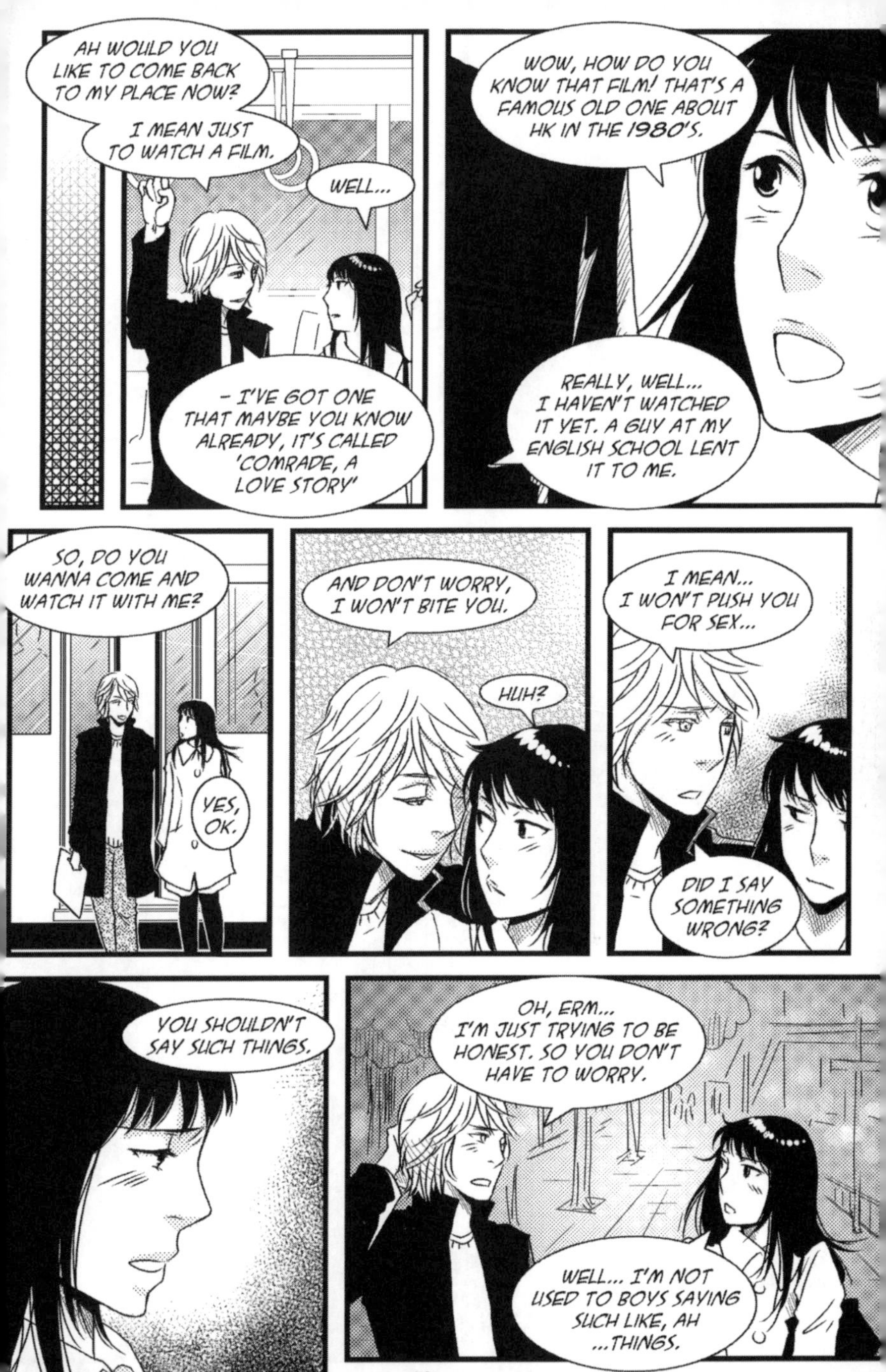
AH WOULD YOU LIKE TO COME BACK TO MY PLACE NOW?
I MEAN JUST TO WATCH A FILM.
WELL...
- I'VE GOT ONE THAT MAYBE YOU KNOW ALREADY, IT'S CALLED 'COMRADE, A LOVE STORY"
WOW, HOW DO YOU KNOW THAT FILM! THAT'S A FAMOUS OLD ONE ABOUT HK IN THE 1980'S.
REALLY, WELL... I HAVEN'T WATCHED IT YET. A GUY AT MY ENGLISH SCHOOL LENT IT TO ME.
SO, DO YOU WANNA COME AND WATCH IT WITH ME?
YES, OK.
AND DON'T WORRY, I WON'T BITE YOU.
HUH?
I MEAN... I WON'T PUSH YOU FOR SEX...
DID I SAY SOMETHING WRONG?
YOU SHOULDN'T SAY SUCH THINGS.
OH, ERM... I'M JUST TRYING TO BE HONEST. SO YOU DON'T HAVE TO WORRY.
WELL... I'M NOT USED TO BOYS SAYING SUCH LIKE, AH ...THINGS.

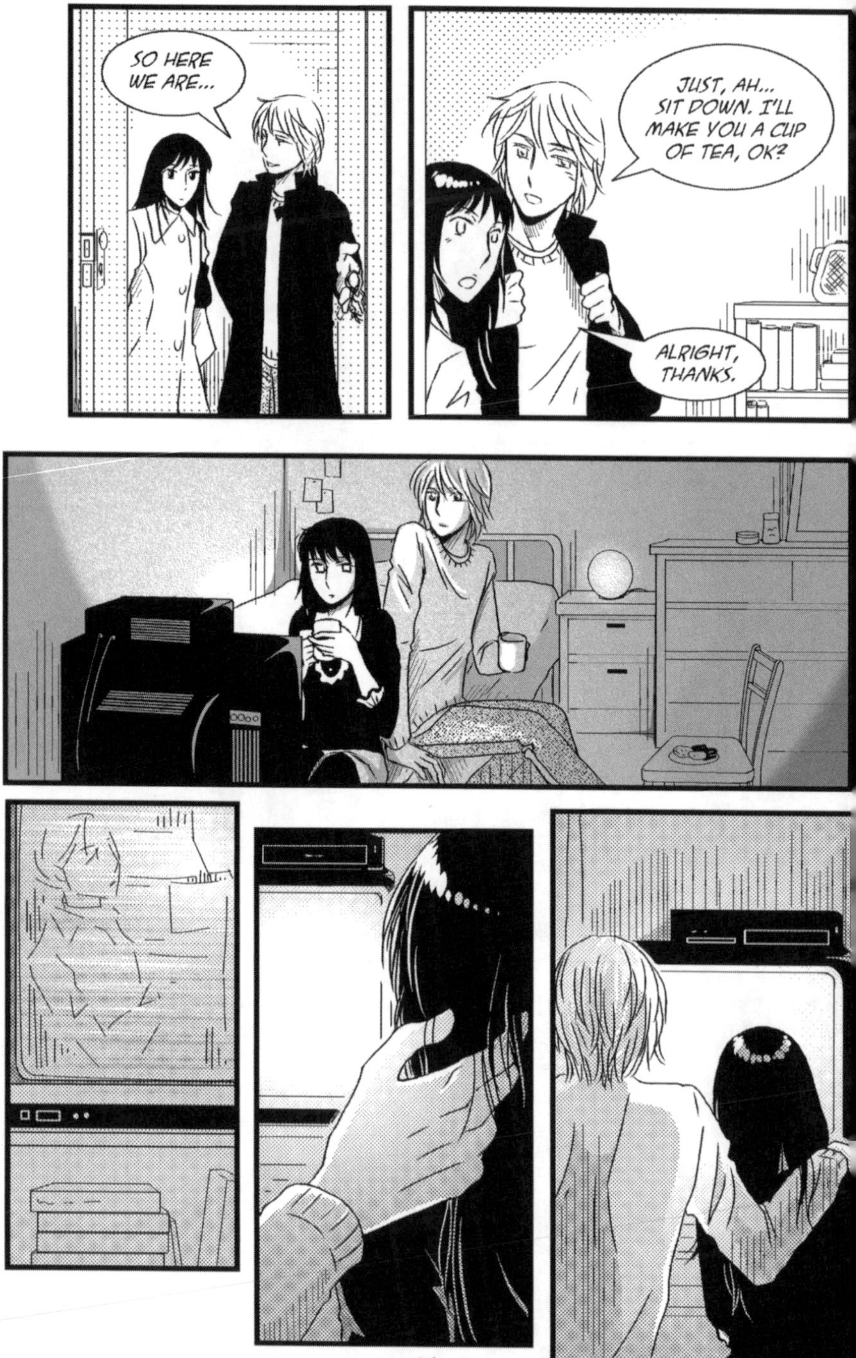
SO HERE WE ARE...
JUST, AH... SIT DOWN. I'LL MAKE YOU A CUP OF TEA, OK?
ALRIGHT, THANKS.

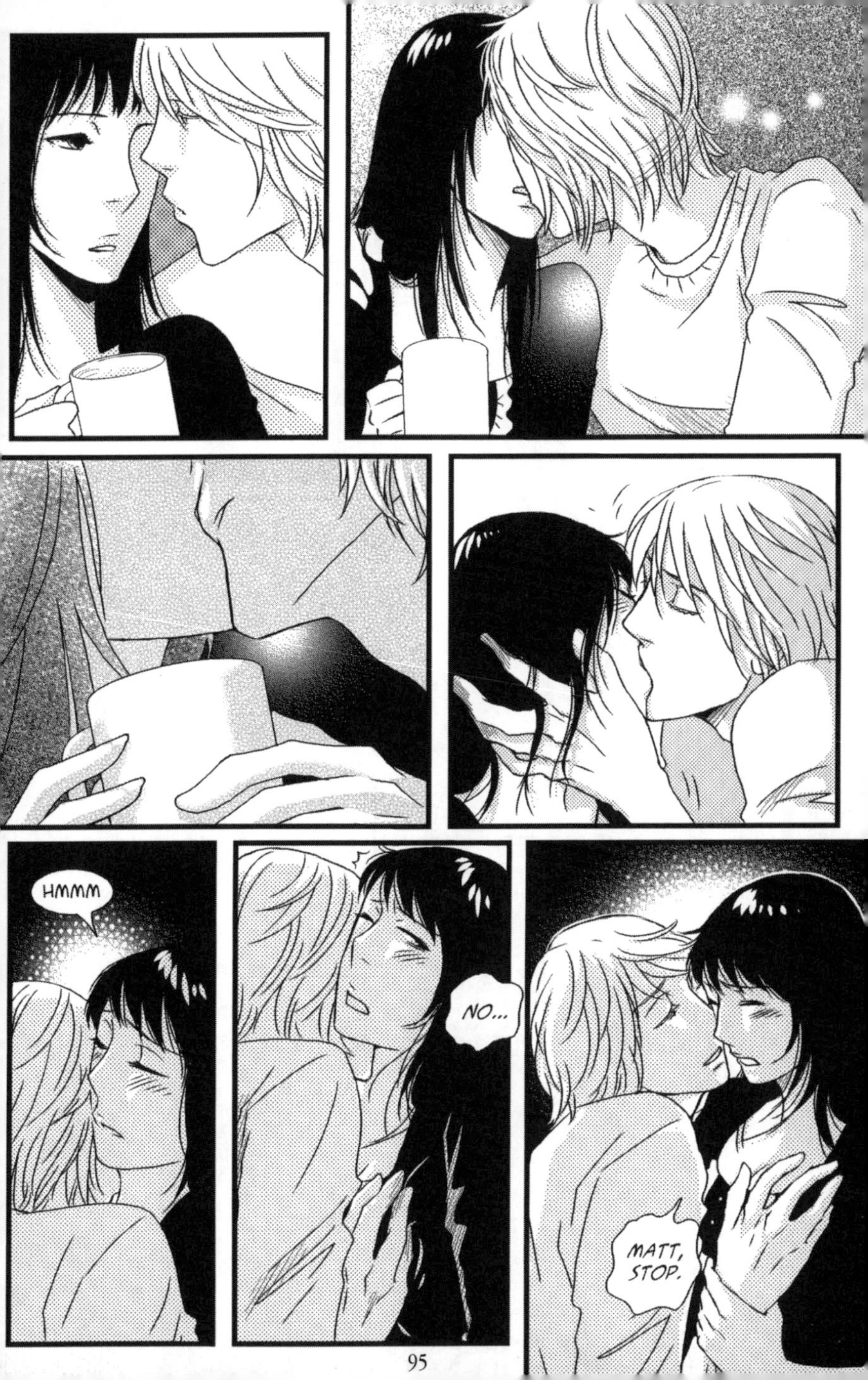
HMMM
NO...
MATT, STOP.

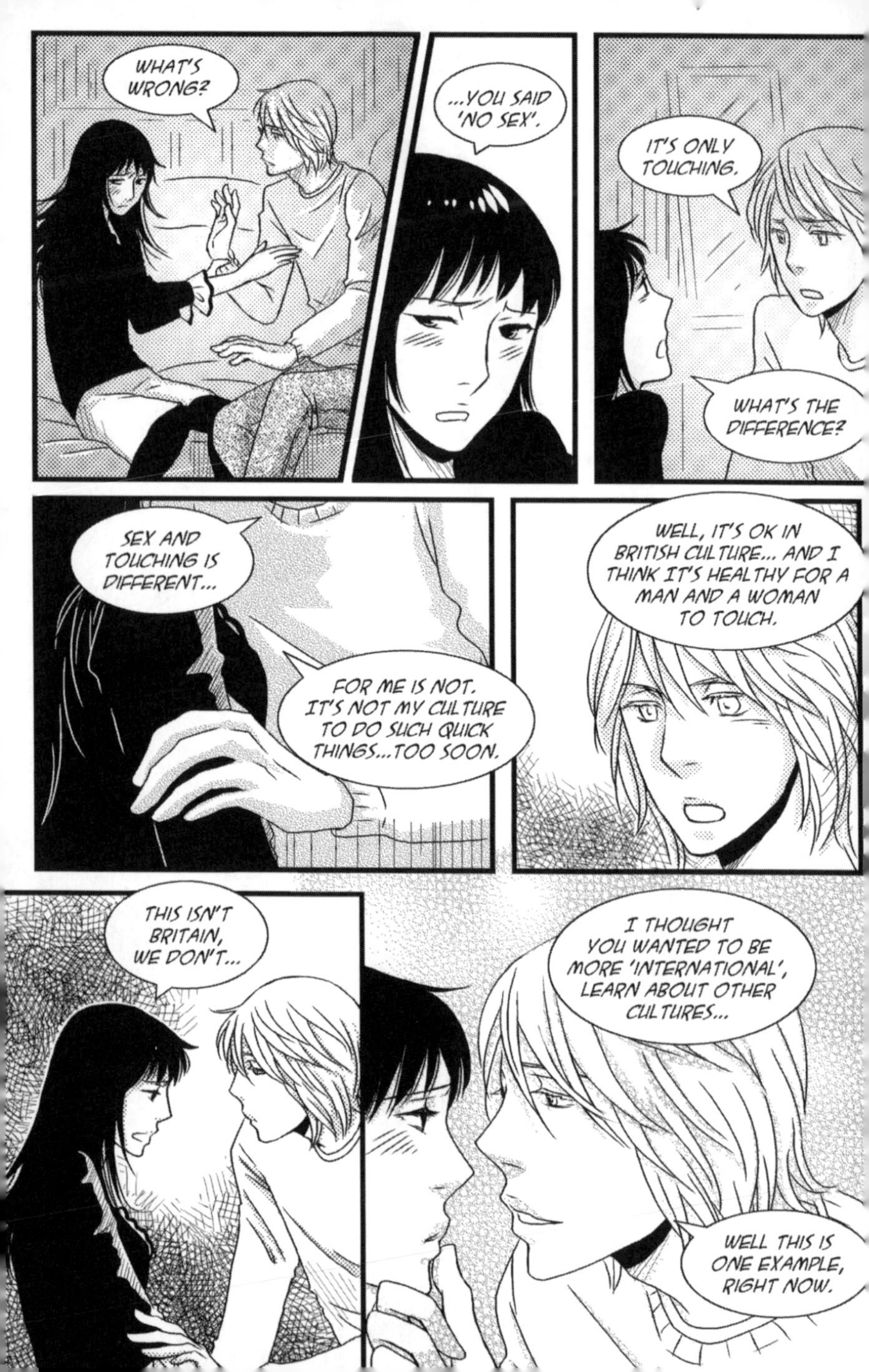
WHAT'S WRONG?
...YOU SAID 'NO SEX'.
IT'S ONLY TOUCHING.
WHAT'S THE DIFFERENCE?
SEX AND TOUCHING IS DIFFERENT...
FOR ME IS NOT. IT'S NOT MY CULTURE TO DO SUCH QUICK THINGS...TOO SOON.
WELL, IT'S OK IN BRITISH CULTURE... AND I THINK IT'S HEALTHY FOR A MAN AND A WOMAN TO TOUCH.
THIS ISN'T BRITAIN, WE DON'T...
I THOUGHT YOU WANTED TO BE MORE 'INTERNATIONAL', LEARN ABOUT OTHER CULTURES...
WELL THIS IS ONE EXAMPLE, RIGHT NOW.

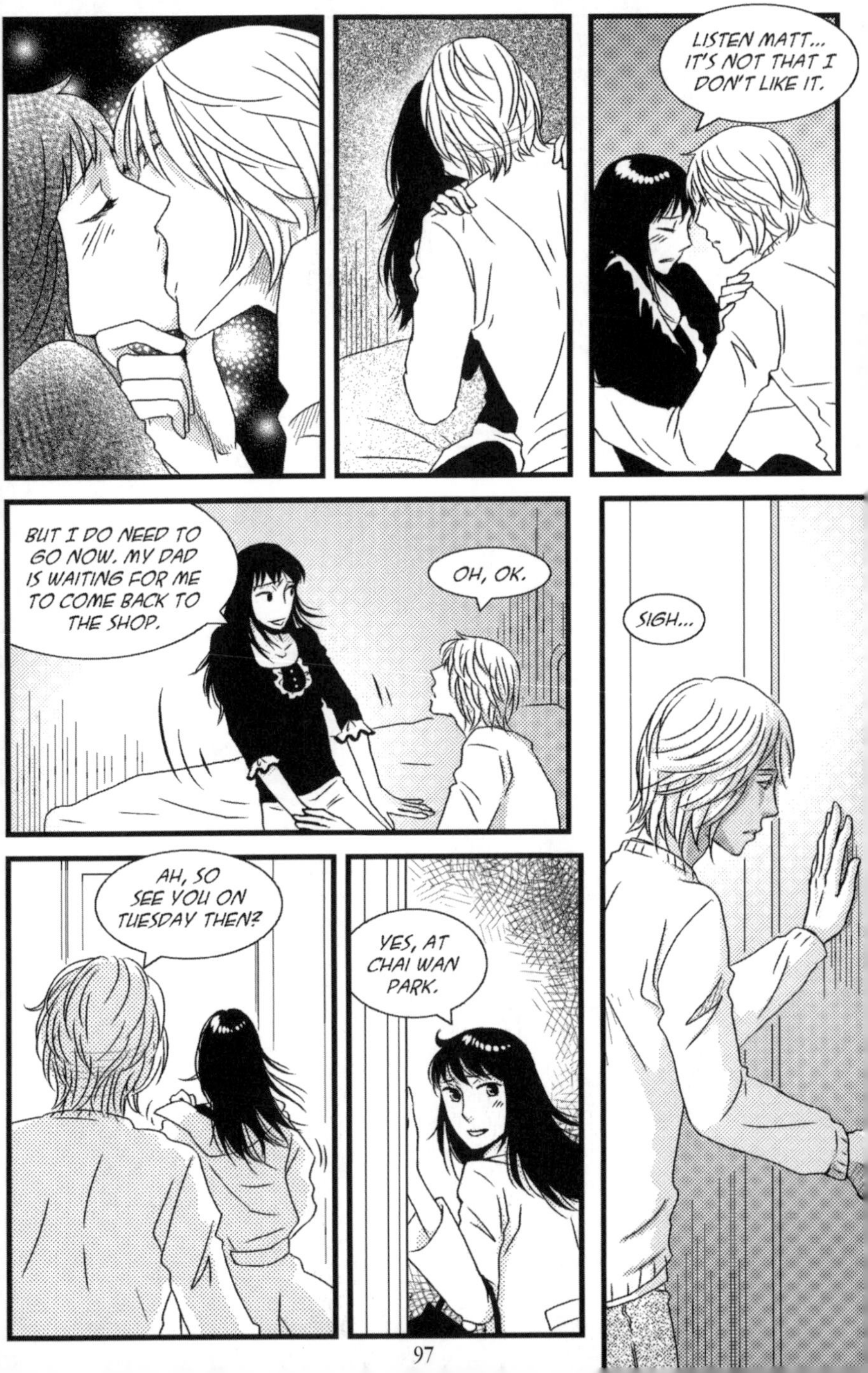
LISTEN MATT... IT'S NOT THAT I DON'T LIKE IT.
BUT I DO NEED TO GO NOW. MY DAD IS WAITING FOR ME TO COME BACK TO THE SHOP.
OH, OK.
SIGH...
AH, SO SEE YOU ON TUESDAY THEN?
YES, AT CHAI WAN PARK.

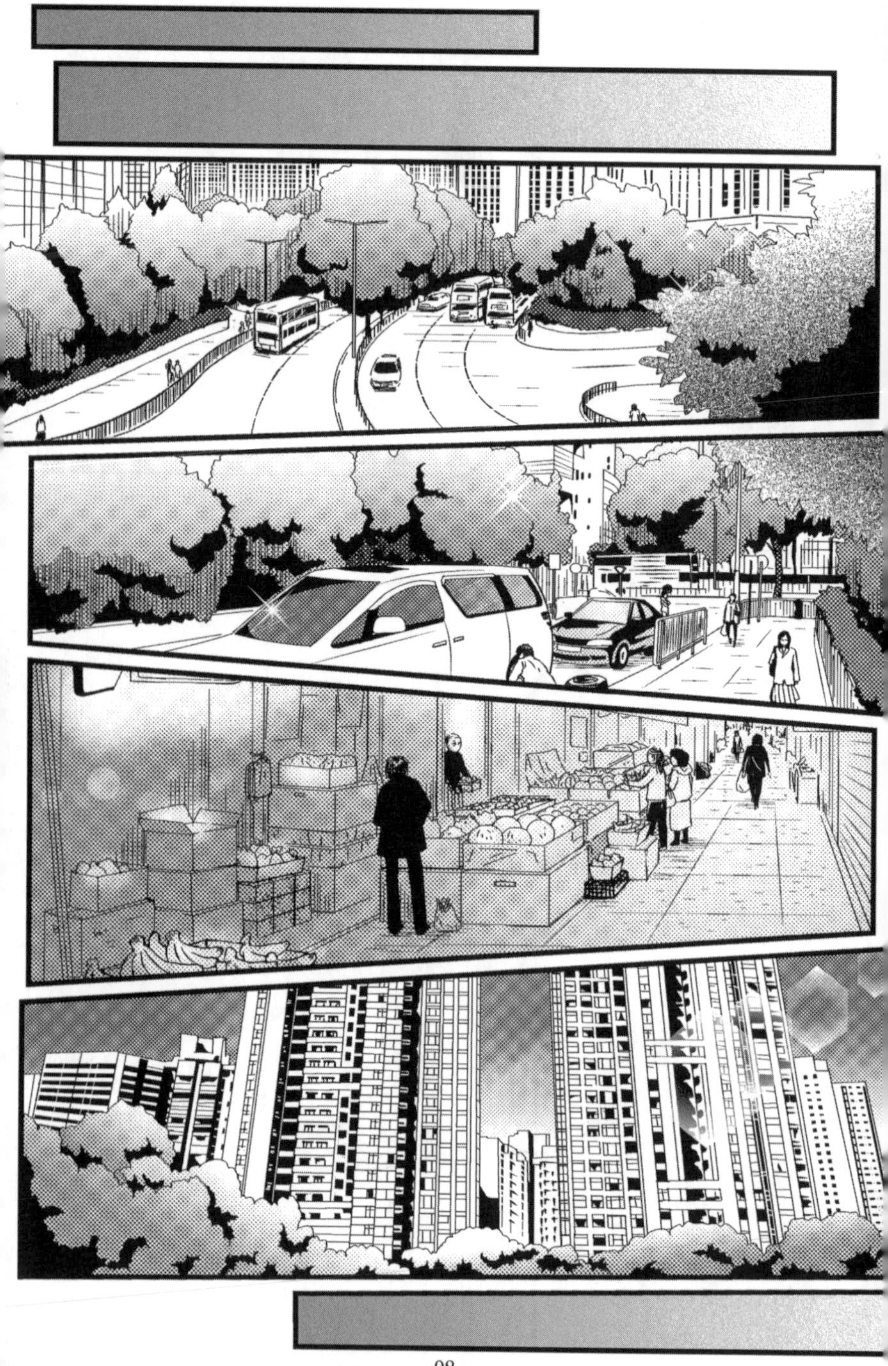

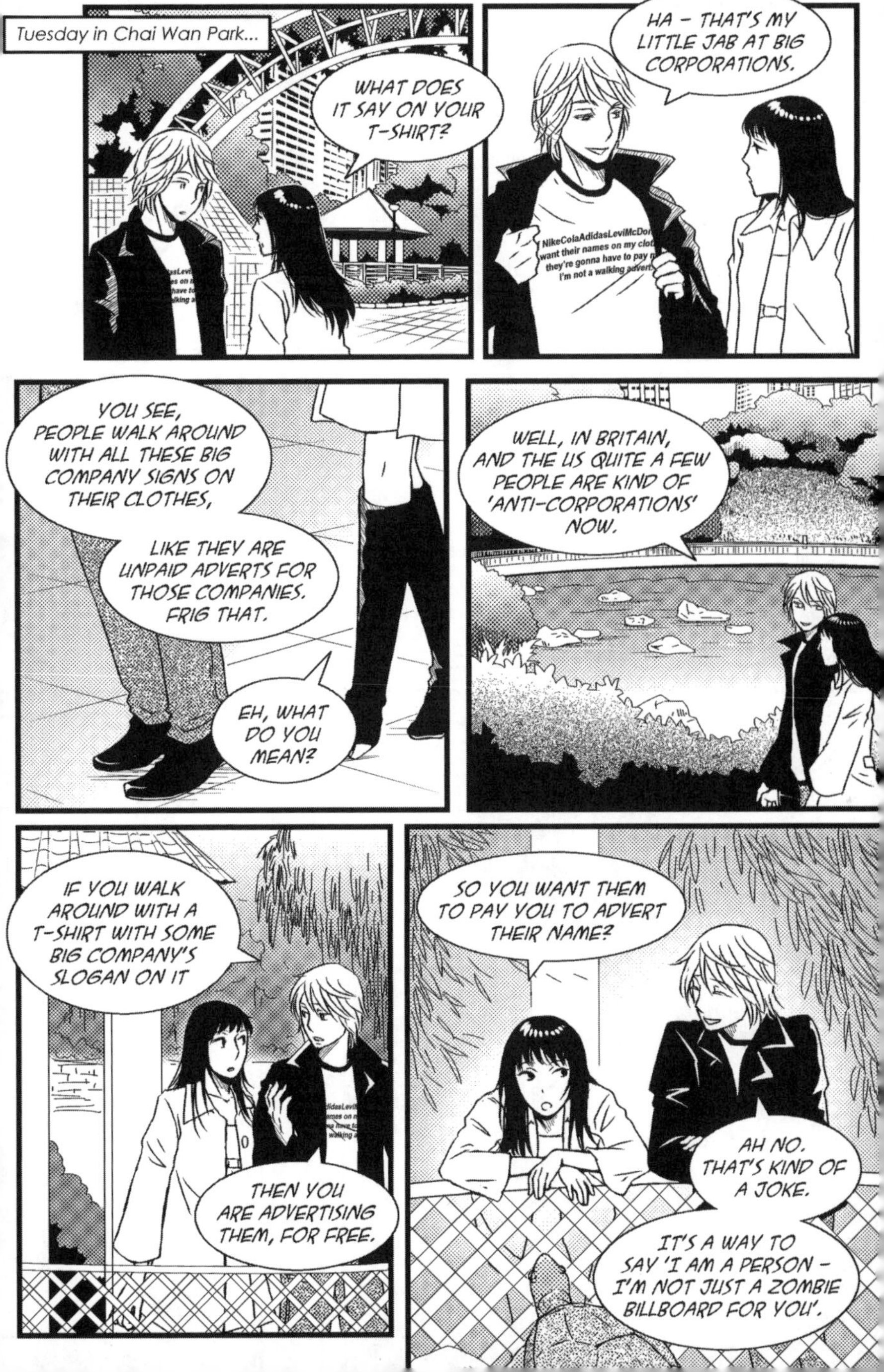
Tuesday in Chai Wan Park...
WHAT DOES IT SAY ON YOUR T-SHIRT?
HA – THAT'S MY LITTLE JAB AT BIG CORPORATIONS.
YOU SEE, PEOPLE WALK AROUND WITH ALL THESE BIG COMPANY SIGNS ON THEIR CLOTHES,
LIKE THEY ARE UNPAID ADVERTS FOR THOSE COMPANIES. FRIG THAT.
EH, WHAT DO YOU MEAN?
WELL, IN BRITAIN, AND THE US QUITE A FEW PEOPLE ARE KIND OF 'ANTI-CORPORATIONS' NOW.
IF YOU WALK AROUND WITH A T-SHIRT WITH SOME BIG COMPANY'S SLOGAN ON IT
THEN YOU ARE ADVERTISING THEM, FOR FREE.
SO YOU WANT THEM TO PAY YOU TO ADVERT THEIR NAME?
AH NO. THAT'S KIND OF A JOKE.
IT'S A WAY TO SAY 'I AM A PERSON – I'M NOT JUST A ZOMBIE BILLBOARD FOR YOU'.

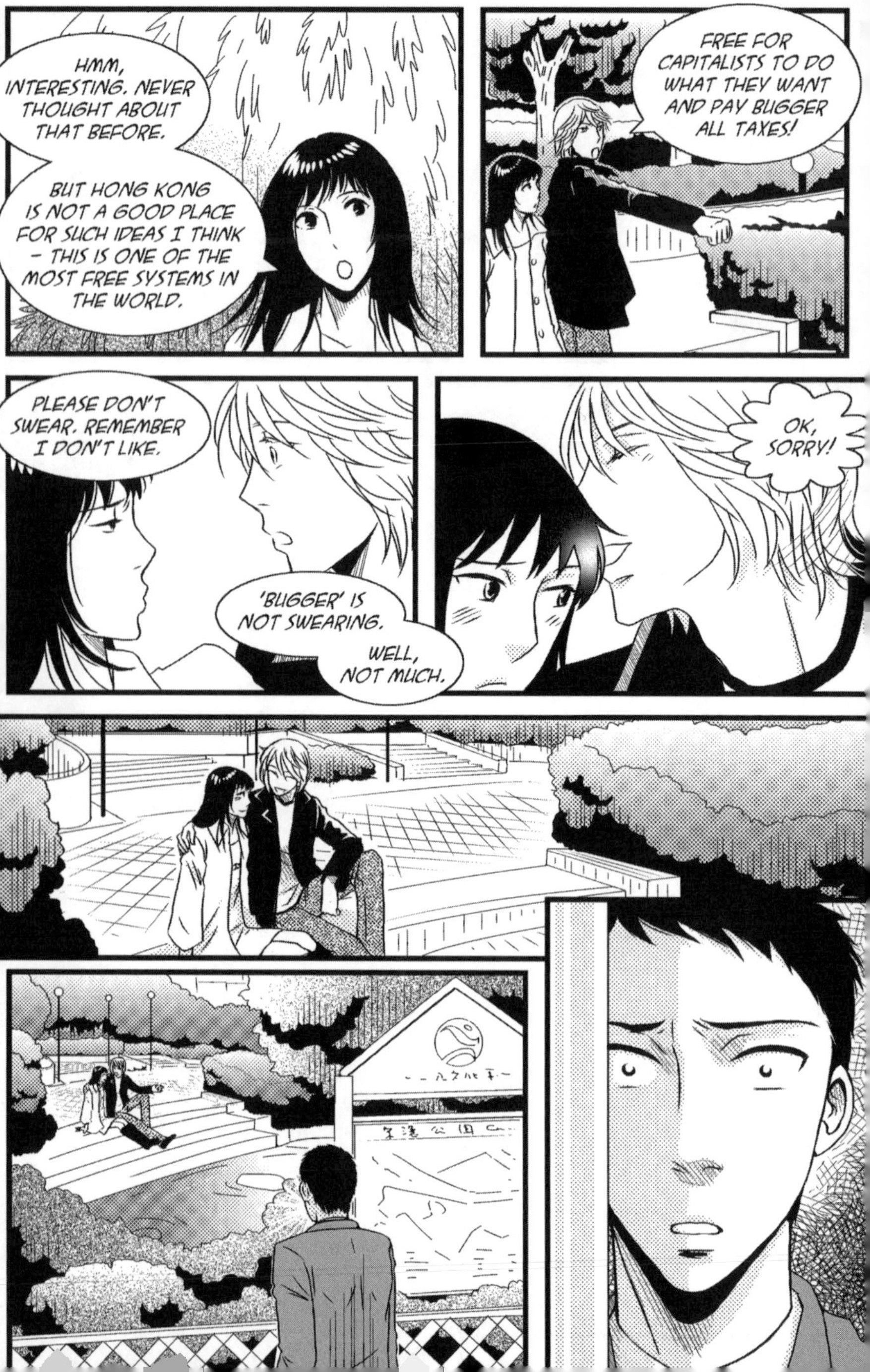
HMM, INTERESTING. NEVER THOUGHT ABOUT THAT BEFORE.
BUT HONG KONG IS NOT A GOOD PLACE FOR SUCH IDEAS I THINK - THIS IS ONE OF THE MOST FREE SYSTEMS IN THE WORLD.
FREE FOR CAPITALISTS TO DO WHAT THEY WANT AND PAY BUGGER ALL TAXES!
PLEASE DON'T SWEAR. REMEMBER I DON'T LIKE.
'BUGGER' IS NOT SWEARING.
WELL, NOT MUCH.
OK, SORRY!

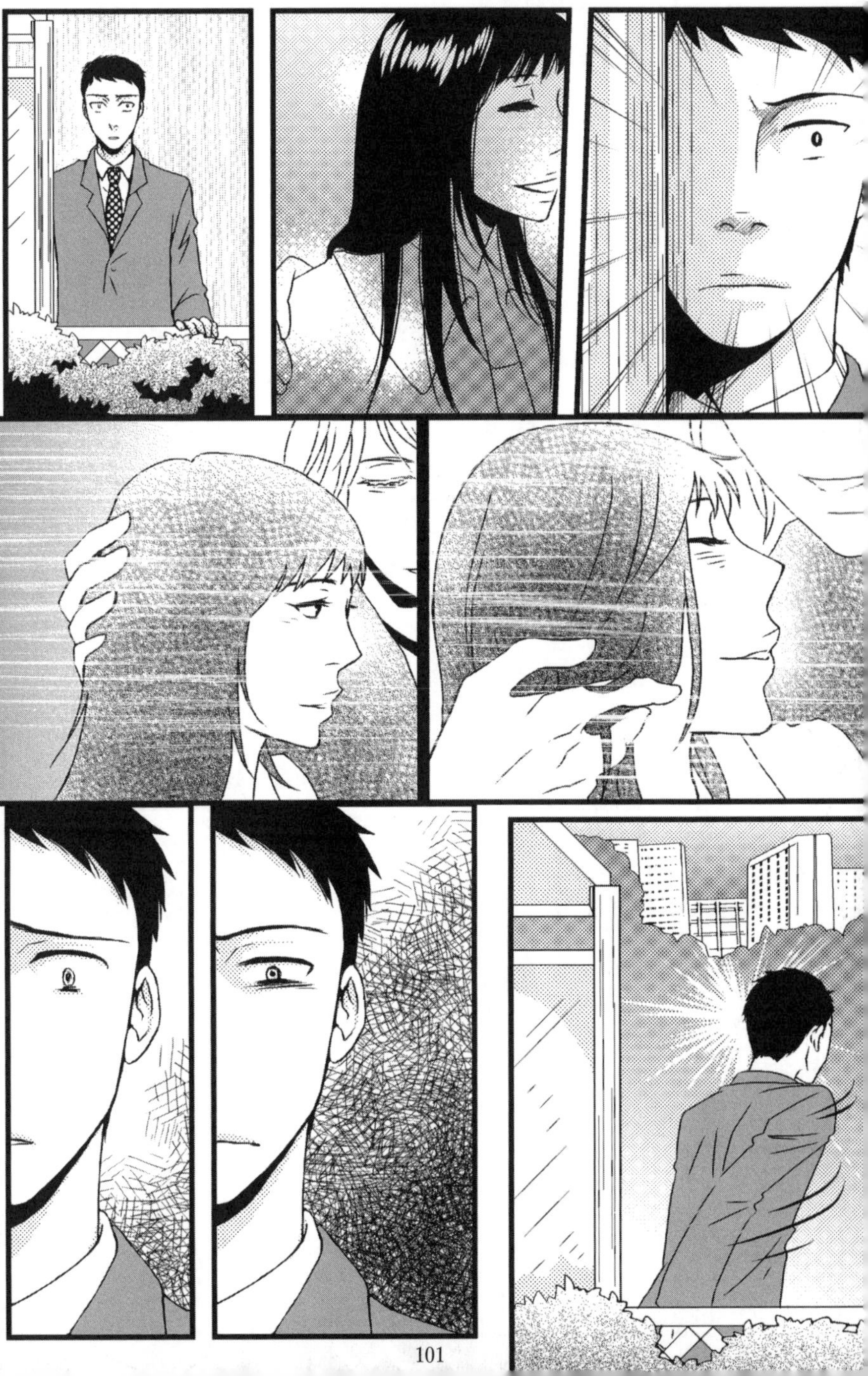

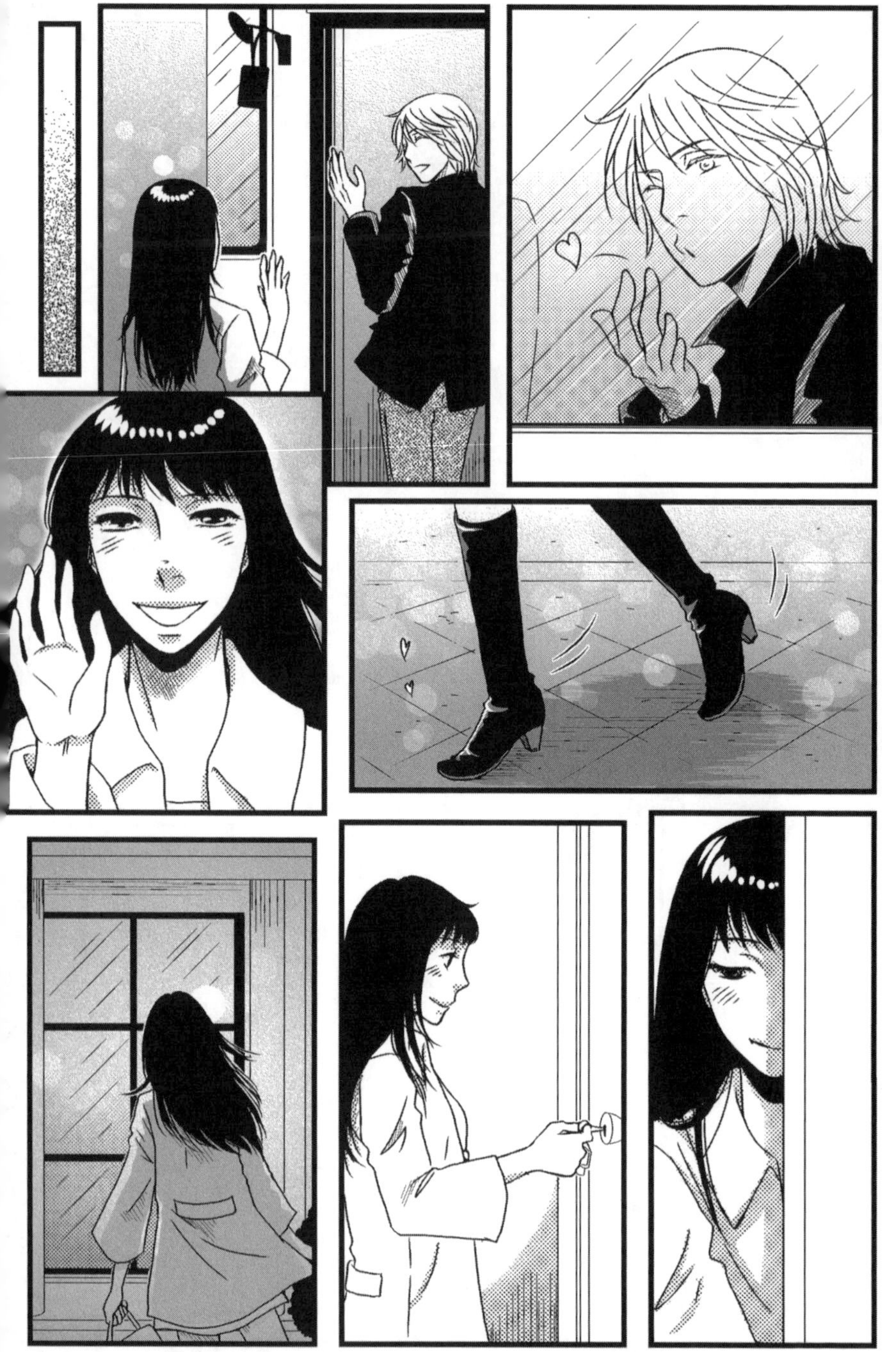

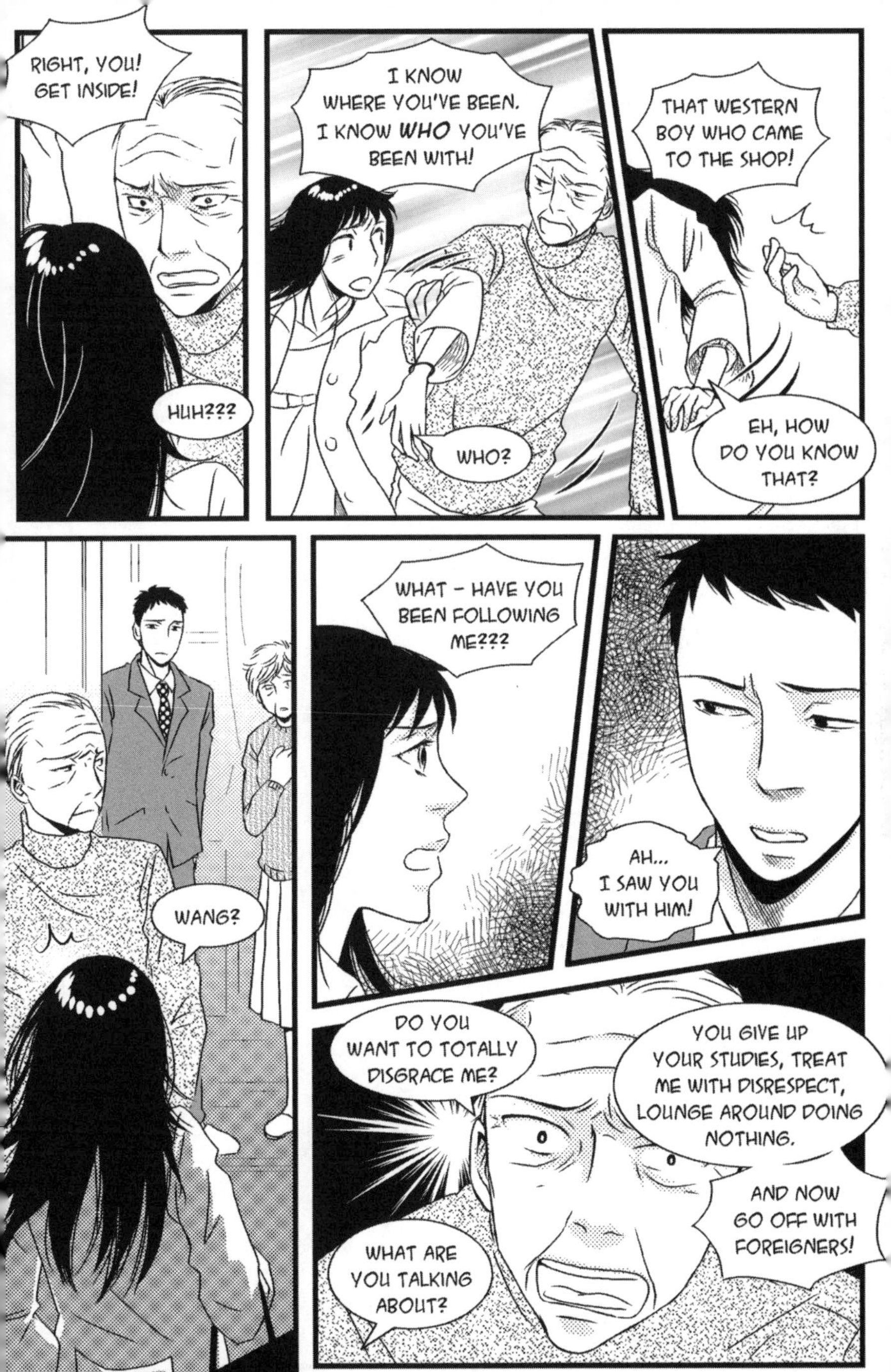
RIGHT, YOU! GET INSIDE!
HUH???
I KNOW WHERE YOU'VE BEEN. I KNOW *WHO* YOU'VE BEEN WITH!
WHO?
THAT WESTERN BOY WHO CAME TO THE SHOP!
EH, HOW DO YOU KNOW THAT?
WANG?
WHAT - HAVE YOU BEEN FOLLOWING ME???
AH... I SAW YOU WITH HIM!
DO YOU WANT TO TOTALLY DISGRACE ME?
YOU GIVE UP YOUR STUDIES, TREAT ME WITH DISRESPECT, LOUNGE AROUND DOING NOTHING.
AND NOW GO OFF WITH FOREIGNERS!
WHAT ARE YOU TALKING ABOUT?

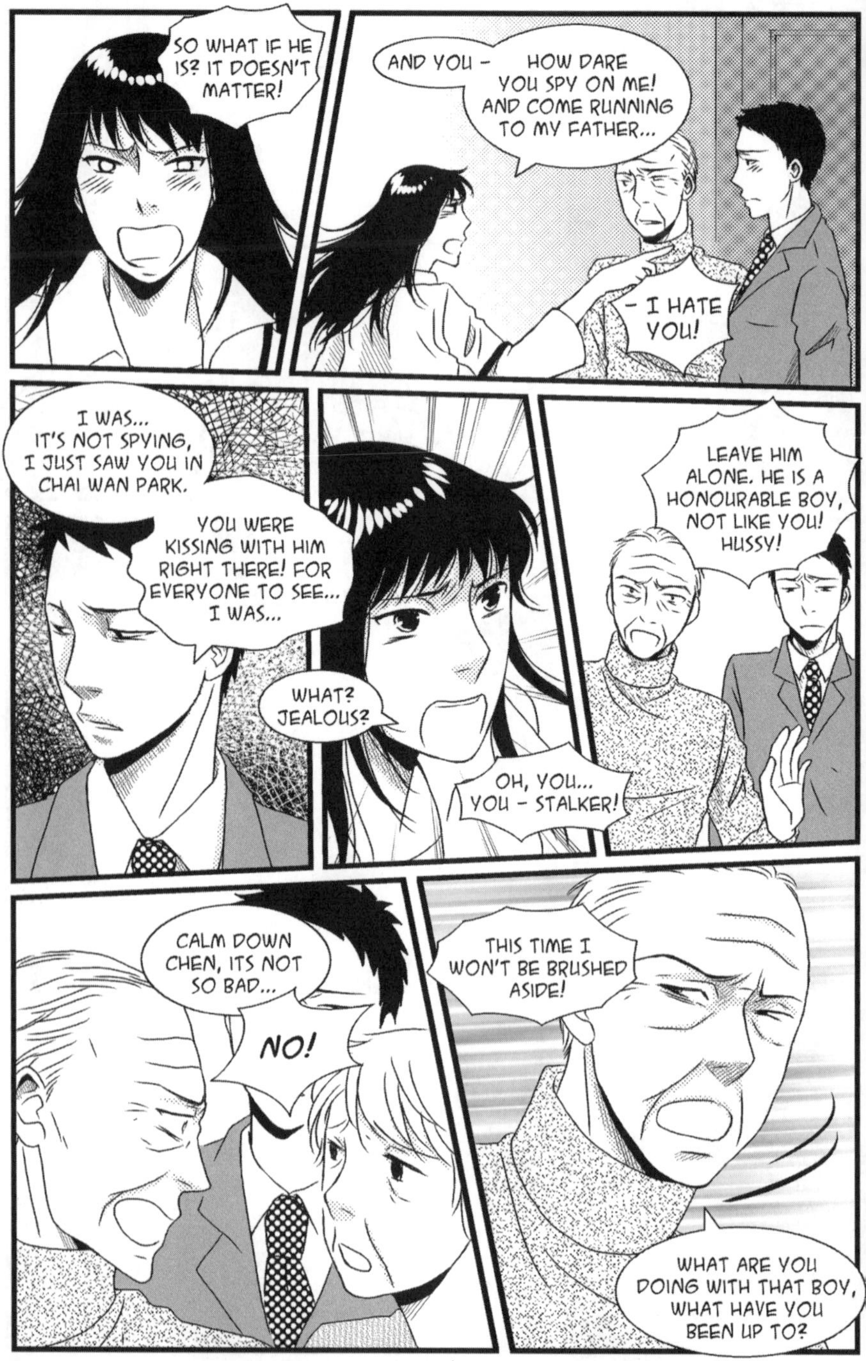

SO WHAT IF HE IS? IT DOESN'T MATTER!
AND YOU -
HOW DARE YOU SPY ON ME! AND COME RUNNING TO MY FATHER...
- I HATE YOU!
I WAS... IT'S NOT SPYING, I JUST SAW YOU IN CHAI WAN PARK.
YOU WERE KISSING WITH HIM RIGHT THERE! FOR EVERYONE TO SEE... I WAS...
WHAT? JEALOUS?
OH, YOU... YOU - STALKER!
LEAVE HIM ALONE. HE IS A HONOURABLE BOY, NOT LIKE YOU! HUSSY!
CALM DOWN CHEN, ITS NOT SO BAD...
NO!
THIS TIME I WON'T BE BRUSHED ASIDE!
WHAT ARE YOU DOING WITH THAT BOY, WHAT HAVE YOU BEEN UP TO?

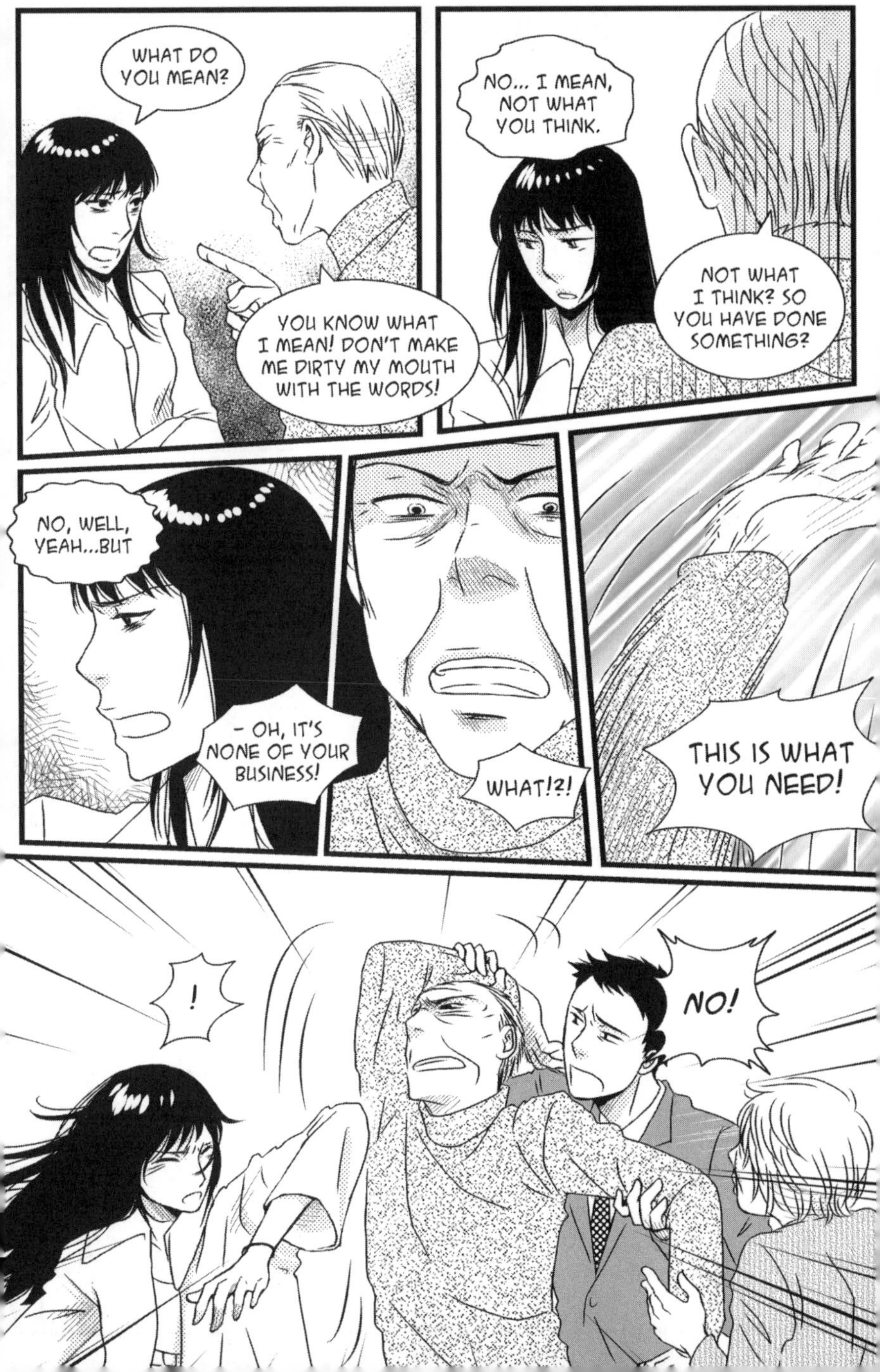
WHAT DO YOU MEAN?
YOU KNOW WHAT I MEAN! DON'T MAKE ME DIRTY MY MOUTH WITH THE WORDS!
NO... I MEAN, NOT WHAT YOU THINK.
NOT WHAT I THINK? SO YOU HAVE DONE SOMETHING?
NO, WELL, YEAH...BUT
- OH, IT'S NONE OF YOUR BUSINESS!
WHAT!?!
THIS IS WHAT YOU NEED!
!
NO!

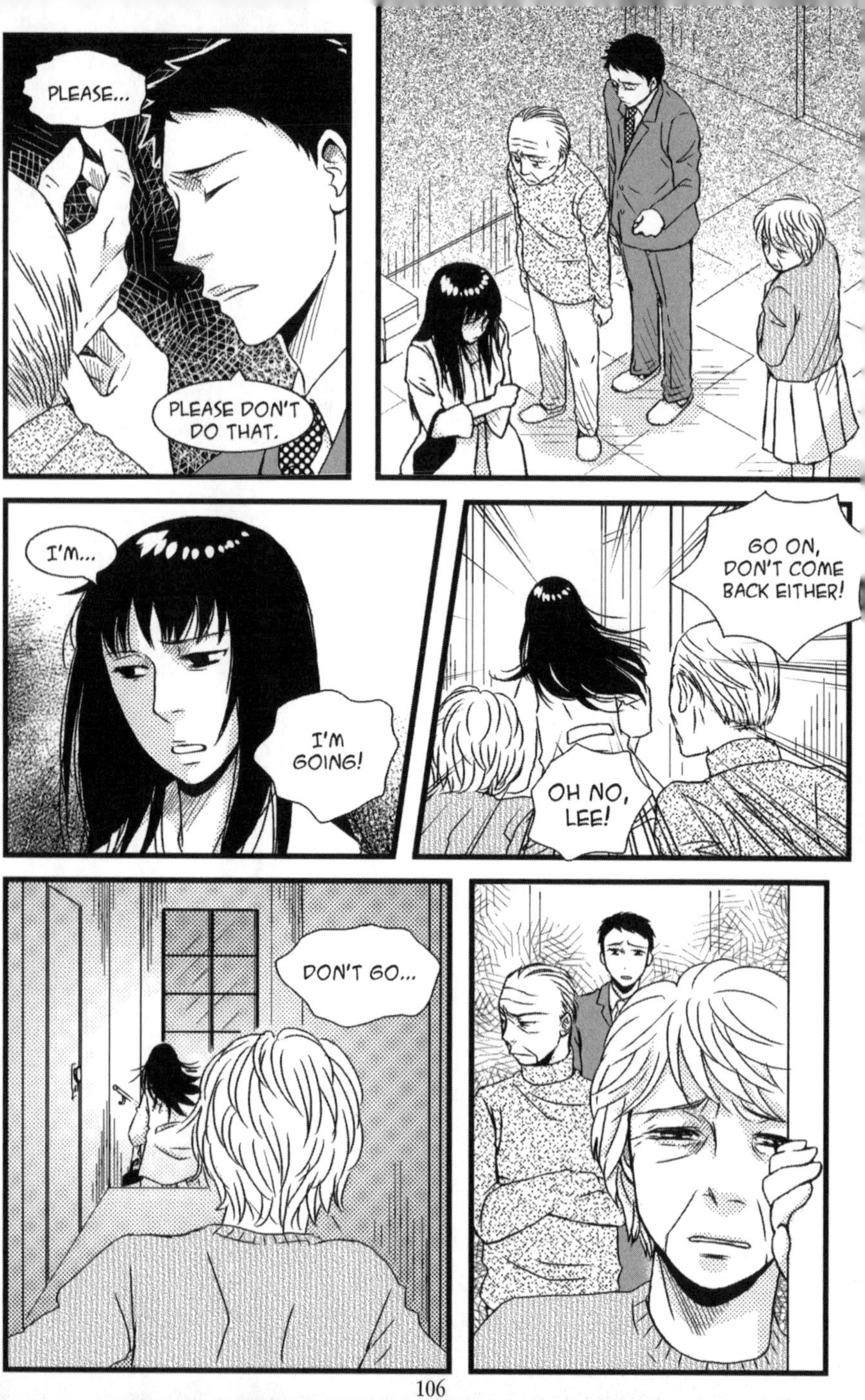
PLEASE...
PLEASE DON'T DO THAT.
I'M...
I'M GOING!
GO ON, DON'T COME BACK EITHER!
OH NO, LEE!
DON'T GO...

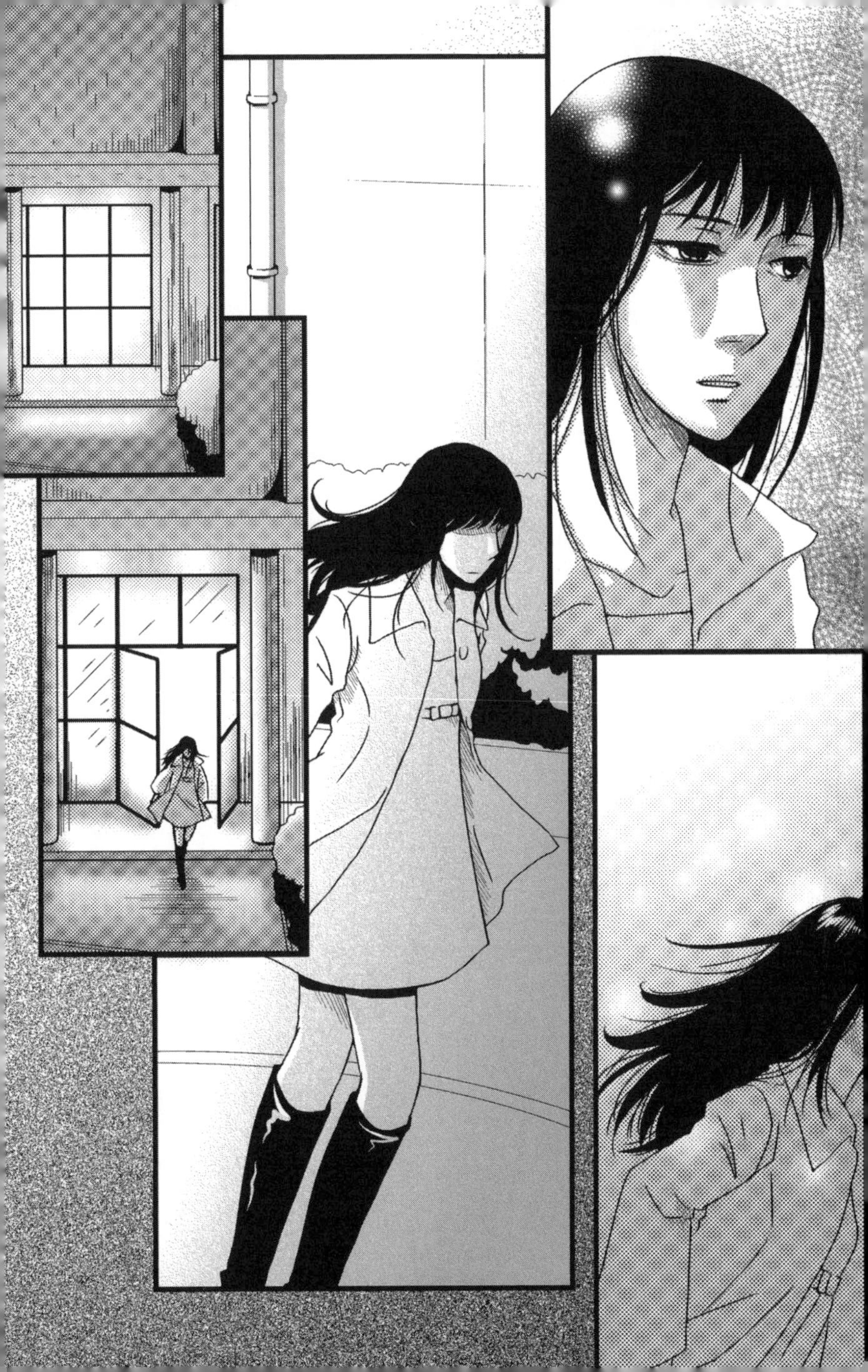

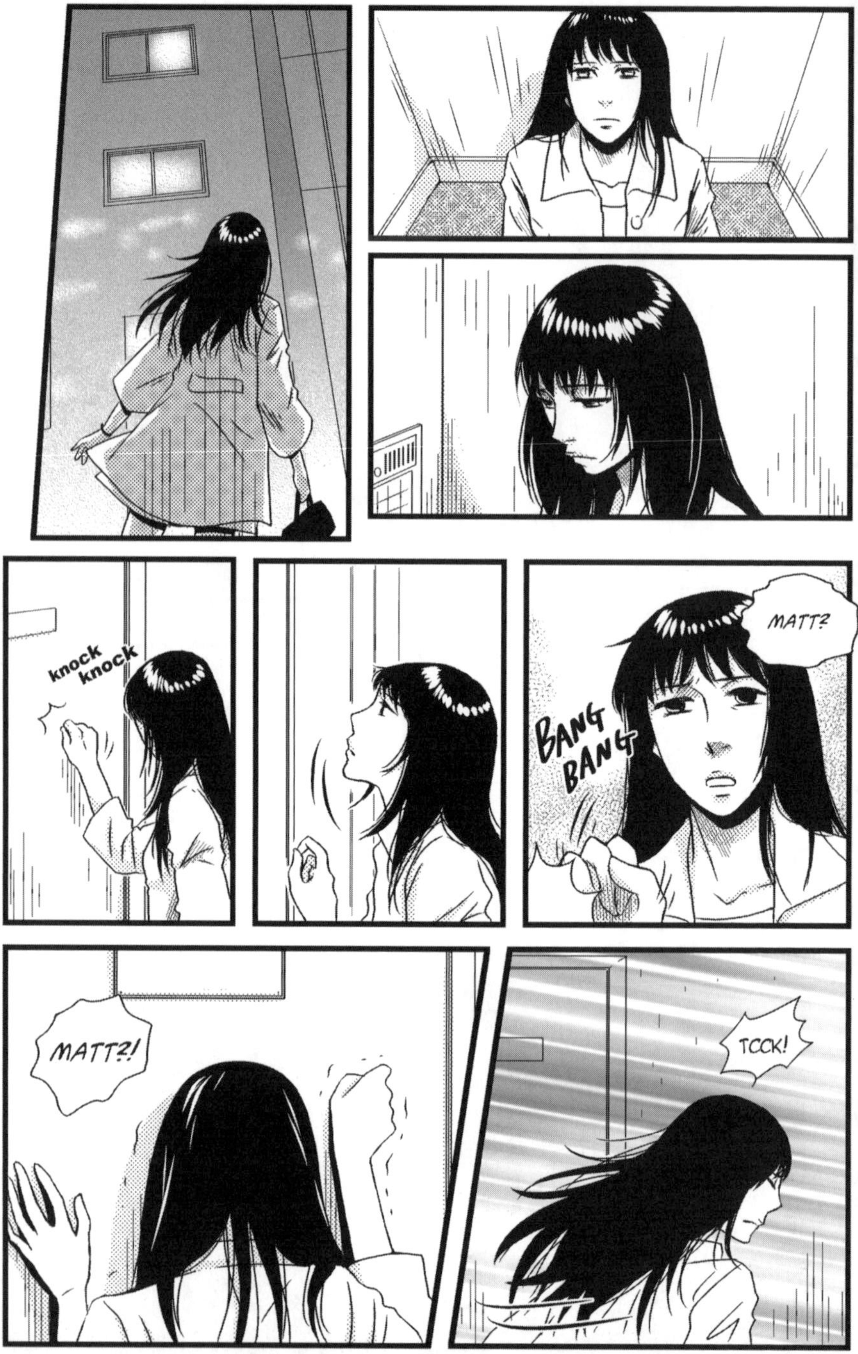
knock knock
MATT?
BANG BANG
MATT?!
TCCK!

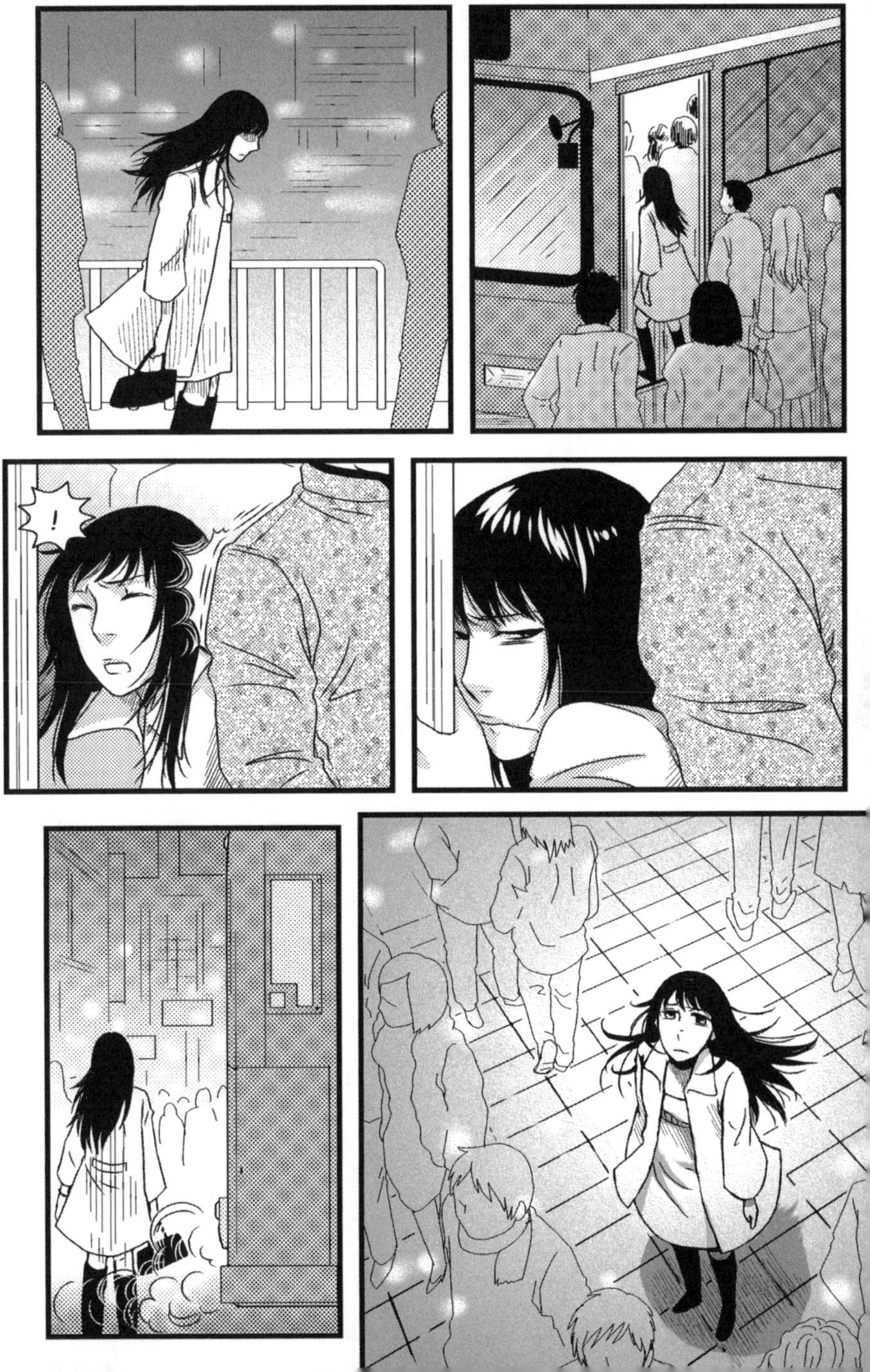
!

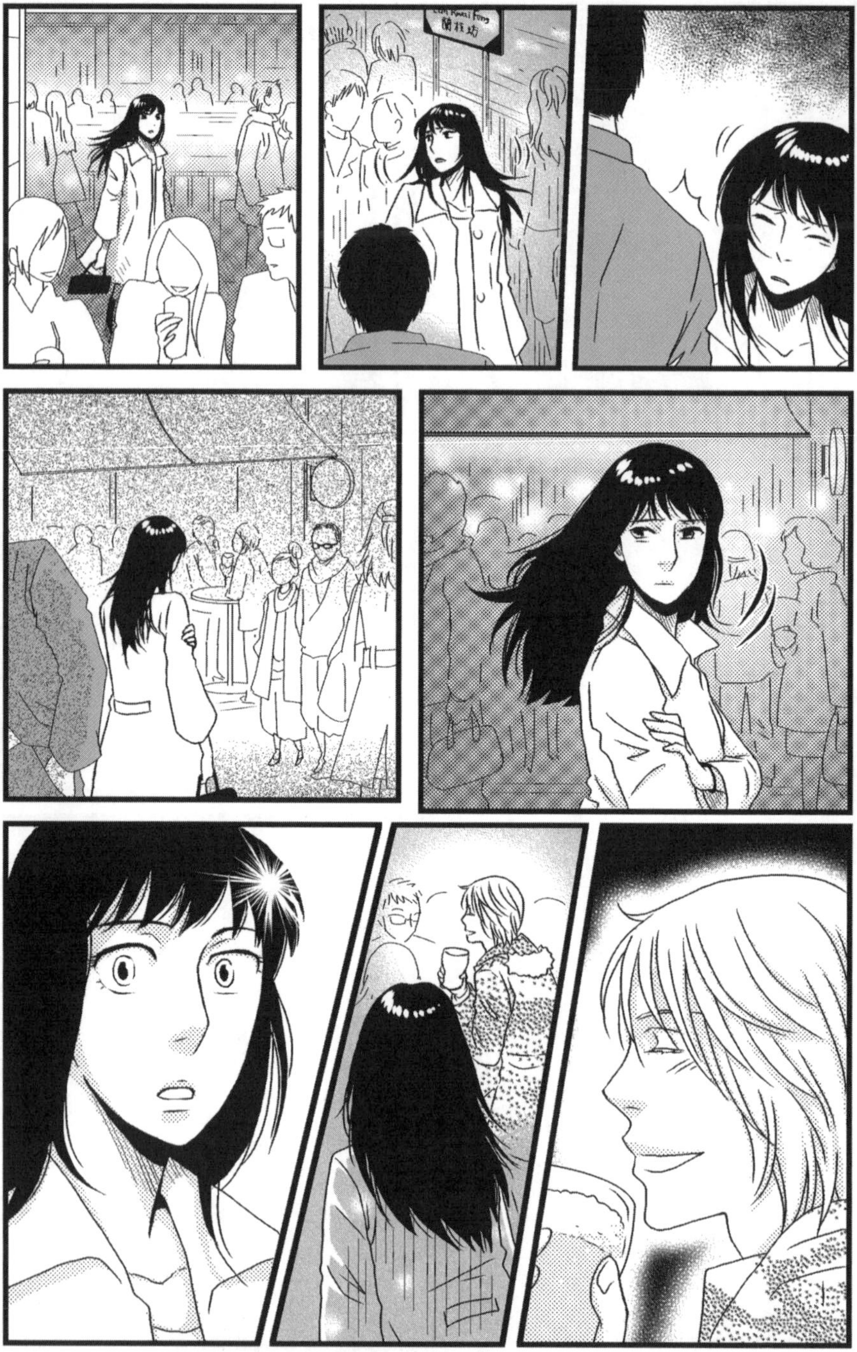

Kwai Fong
蘭桂坊

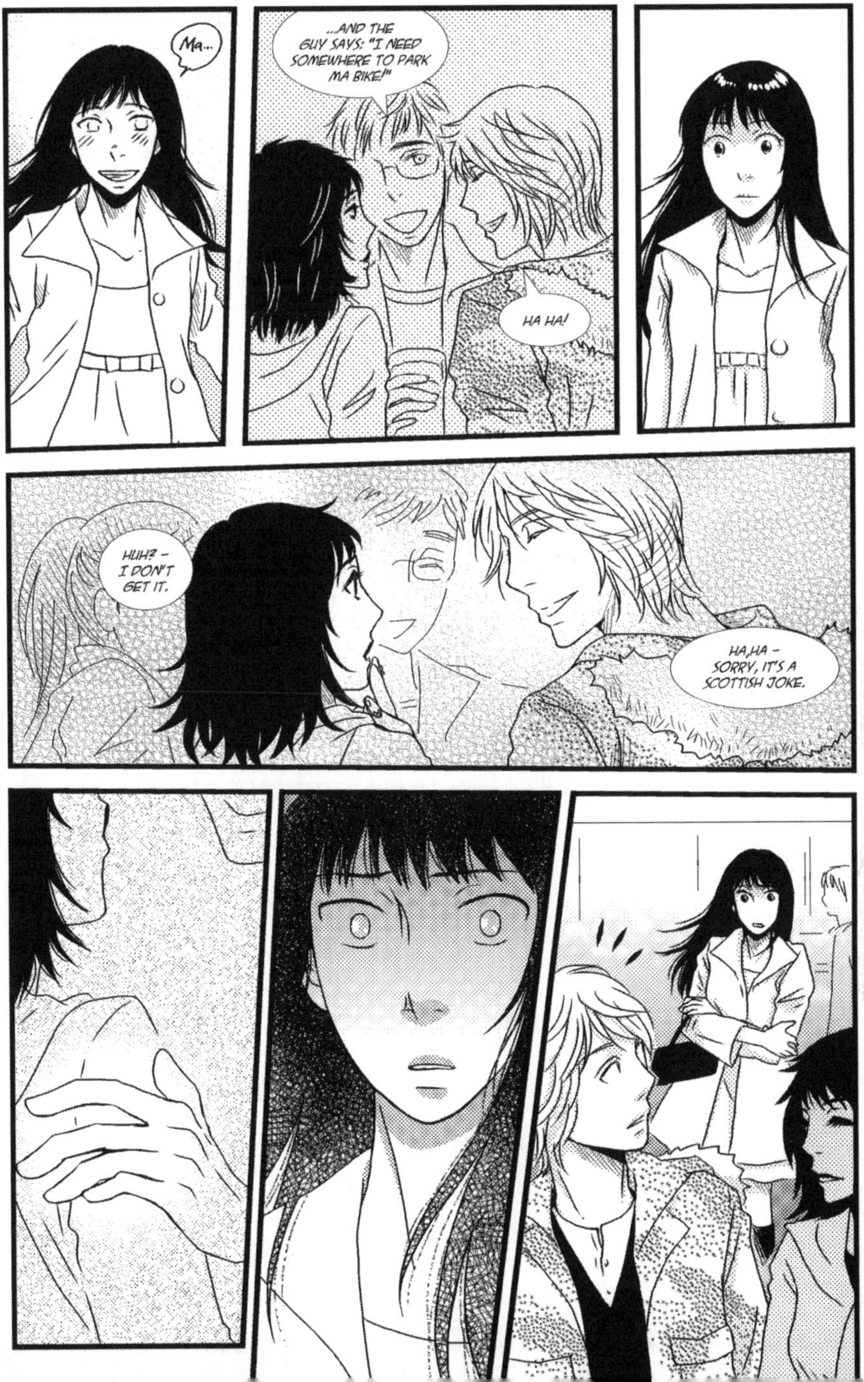
Ma...
...AND THE GUY SAYS: "I NEED SOMEWHERE TO PARK MA BIKE!"
HA HA!
HUH? - I DON'T GET IT.
HA,HA - SORRY, IT'S A SCOTTISH JOKE.

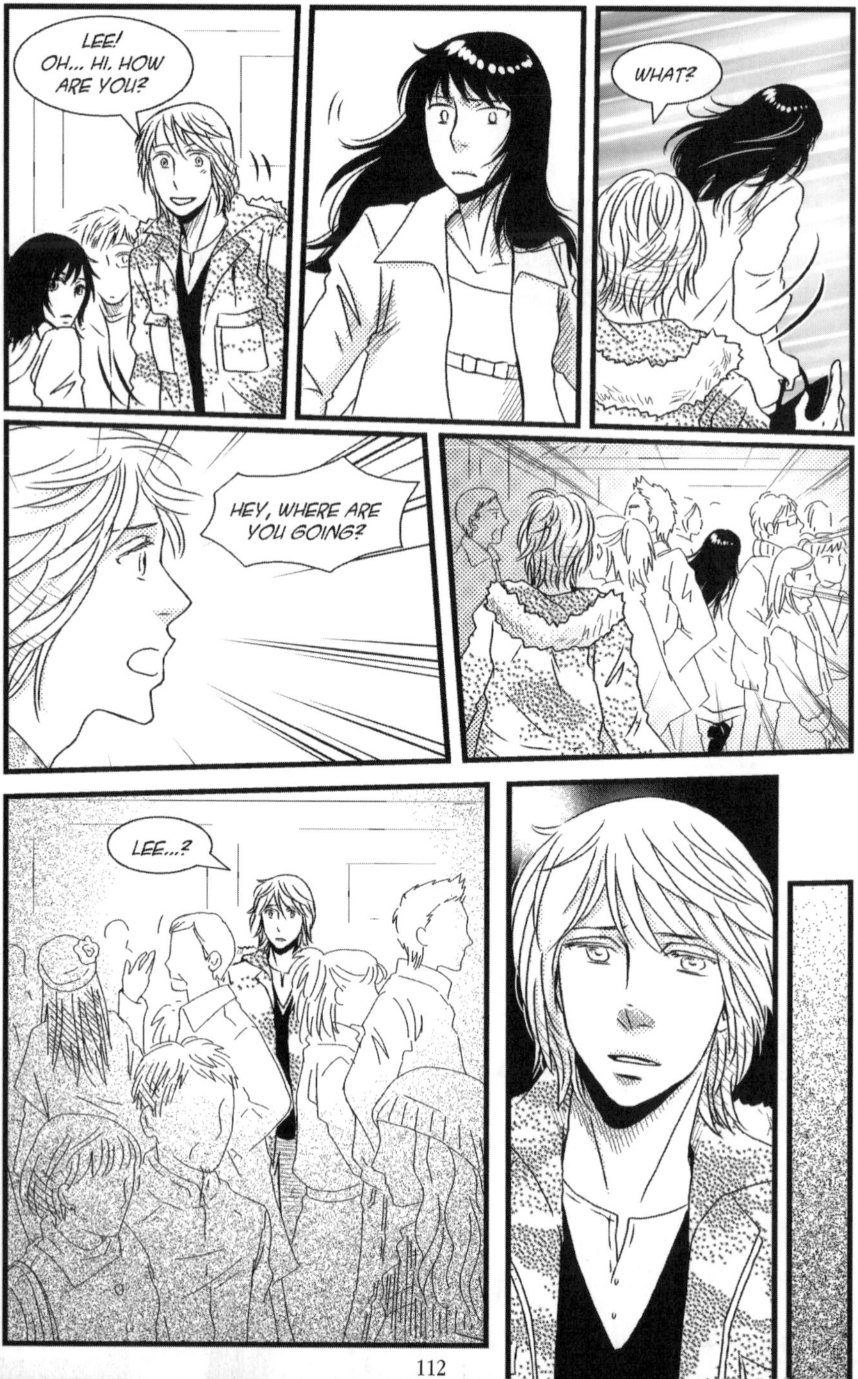
LEE!
OH... HI. HOW ARE YOU?
WHAT?
HEY, WHERE ARE YOU GOING?
LEE...?

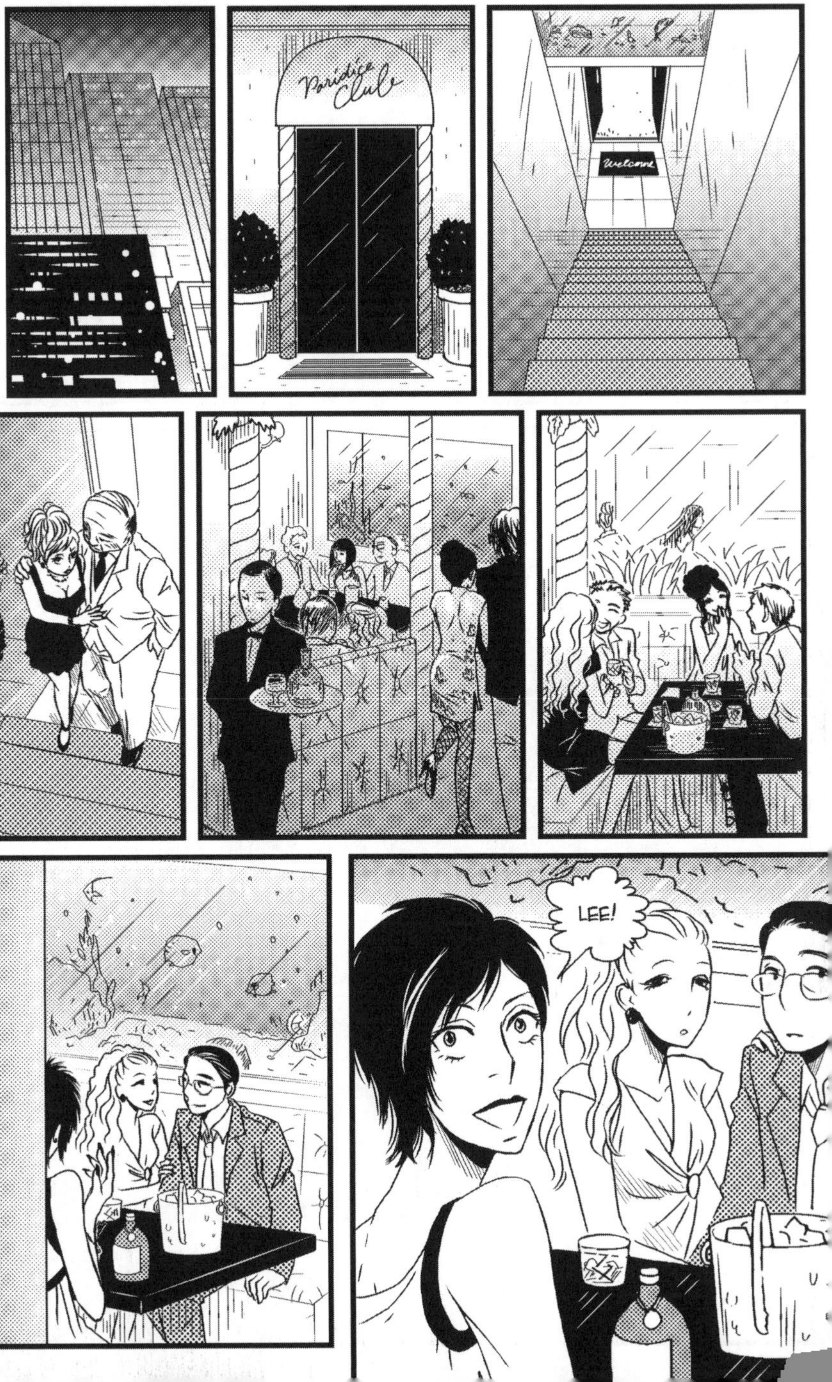
Paradise Club
Welcome
LEE!

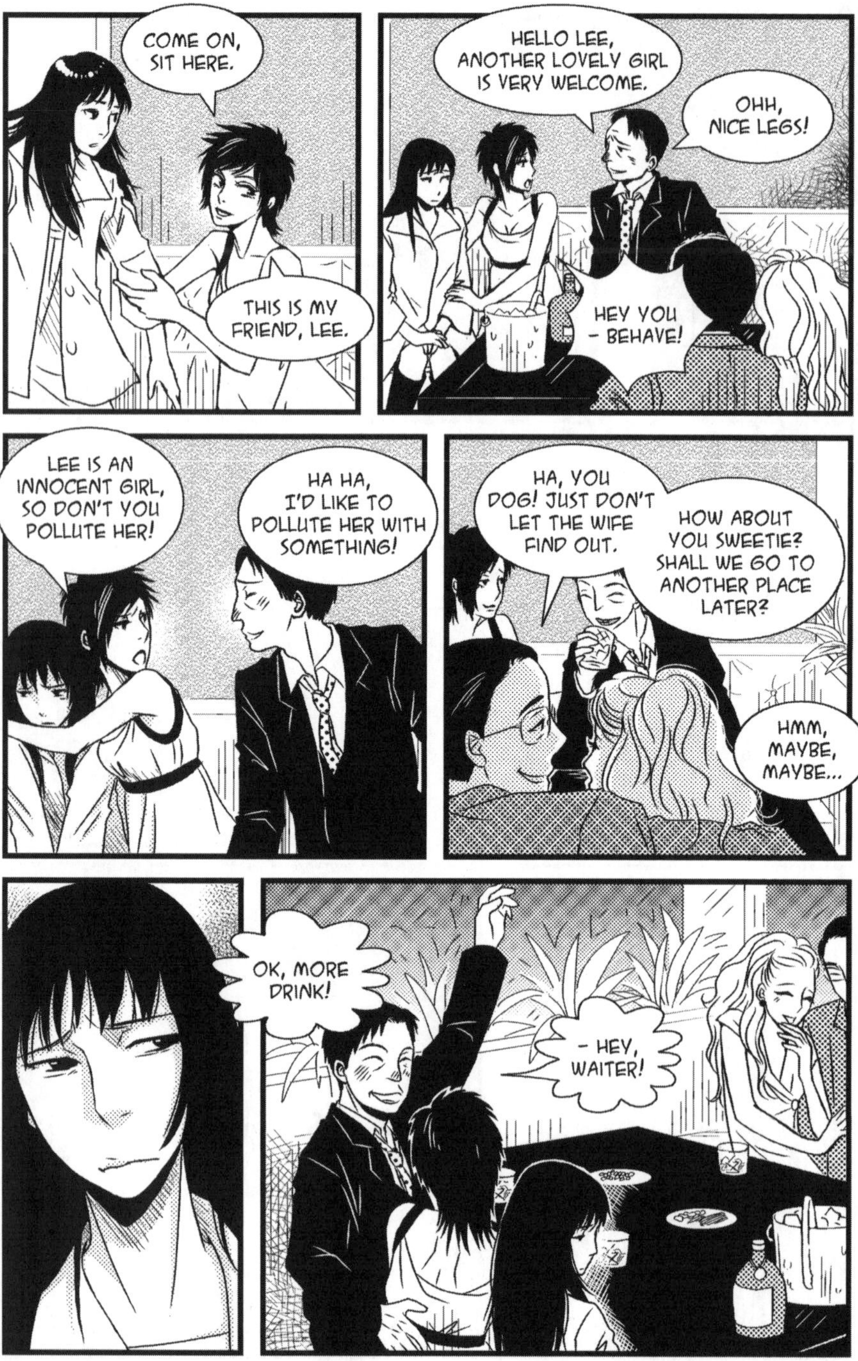
COME ON, SIT HERE.
THIS IS MY FRIEND, LEE.
HELLO LEE, ANOTHER LOVELY GIRL IS VERY WELCOME.
OHH, NICE LEGS!
HEY YOU - BEHAVE!
LEE IS AN INNOCENT GIRL, SO DON'T YOU POLLUTE HER!
HA HA, I'D LIKE TO POLLUTE HER WITH SOMETHING!
HA, YOU DOG! JUST DON'T LET THE WIFE FIND OUT.
HOW ABOUT YOU SWEETIE? SHALL WE GO TO ANOTHER PLACE LATER?
HMM, MAYBE, MAYBE...
OK, MORE DRINK!
- HEY, WAITER!

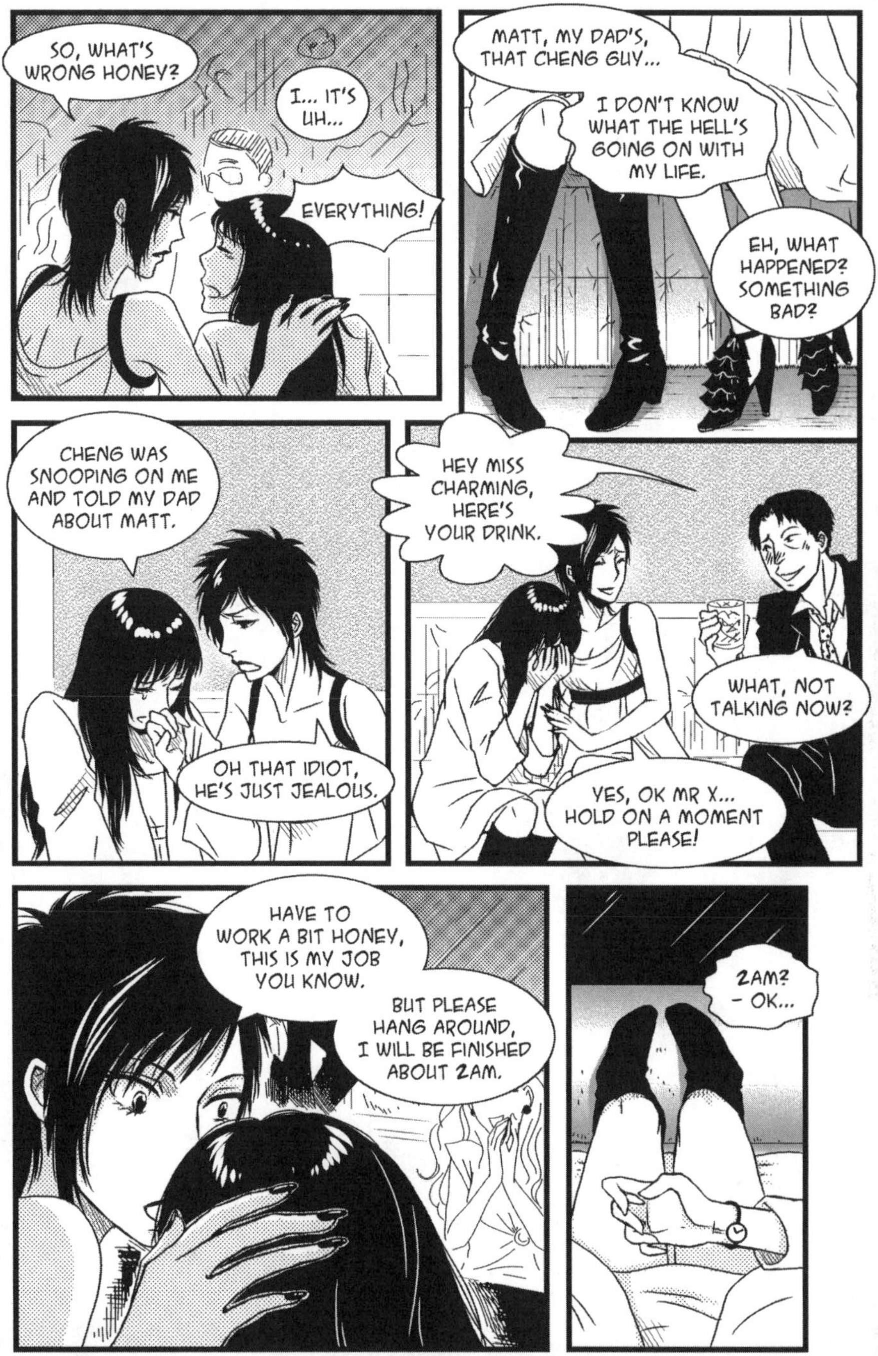
SO, WHAT'S WRONG HONEY?
I... IT'S UH...
EVERYTHING!
MATT, MY DAD'S, THAT CHENG GUY...
I DON'T KNOW WHAT THE HELL'S GOING ON WITH MY LIFE.
EH, WHAT HAPPENED? SOMETHING BAD?
CHENG WAS SNOOPING ON ME AND TOLD MY DAD ABOUT MATT.
OH THAT IDIOT, HE'S JUST JEALOUS.
HEY MISS CHARMING, HERE'S YOUR DRINK.
WHAT, NOT TALKING NOW?
YES, OK MR X... HOLD ON A MOMENT PLEASE!
HAVE TO WORK A BIT HONEY, THIS IS MY JOB YOU KNOW.
BUT PLEASE HANG AROUND, I WILL BE FINISHED ABOUT 2AM.
2AM? - OK...

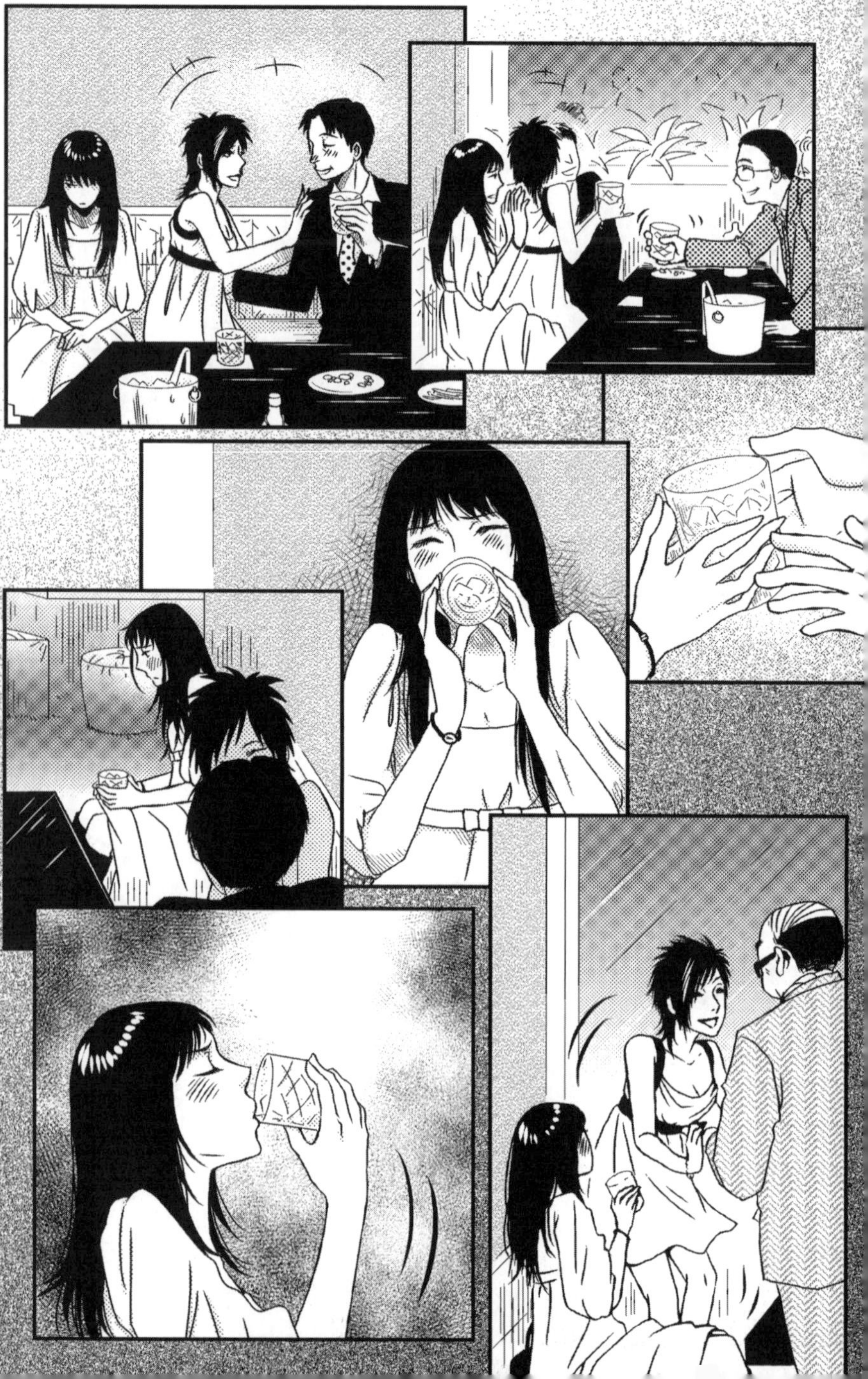

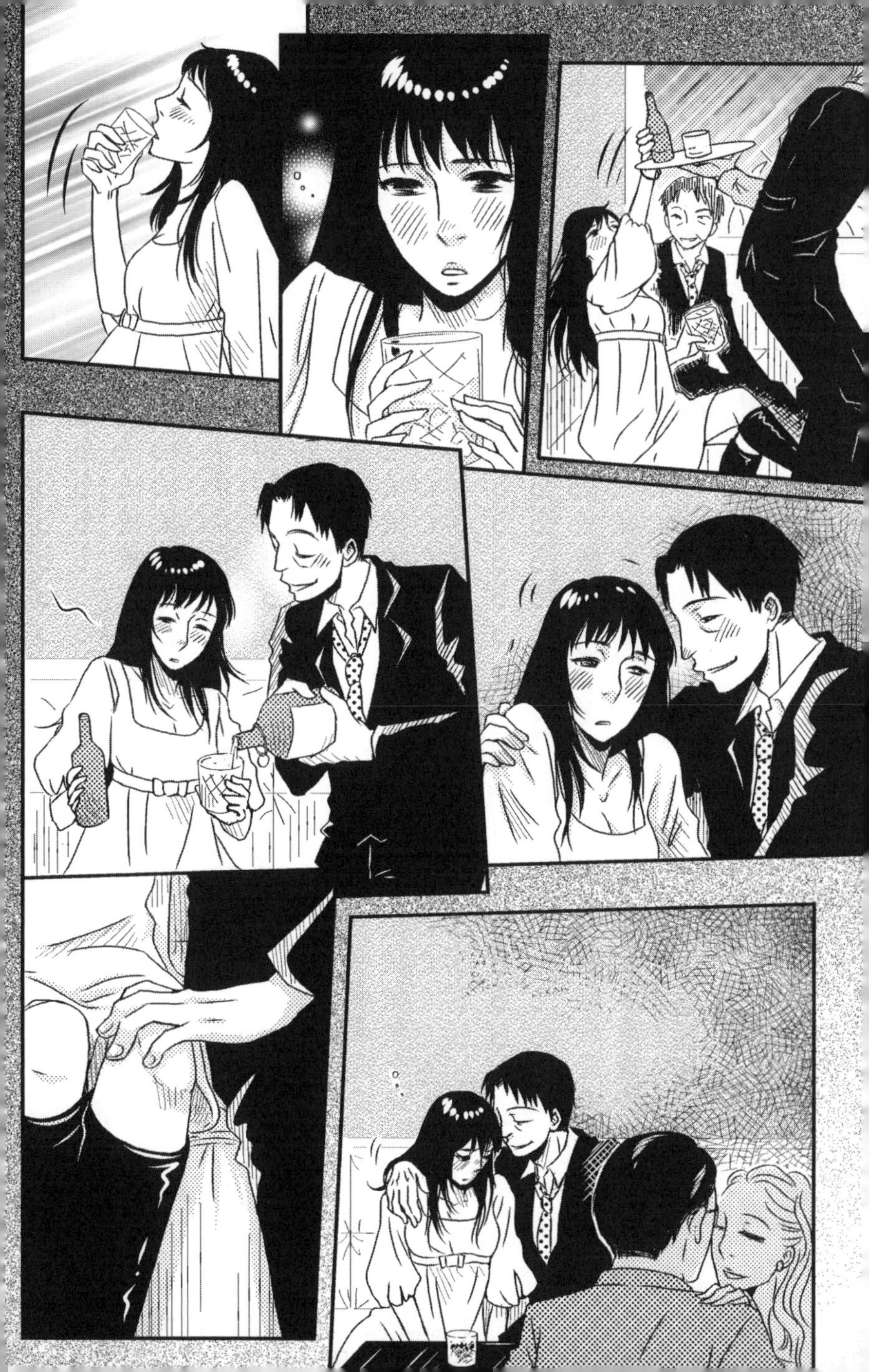

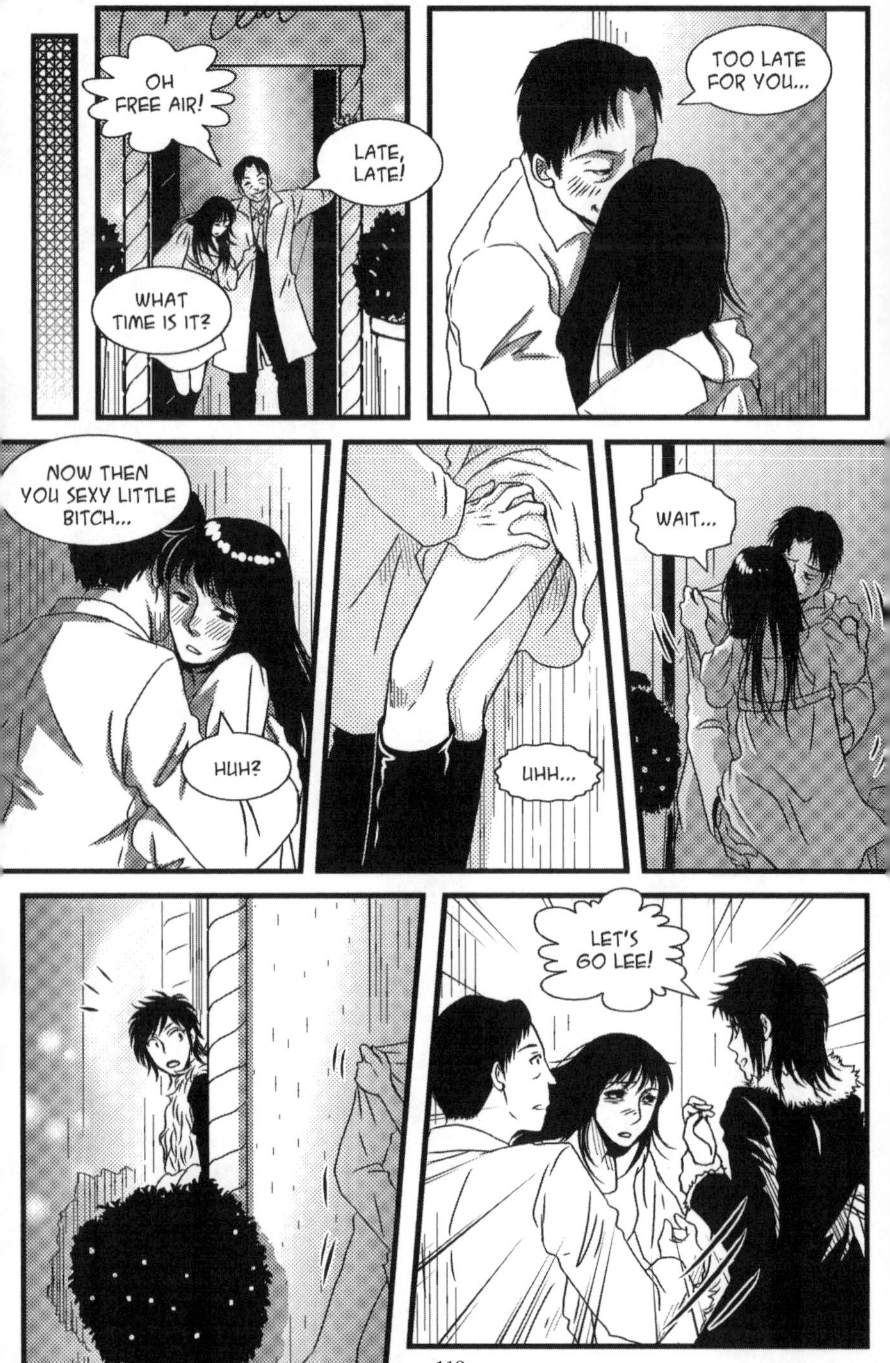
OH FREE AIR!
LATE, LATE!
WHAT TIME IS IT?
TOO LATE FOR YOU...
NOW THEN YOU SEXY LITTLE BITCH...
HUH?
UHH...
WAIT...
LET'S GO LEE!

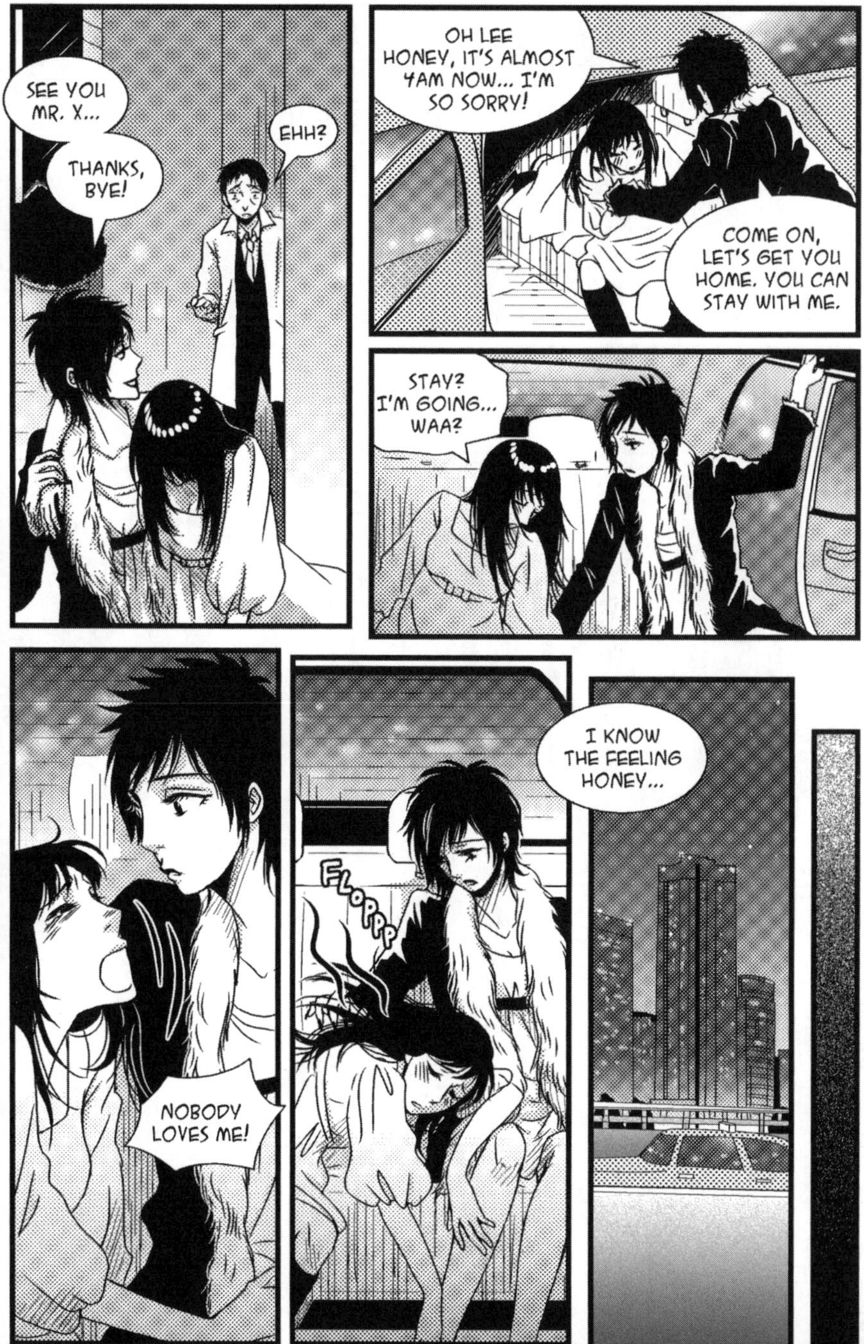
SEE YOU MR. X...
THANKS, BYE!
EHH?
OH LEE HONEY, IT'S ALMOST 4AM NOW... I'M SO SORRY!
COME ON, LET'S GET YOU HOME. YOU CAN STAY WITH ME.
STAY? I'M GOING... WAA?
NOBODY LOVES ME!
FLOPPP
I KNOW THE FEELING HONEY...

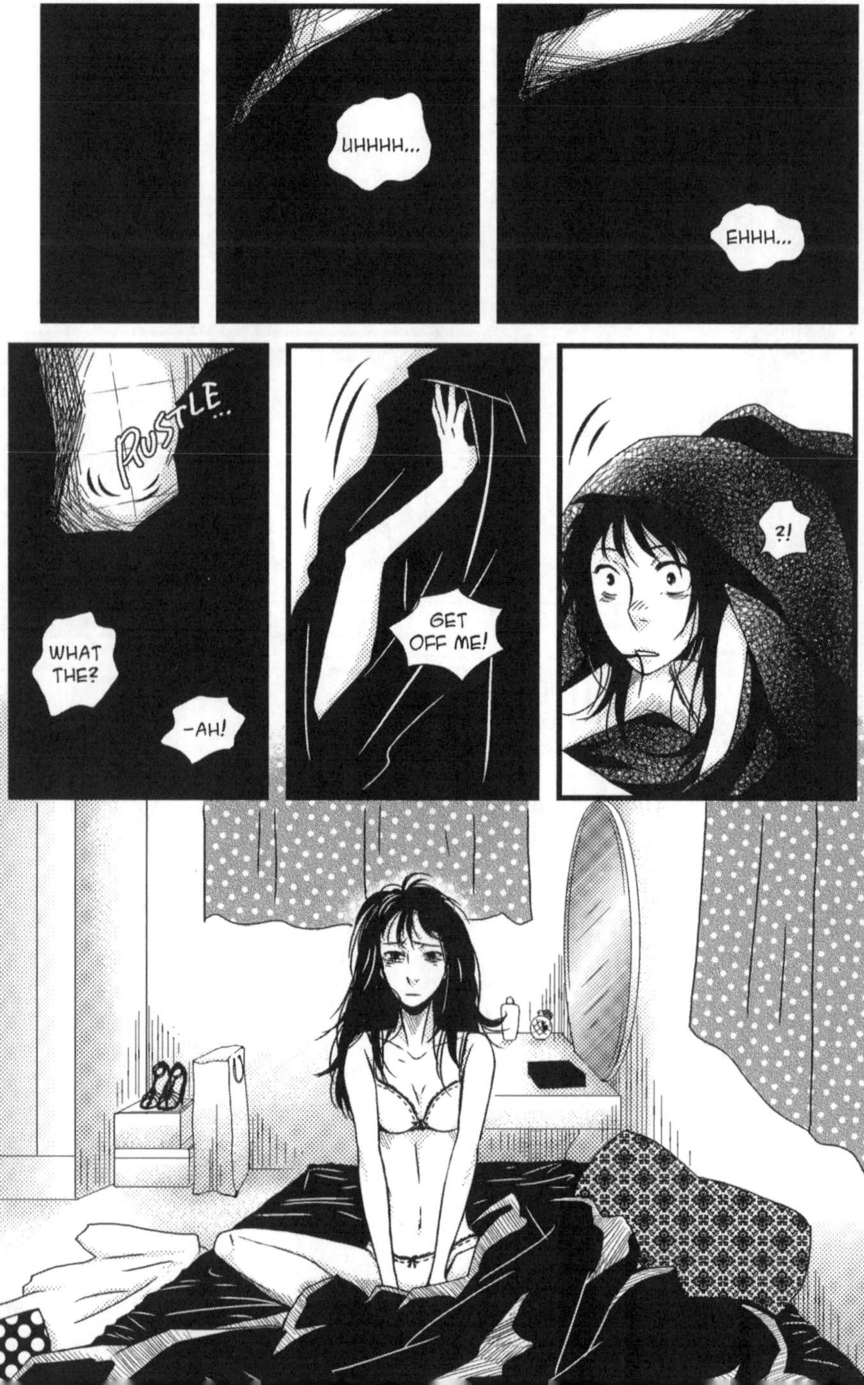
UHHHH...
EHHH...
RUSTLE...
WHAT THE?
-AH!
GET OFF ME!
?!

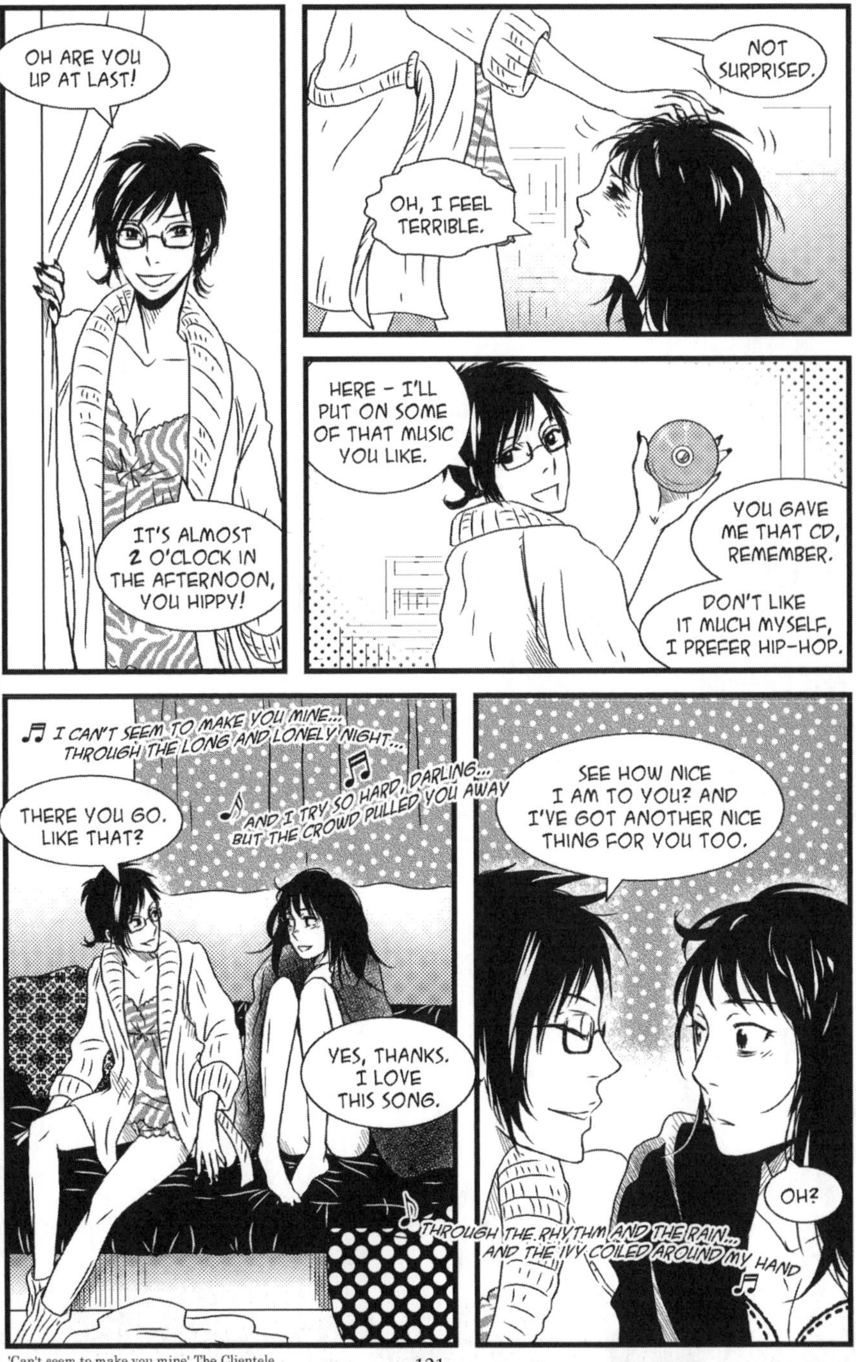
OH ARE YOU UP AT LAST!
IT'S ALMOST 2 O'CLOCK IN THE AFTERNOON, YOU HIPPY!
NOT SURPRISED.
OH, I FEEL TERRIBLE.
HERE - I'LL PUT ON SOME OF THAT MUSIC YOU LIKE.
YOU GAVE ME THAT CD, REMEMBER.
DON'T LIKE IT MUCH MYSELF, I PREFER HIP-HOP.
I CAN'T SEEM TO MAKE YOU MINE... THROUGH THE LONG AND LONELY NIGHT...
AND I TRY SO HARD, DARLING... BUT THE CROWD PULLED YOU AWAY
THERE YOU GO. LIKE THAT?
YES, THANKS. I LOVE THIS SONG.
SEE HOW NICE I AM TO YOU? AND I'VE GOT ANOTHER NICE THING FOR YOU TOO.
OH?
THROUGH THE RHYTHM AND THE RAIN... AND THE IVY COILED AROUND MY HAND

'Can't seem to make you mine' The Clientele

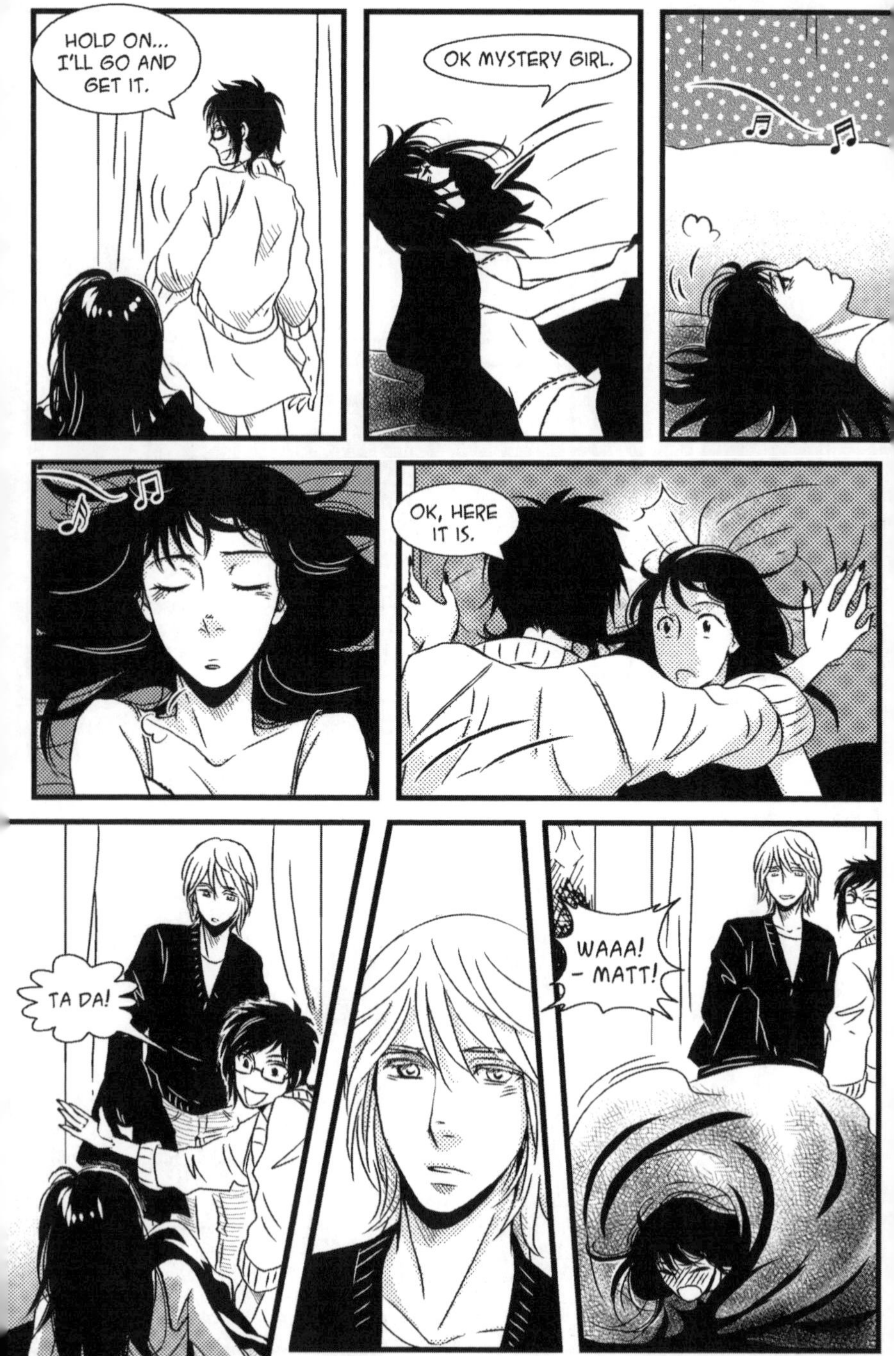
HOLD ON... I'LL GO AND GET IT.
OK MYSTERY GIRL.
OK, HERE IT IS.
TA DA!
WAAA! - MATT!

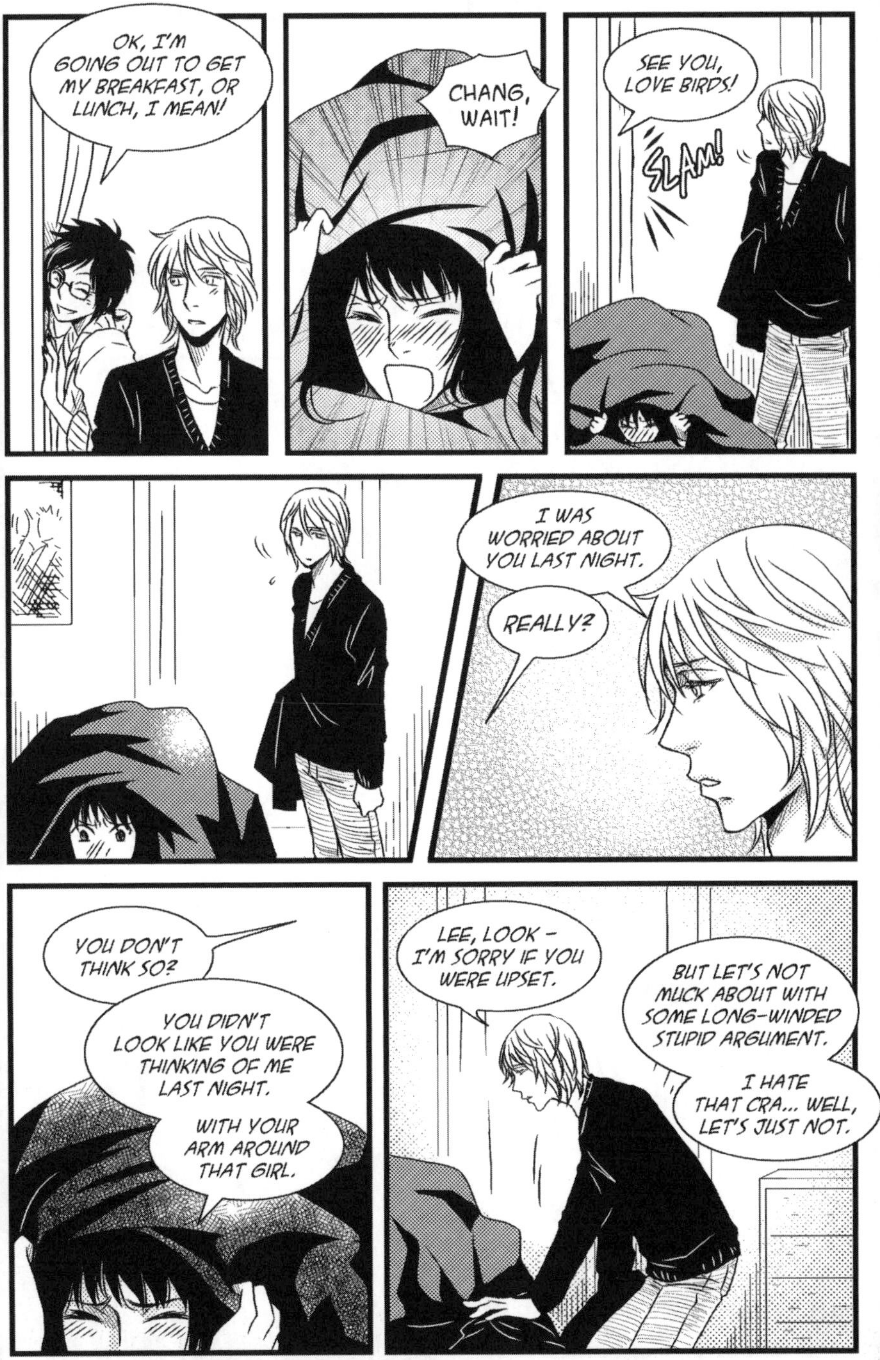

OK, I'M GOING OUT TO GET MY BREAKFAST, OR LUNCH, I MEAN!
CHANG, WAIT!
SEE YOU, LOVE BIRDS!
SLAM!
I WAS WORRIED ABOUT YOU LAST NIGHT.
REALLY?
YOU DON'T THINK SO?
YOU DIDN'T LOOK LIKE YOU WERE THINKING OF ME LAST NIGHT.
WITH YOUR ARM AROUND THAT GIRL.
LEE, LOOK - I'M SORRY IF YOU WERE UPSET.
BUT LET'S NOT MUCK ABOUT WITH SOME LONG-WINDED STUPID ARGUMENT.
I HATE THAT CRA... WELL, LET'S JUST NOT.

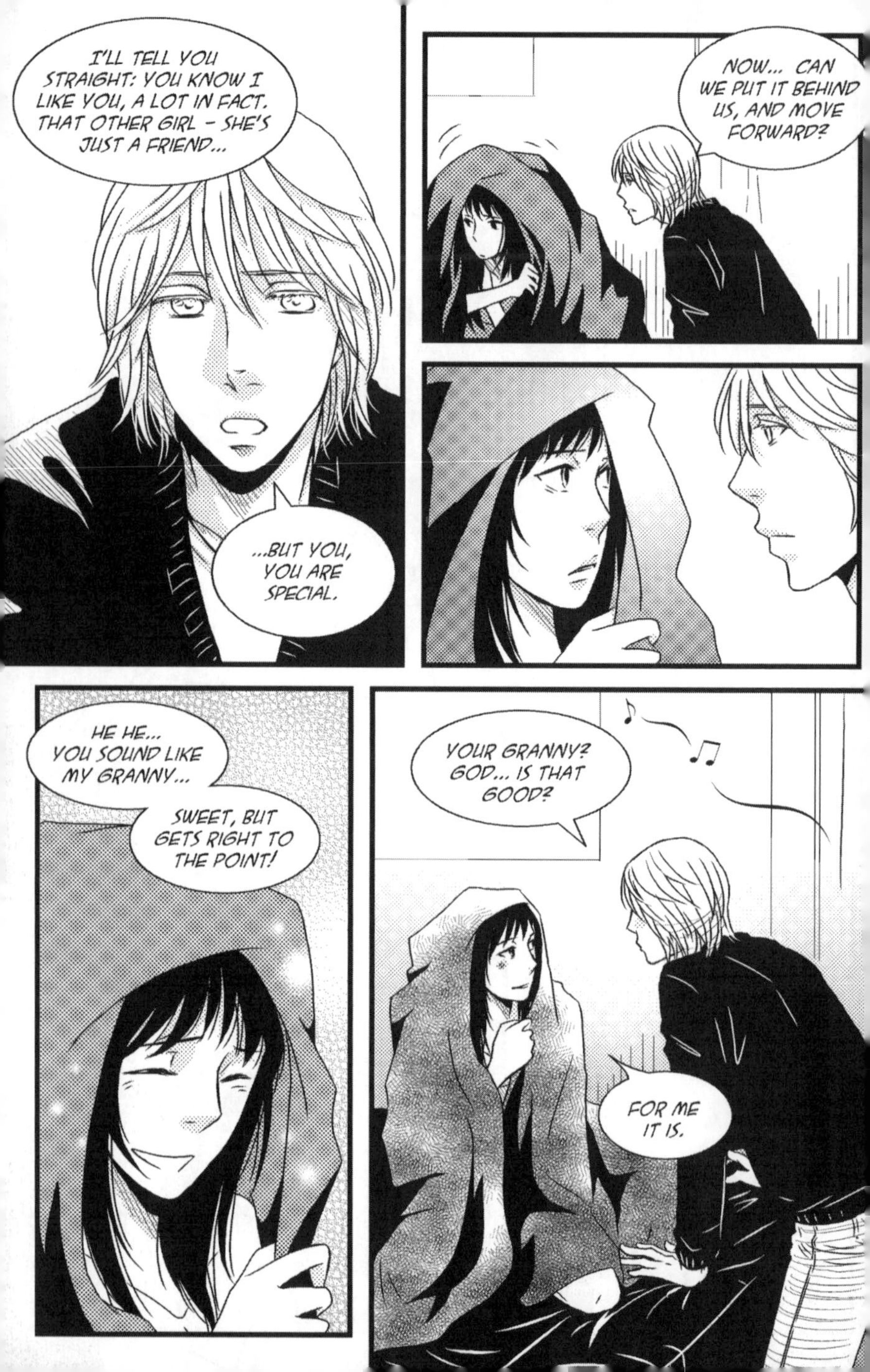
I'LL TELL YOU STRAIGHT: YOU KNOW I LIKE YOU, A LOT IN FACT. THAT OTHER GIRL – SHE'S JUST A FRIEND...
...BUT YOU, YOU ARE SPECIAL.
NOW... CAN WE PUT IT BEHIND US, AND MOVE FORWARD?
HE HE... YOU SOUND LIKE MY GRANNY...
SWEET, BUT GETS RIGHT TO THE POINT!
YOUR GRANNY? GOD... IS THAT GOOD?
FOR ME IT IS.

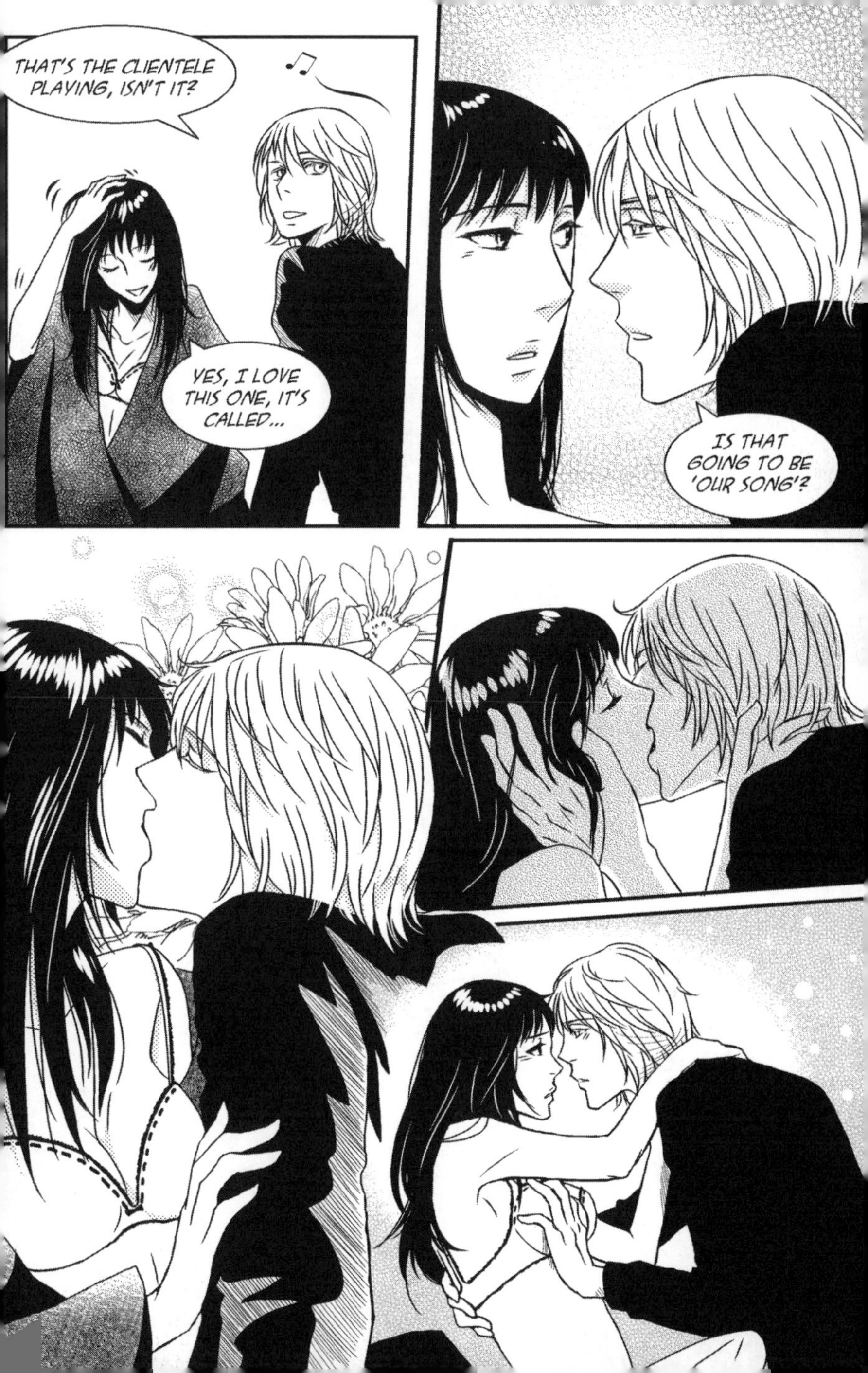
THAT'S THE CLIENTELE PLAYING, ISN'T IT?
YES, I LOVE THIS ONE, IT'S CALLED...
IS THAT GOING TO BE 'OUR SONG'?

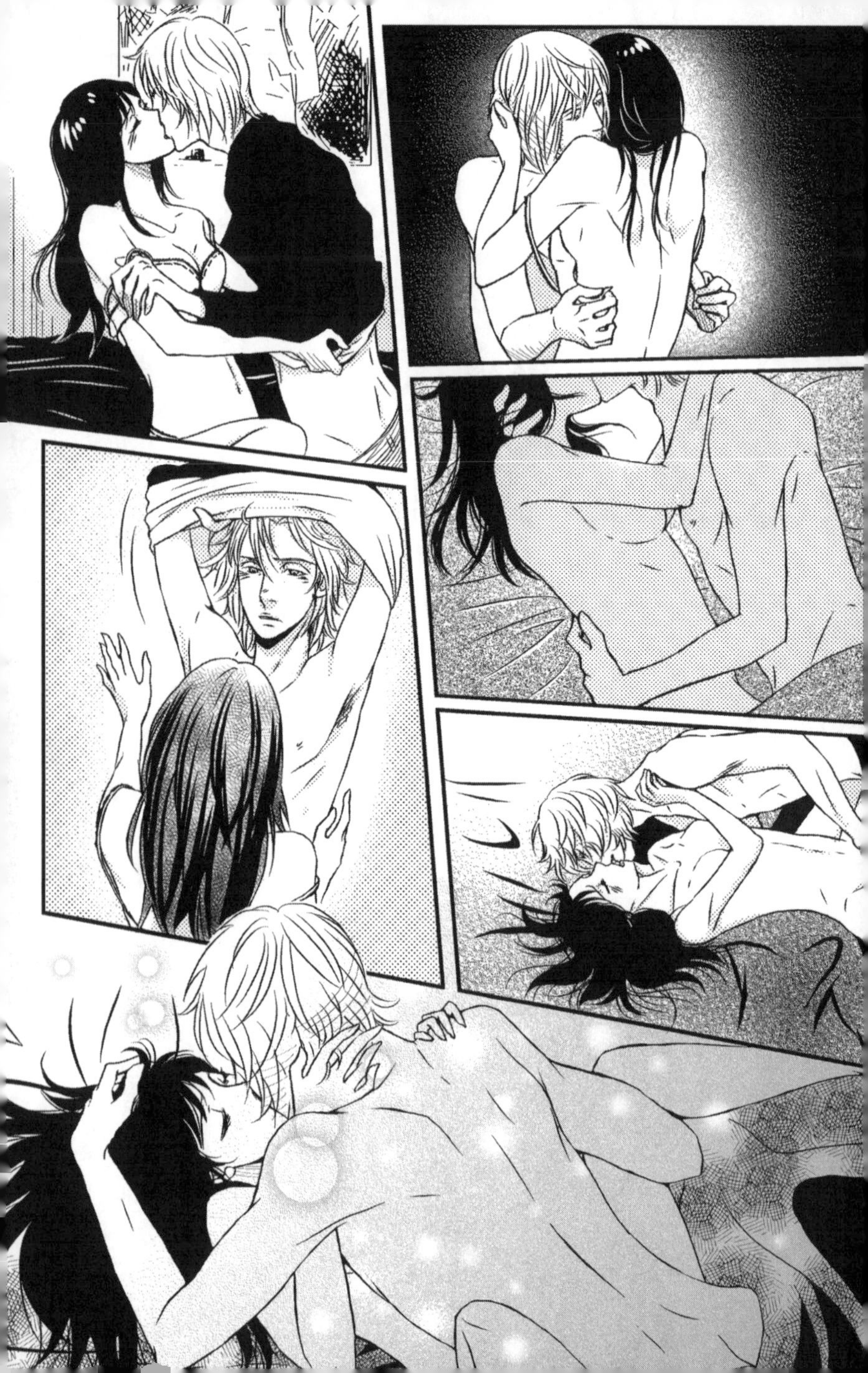

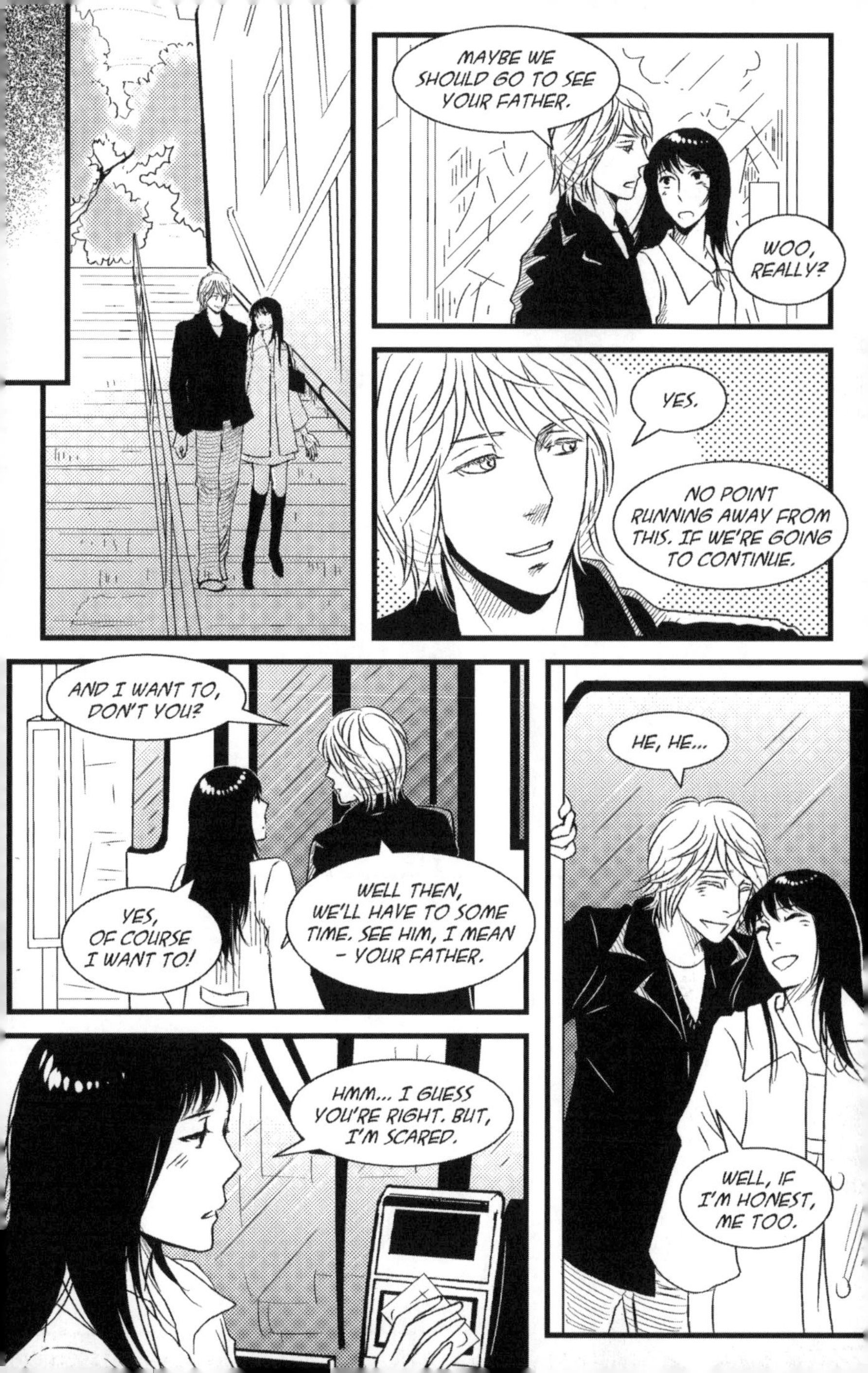
MAYBE WE SHOULD GO TO SEE YOUR FATHER.
WOO, REALLY?
YES.
NO POINT RUNNING AWAY FROM THIS. IF WE'RE GOING TO CONTINUE.
AND I WANT TO, DON'T YOU?
YES, OF COURSE I WANT TO!
WELL THEN, WE'LL HAVE TO SOME TIME. SEE HIM, I MEAN - YOUR FATHER.
HMM... I GUESS YOU'RE RIGHT. BUT, I'M SCARED.
HE, HE...
WELL, IF I'M HONEST, ME TOO.

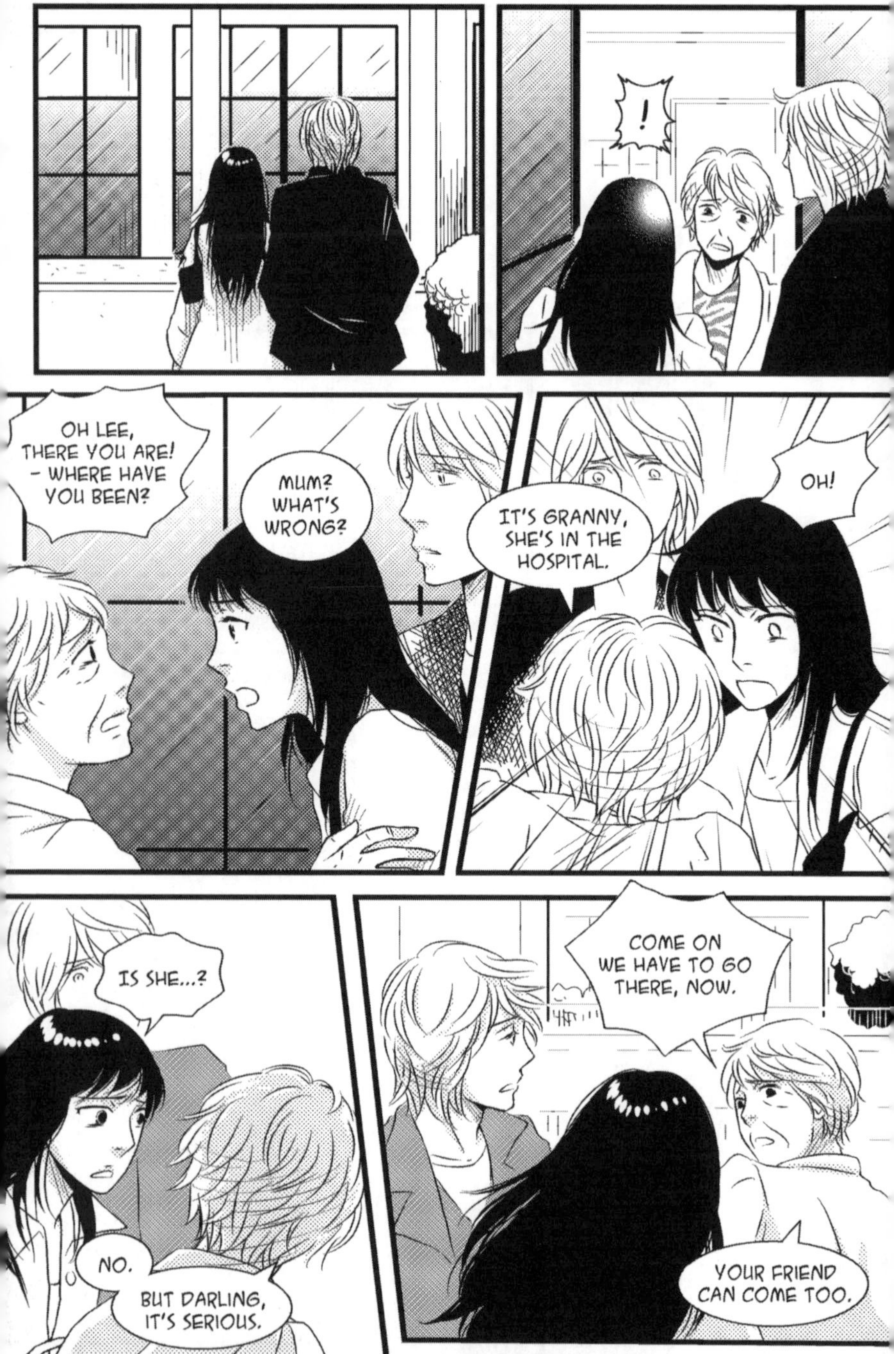
!
OH LEE, THERE YOU ARE! - WHERE HAVE YOU BEEN?
MUM? WHAT'S WRONG?
IT'S GRANNY, SHE'S IN THE HOSPITAL.
OH!
IS SHE...?
NO.
BUT DARLING, IT'S SERIOUS.
COME ON WE HAVE TO GO THERE, NOW.
YOUR FRIEND CAN COME TOO.

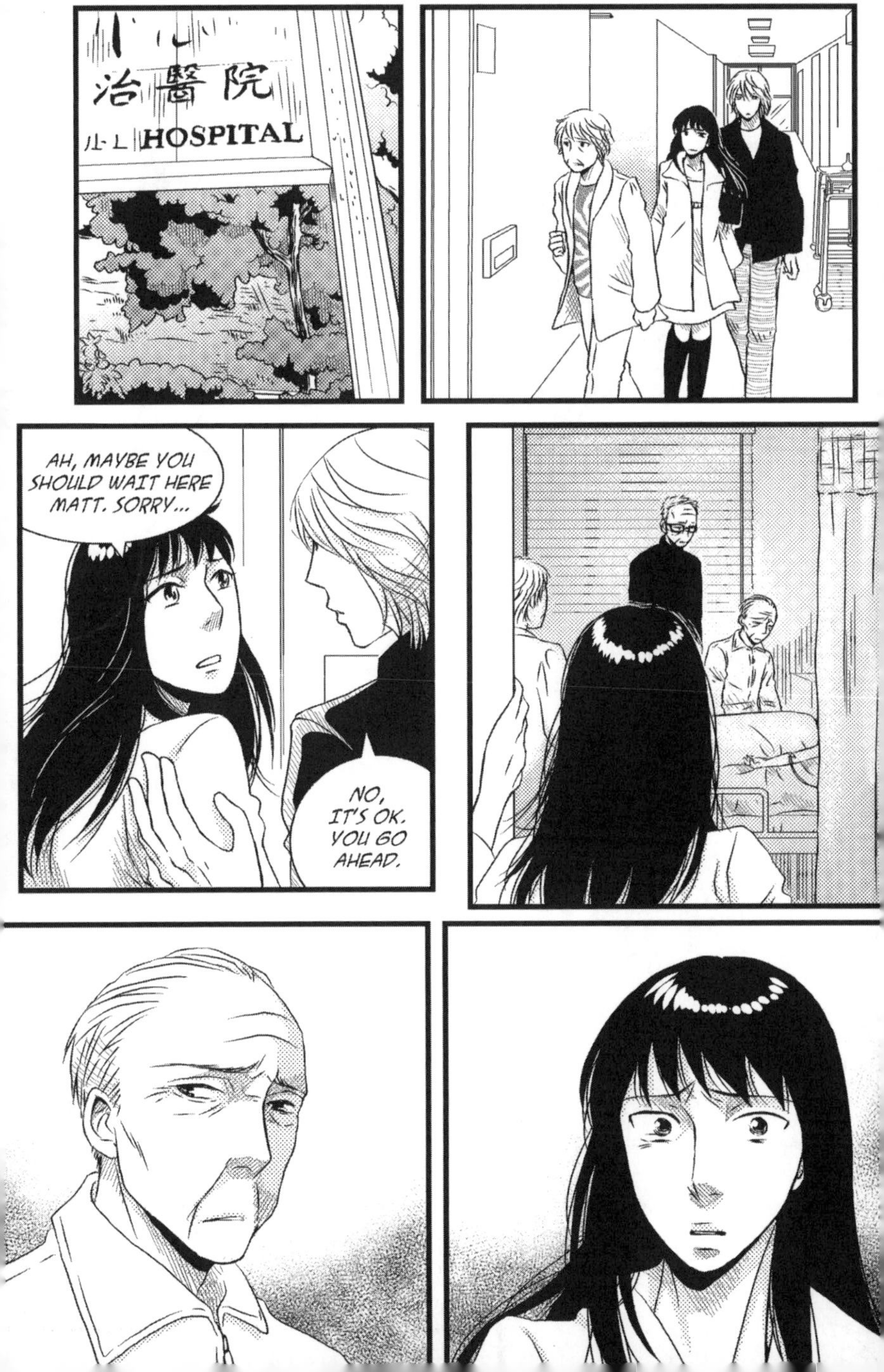
治醫院
HOSPITAL
AH, MAYBE YOU SHOULD WAIT HERE MATT. SORRY...
NO, IT'S OK. YOU GO AHEAD.

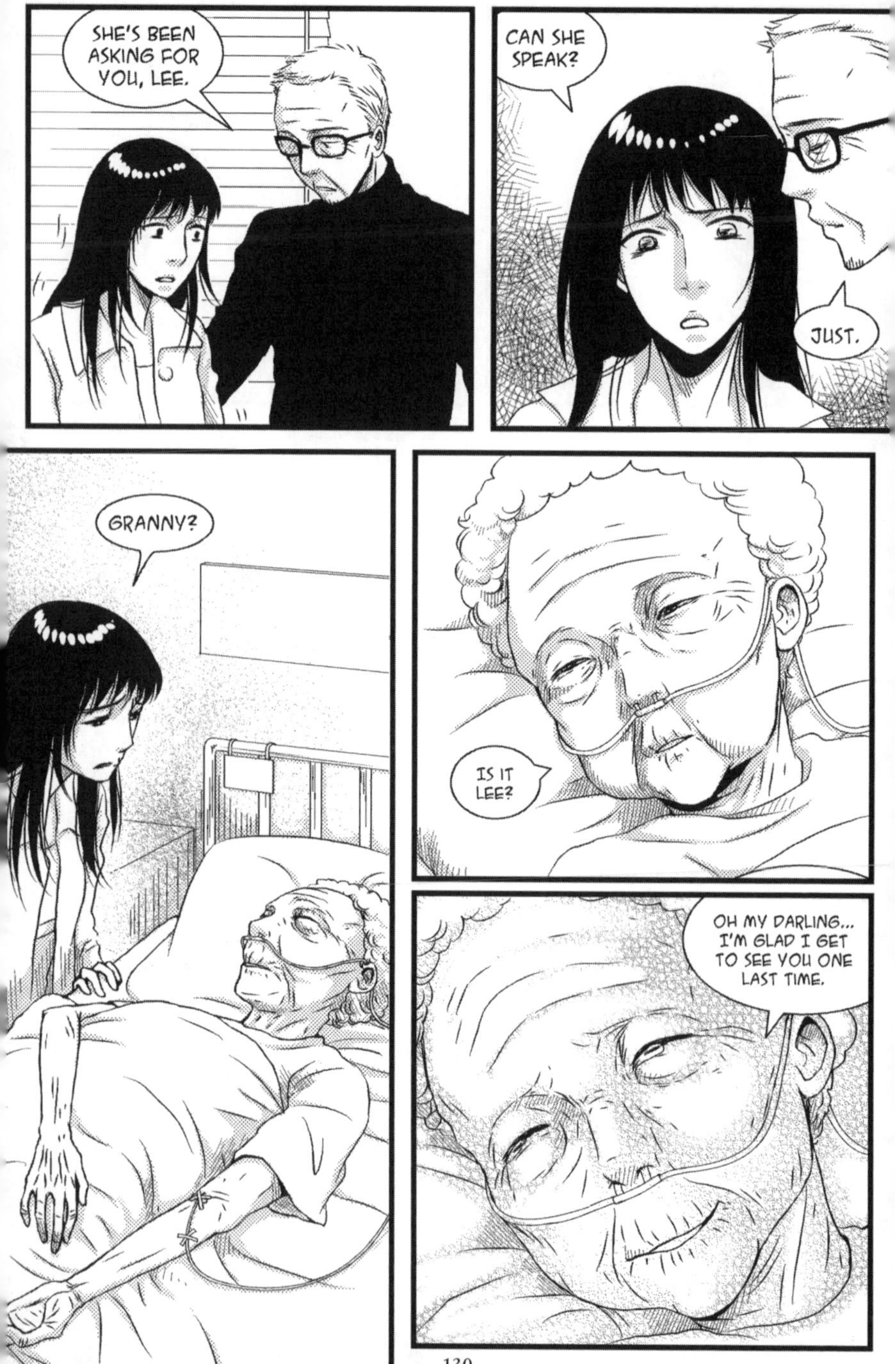
SHE'S BEEN ASKING FOR YOU, LEE.
CAN SHE SPEAK?
JUST.
GRANNY?
IS IT LEE?
OH MY DARLING... I'M GLAD I GET TO SEE YOU ONE LAST TIME.

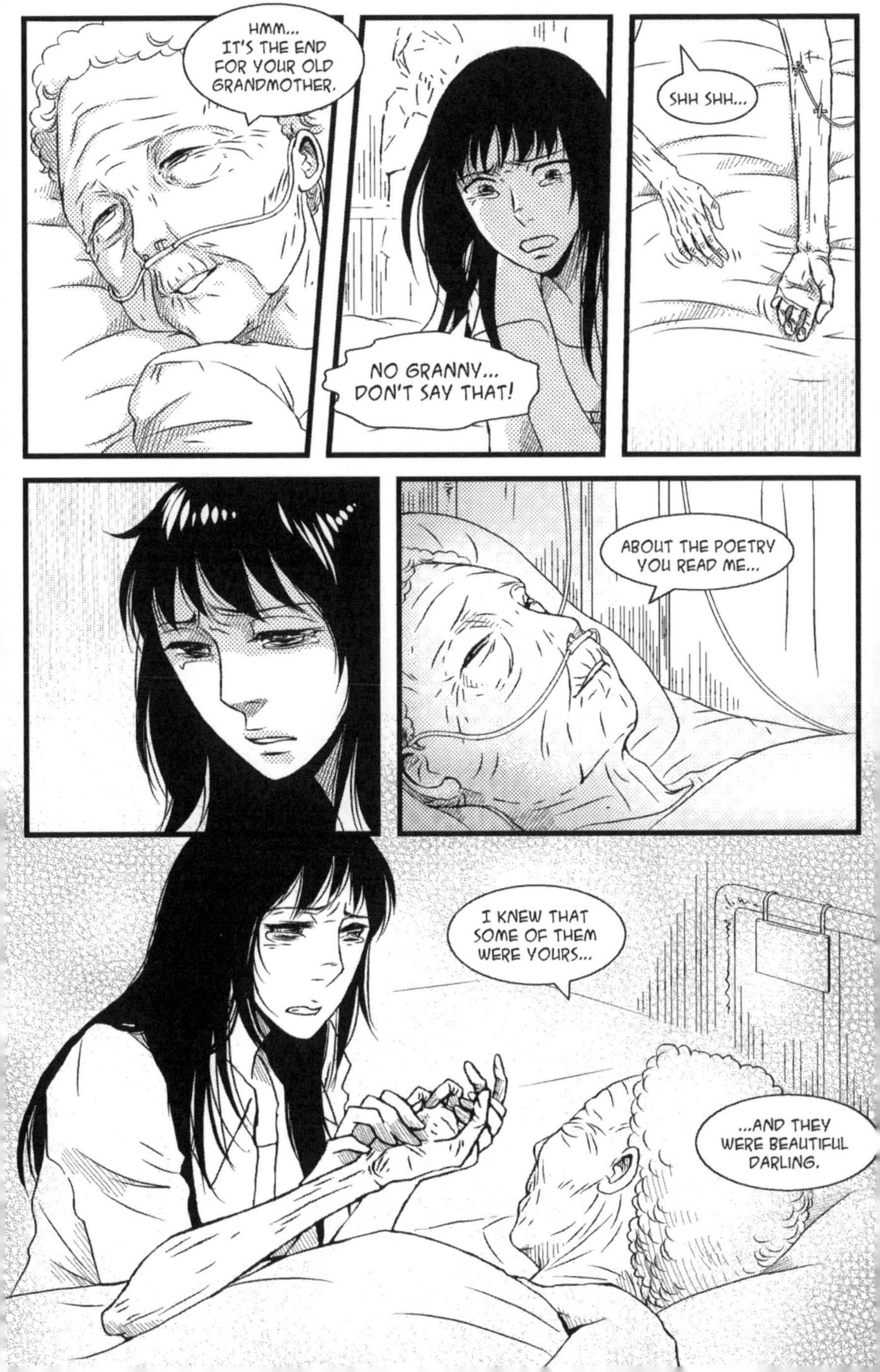
HMM...
IT'S THE END
FOR YOUR OLD
GRANDMOTHER.
NO GRANNY...
DON'T SAY THAT!
SHH SHH...
ABOUT THE POETRY
YOU READ ME...
I KNEW THAT
SOME OF THEM
WERE YOURS...
...AND THEY
WERE BEAUTIFUL
DARLING.

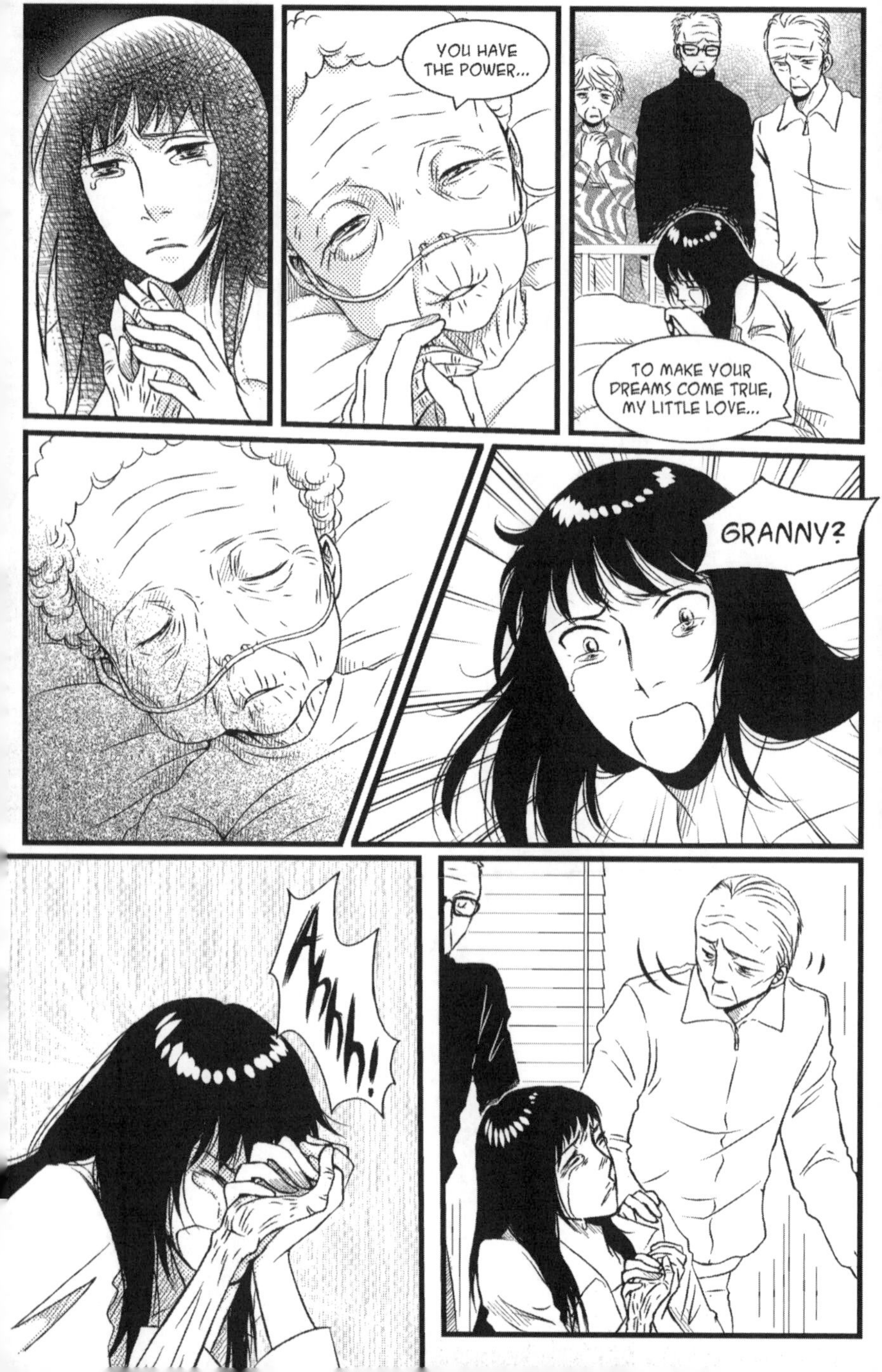
YOU HAVE THE POWER...
TO MAKE YOUR DREAMS COME TRUE, MY LITTLE LOVE...
GRANNY?
Ahhh!

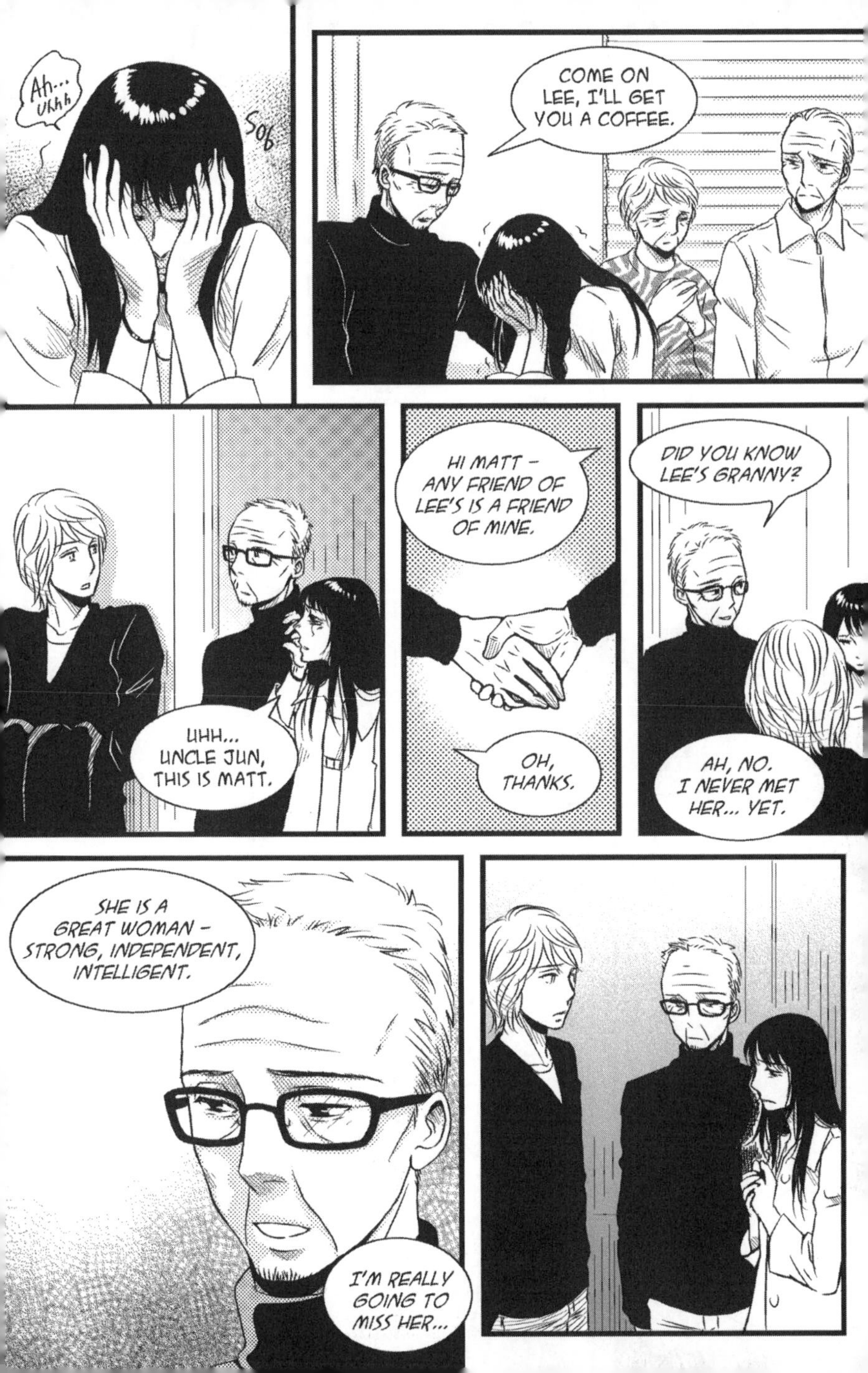
Ah... Uhhh
Sob
COME ON LEE, I'LL GET YOU A COFFEE.
UHH... UNCLE JUN, THIS IS MATT.
HI MATT - ANY FRIEND OF LEE'S IS A FRIEND OF MINE.
OH, THANKS.
DID YOU KNOW LEE'S GRANNY?
AH, NO. I NEVER MET HER... YET.
SHE IS A GREAT WOMAN - STRONG, INDEPENDENT, INTELLIGENT.
I'M REALLY GOING TO MISS HER...

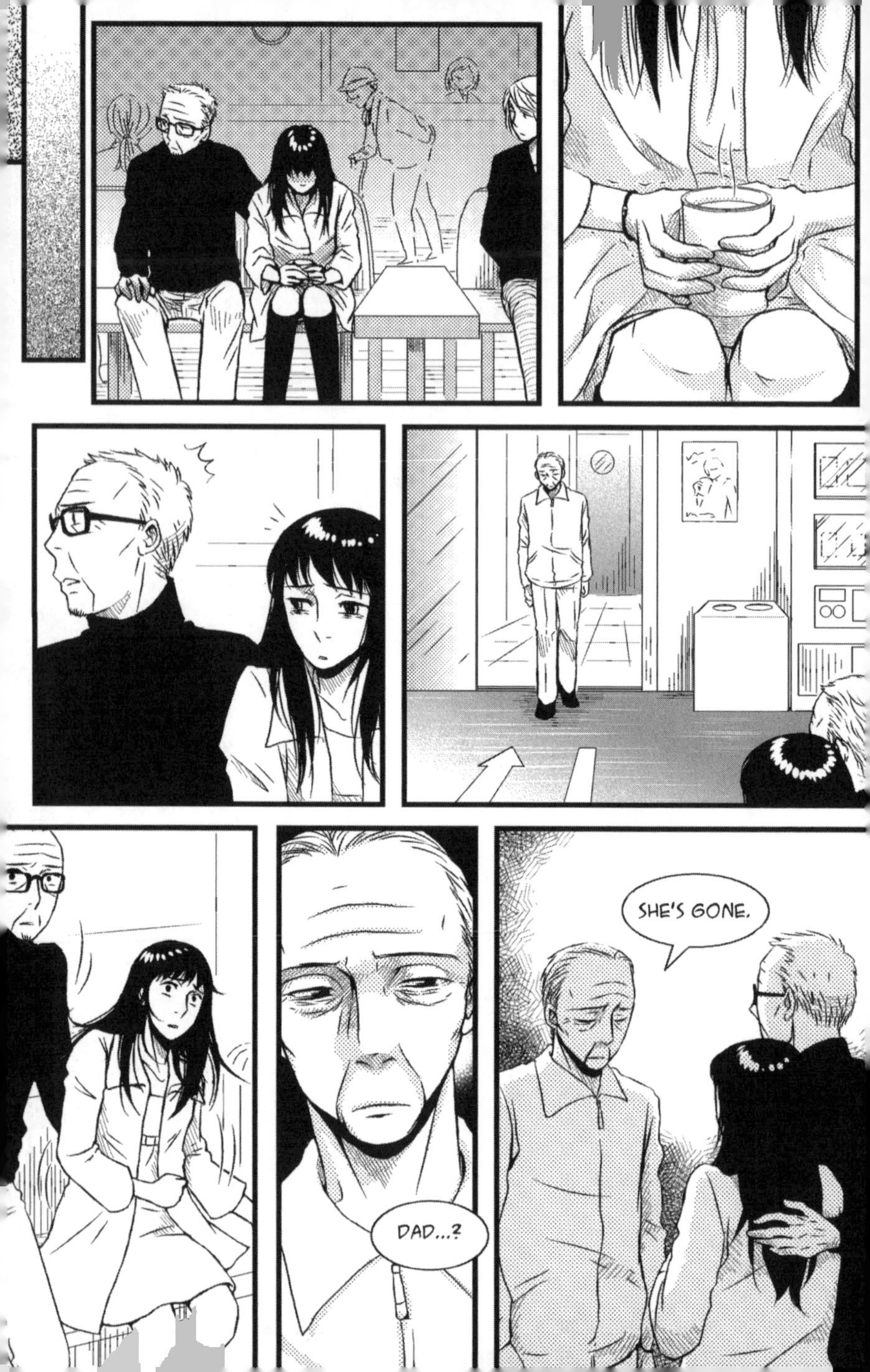
DAD...?
SHE'S GONE.

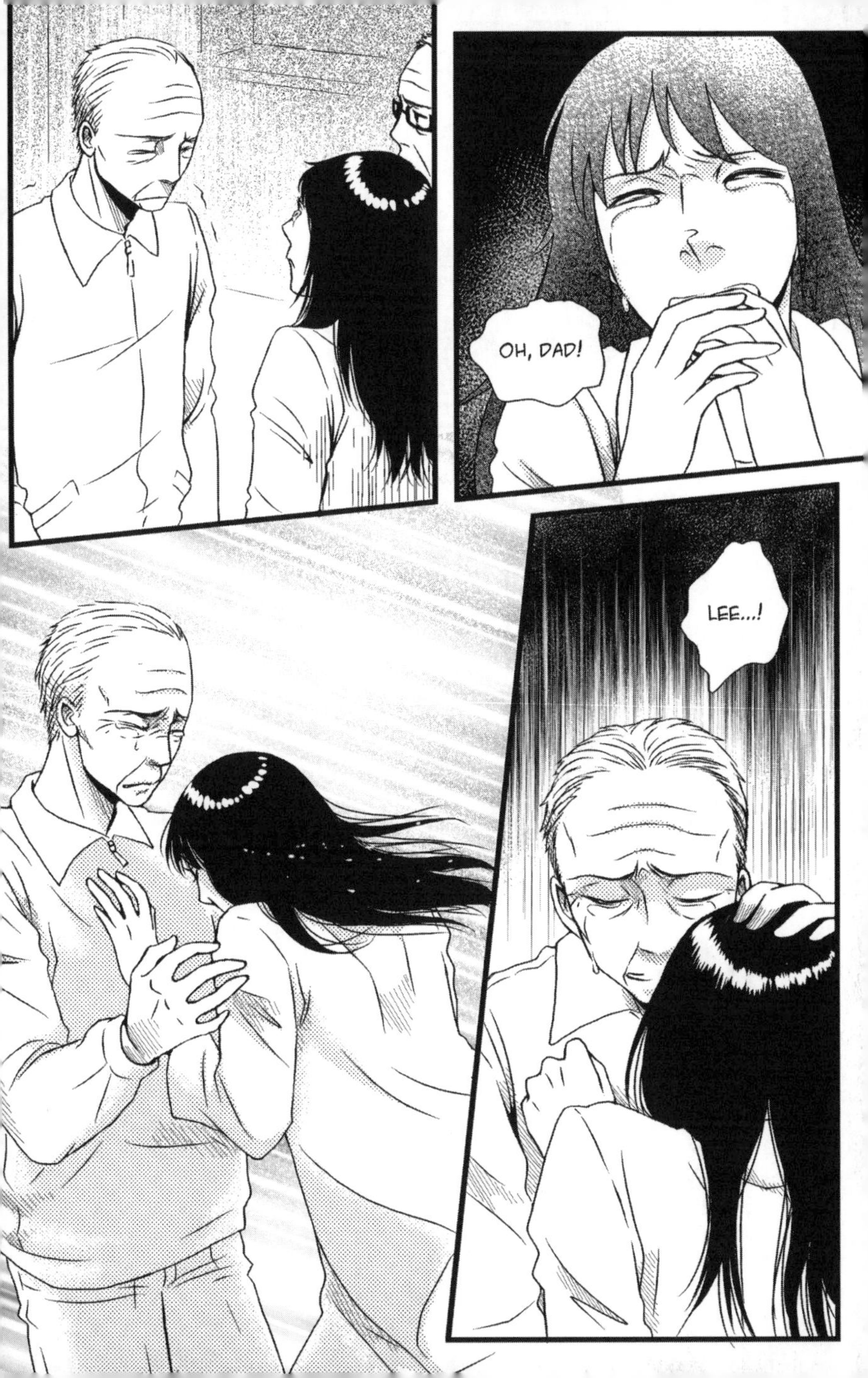
OH, DAD!
LEE...!

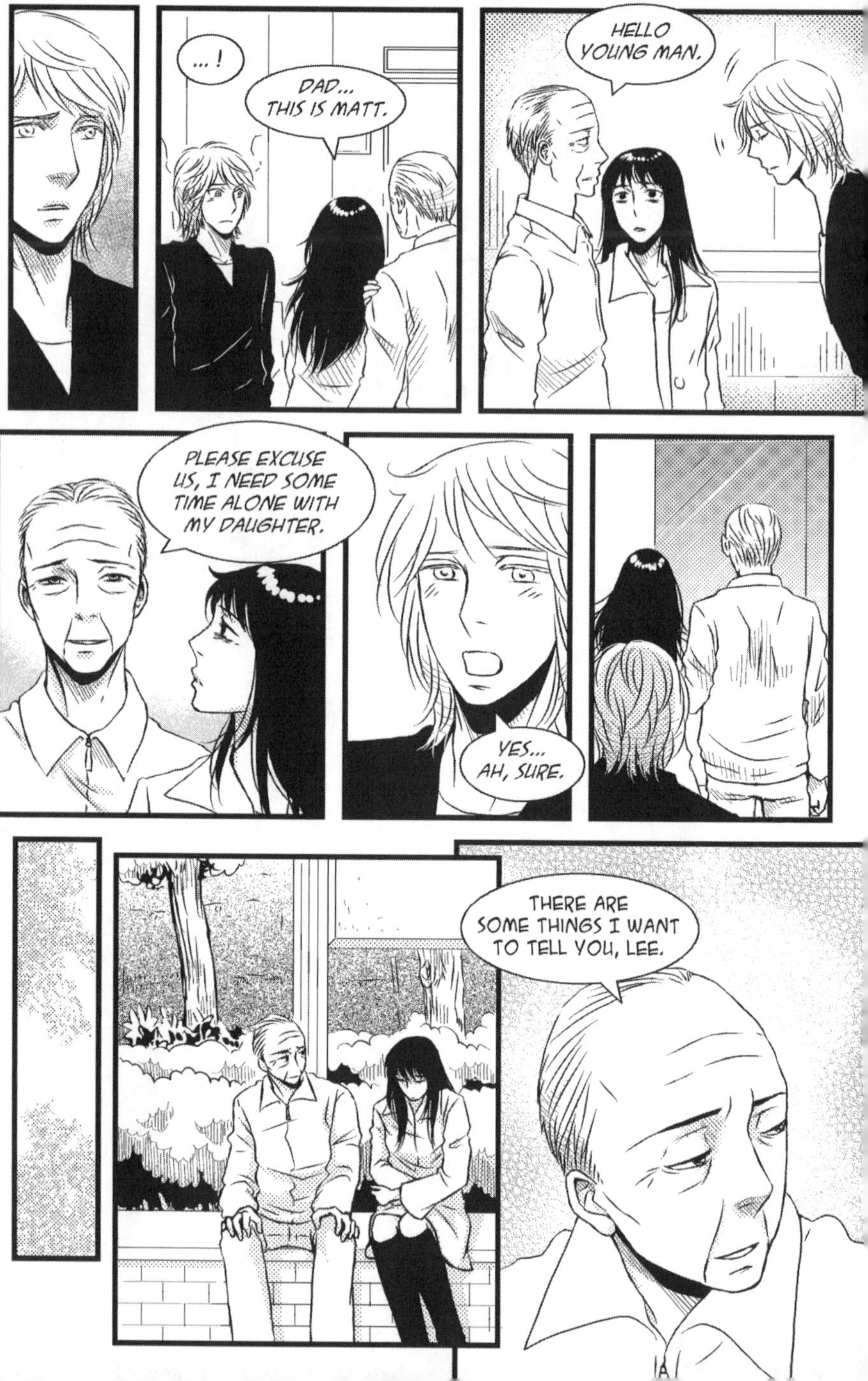
...!
DAD... THIS IS MATT.
HELLO YOUNG MAN.
PLEASE EXCUSE US, I NEED SOME TIME ALONE WITH MY DAUGHTER.
YES... AH, SURE.
THERE ARE SOME THINGS I WANT TO TELL YOU, LEE.

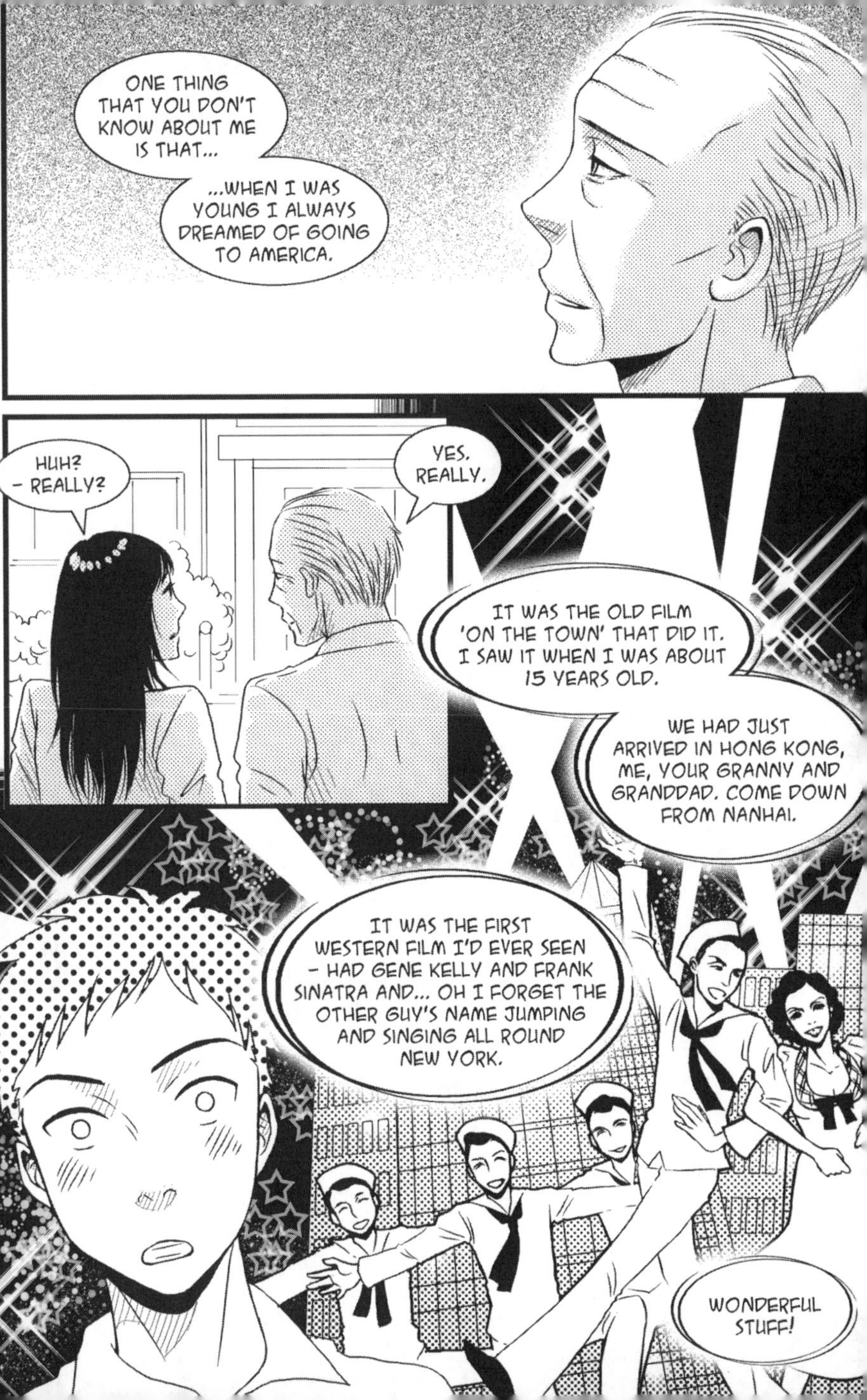
ONE THING THAT YOU DON'T KNOW ABOUT ME IS THAT...
...WHEN I WAS YOUNG I ALWAYS DREAMED OF GOING TO AMERICA.
HUH? - REALLY?
YES. REALLY.
IT WAS THE OLD FILM 'ON THE TOWN' THAT DID IT. I SAW IT WHEN I WAS ABOUT 15 YEARS OLD.
WE HAD JUST ARRIVED IN HONG KONG, ME, YOUR GRANNY AND GRANDDAD. COME DOWN FROM NANHAI.
IT WAS THE FIRST WESTERN FILM I'D EVER SEEN - HAD GENE KELLY AND FRANK SINATRA AND... OH I FORGET THE OTHER GUY'S NAME JUMPING AND SINGING ALL ROUND NEW YORK.
WONDERFUL STUFF!

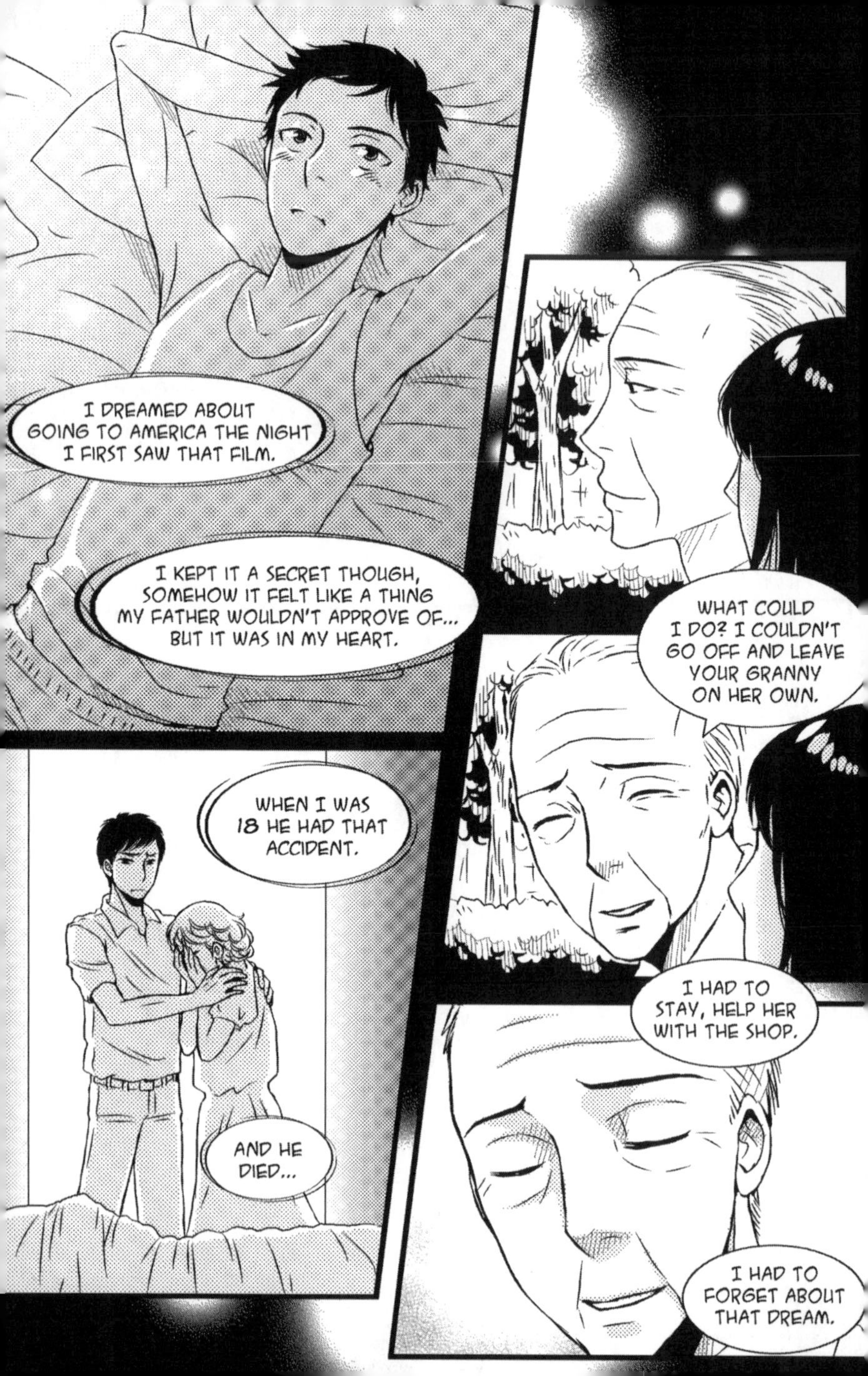
I DREAMED ABOUT GOING TO AMERICA THE NIGHT I FIRST SAW THAT FILM.
I KEPT IT A SECRET THOUGH, SOMEHOW IT FELT LIKE A THING MY FATHER WOULDN'T APPROVE OF... BUT IT WAS IN MY HEART.
WHAT COULD I DO? I COULDN'T GO OFF AND LEAVE YOUR GRANNY ON HER OWN.
WHEN I WAS 18 HE HAD THAT ACCIDENT.
AND HE DIED...
I HAD TO STAY, HELP HER WITH THE SHOP.
I HAD TO FORGET ABOUT THAT DREAM.

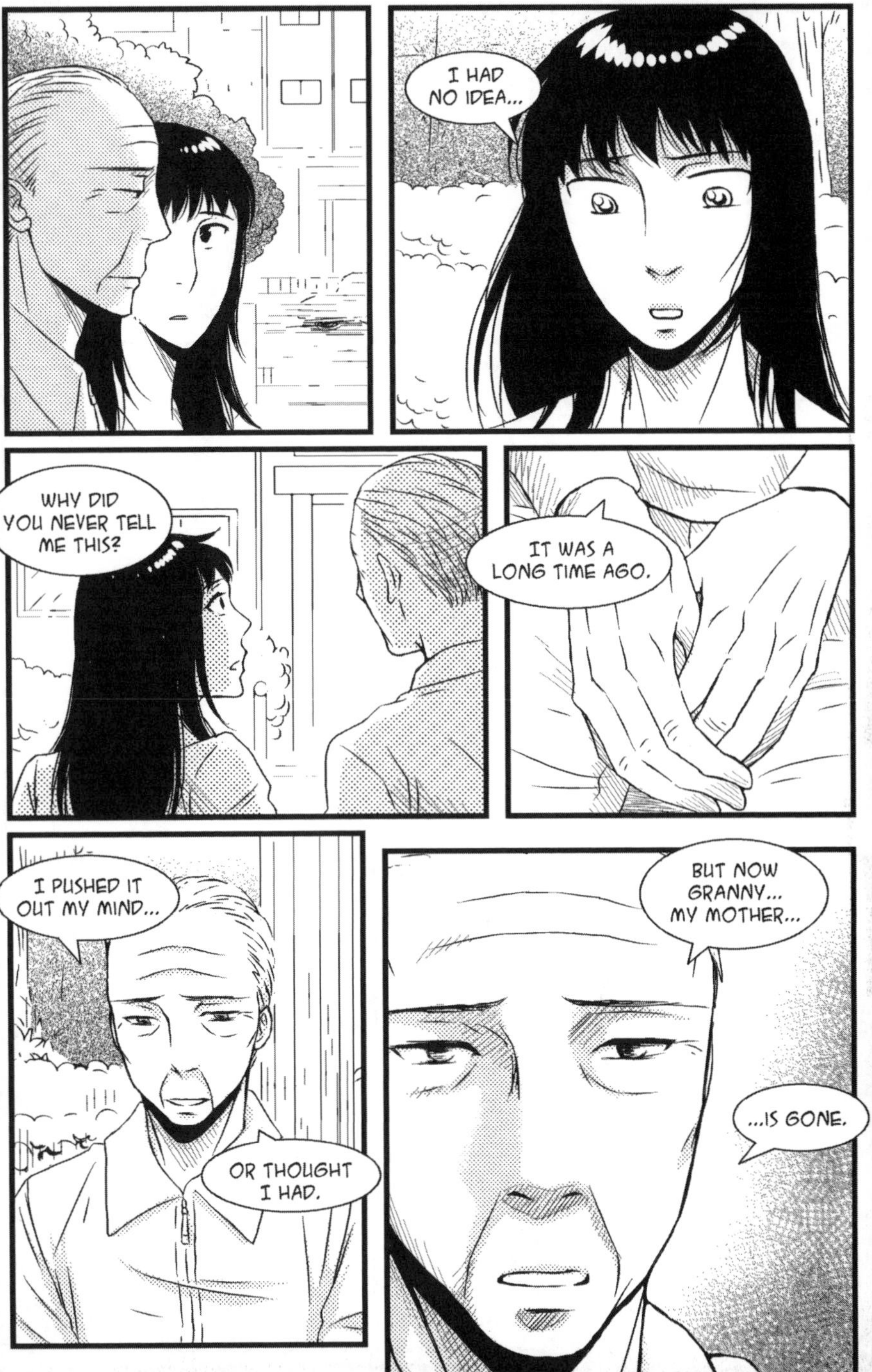
I HAD NO IDEA...
WHY DID YOU NEVER TELL ME THIS?
IT WAS A LONG TIME AGO.
I PUSHED IT OUT MY MIND...
OR THOUGHT I HAD.
BUT NOW GRANNY... MY MOTHER...
...IS GONE.

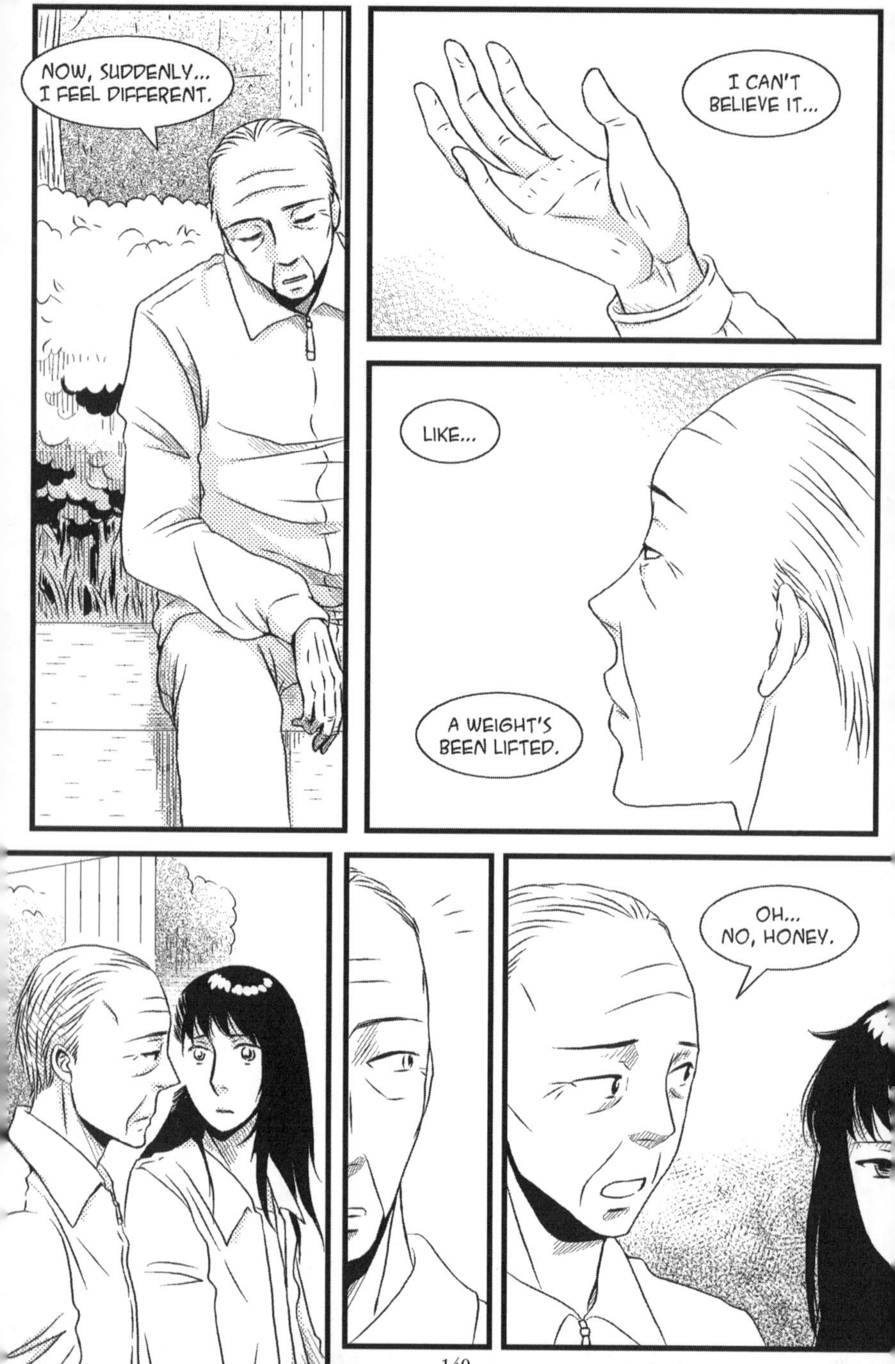
NOW, SUDDENLY... I FEEL DIFFERENT.
I CAN'T BELIEVE IT...
LIKE...
A WEIGHT'S BEEN LIFTED.
OH... NO, HONEY.

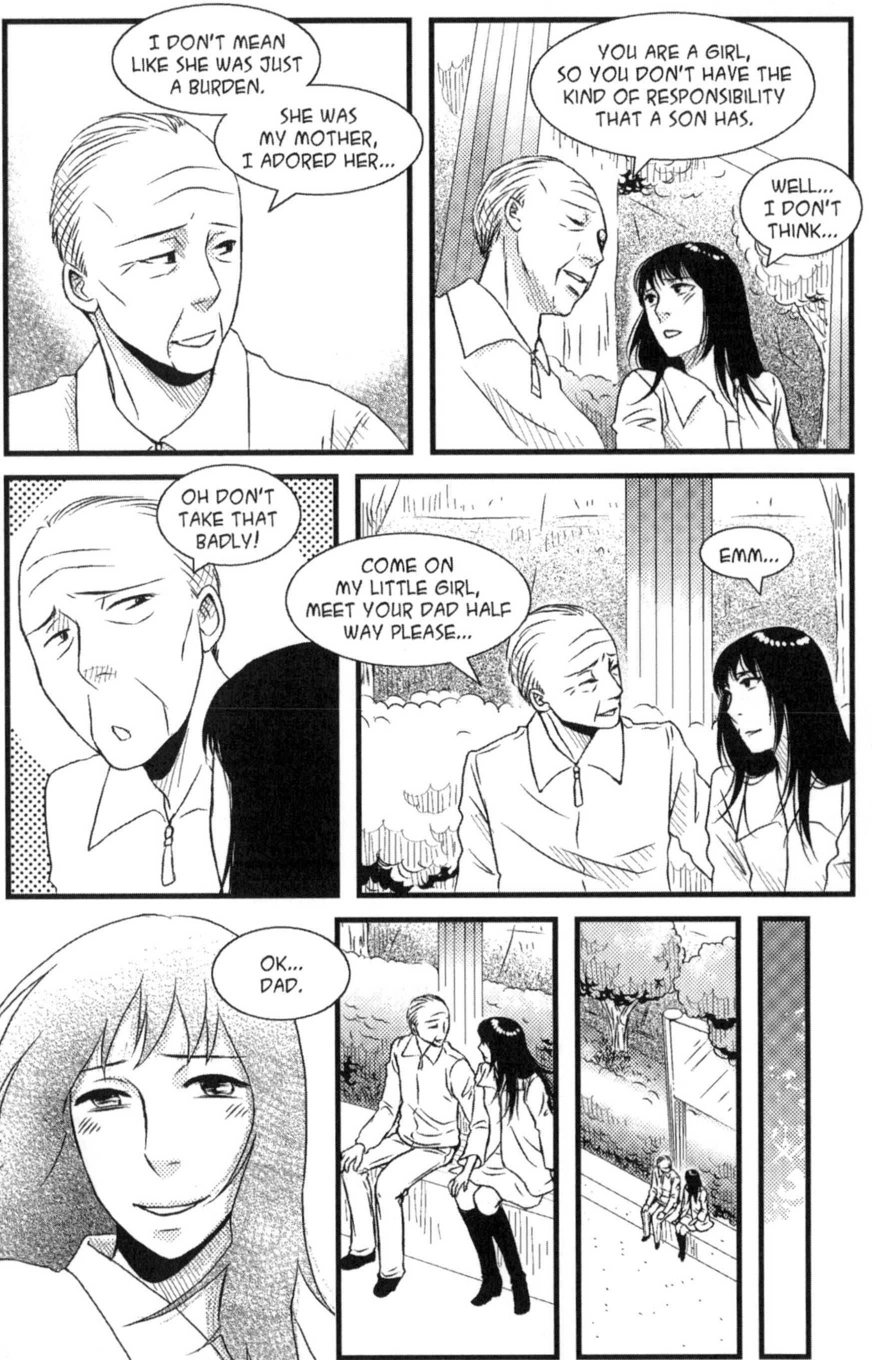
I DON'T MEAN LIKE SHE WAS JUST A BURDEN.
SHE WAS MY MOTHER, I ADORED HER...
YOU ARE A GIRL, SO YOU DON'T HAVE THE KIND OF RESPONSIBILITY THAT A SON HAS.
WELL... I DON'T THINK...
OH DON'T TAKE THAT BADLY!
COME ON MY LITTLE GIRL, MEET YOUR DAD HALF WAY PLEASE...
EMM...
OK... DAD.

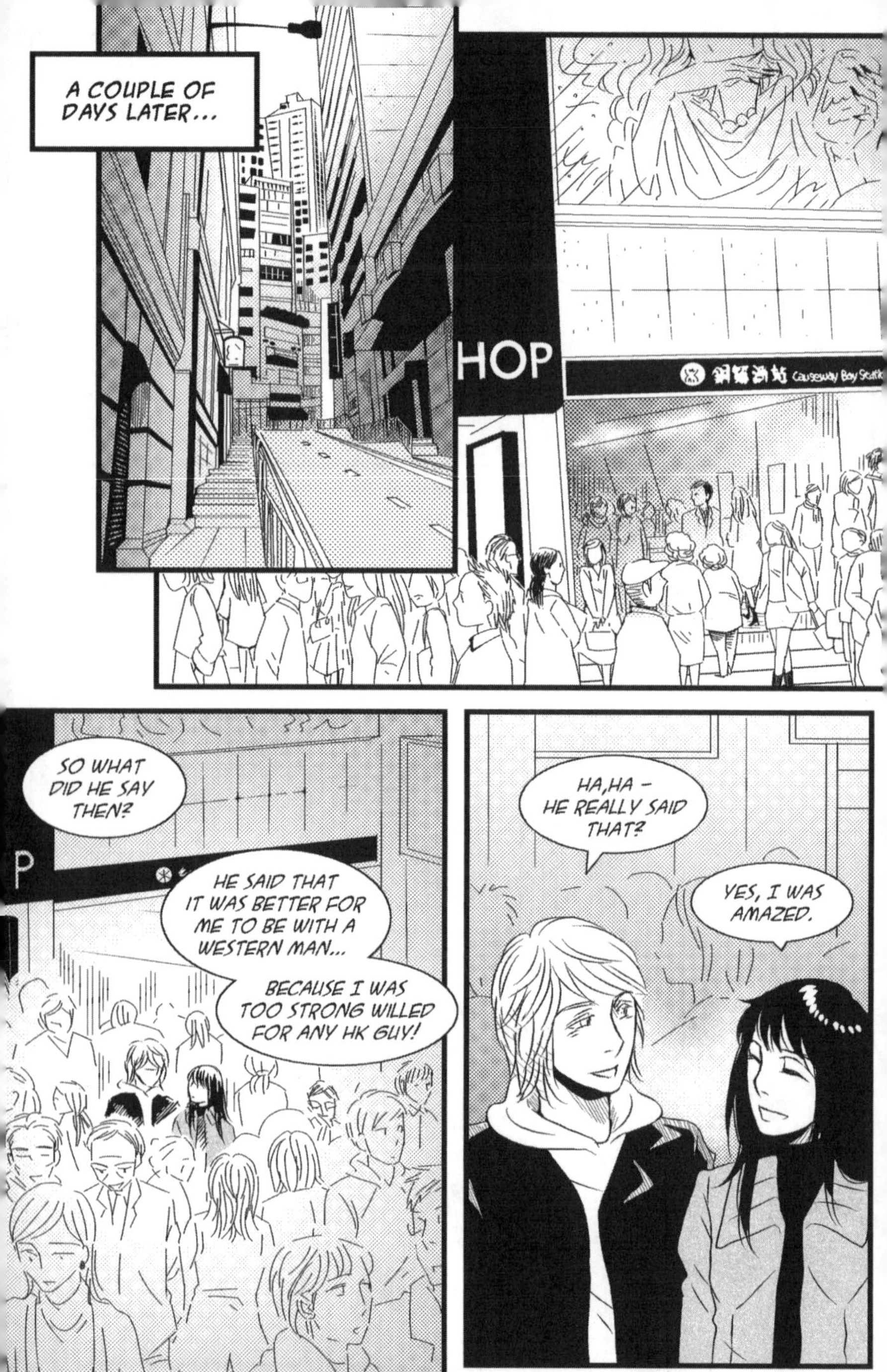
A COUPLE OF DAYS LATER...
HOP
SO WHAT DID HE SAY THEN?
HE SAID THAT IT WAS BETTER FOR ME TO BE WITH A WESTERN MAN...
BECAUSE I WAS TOO STRONG WILLED FOR ANY HK GUY!
HA,HA – HE REALLY SAID THAT?
YES, I WAS AMAZED.

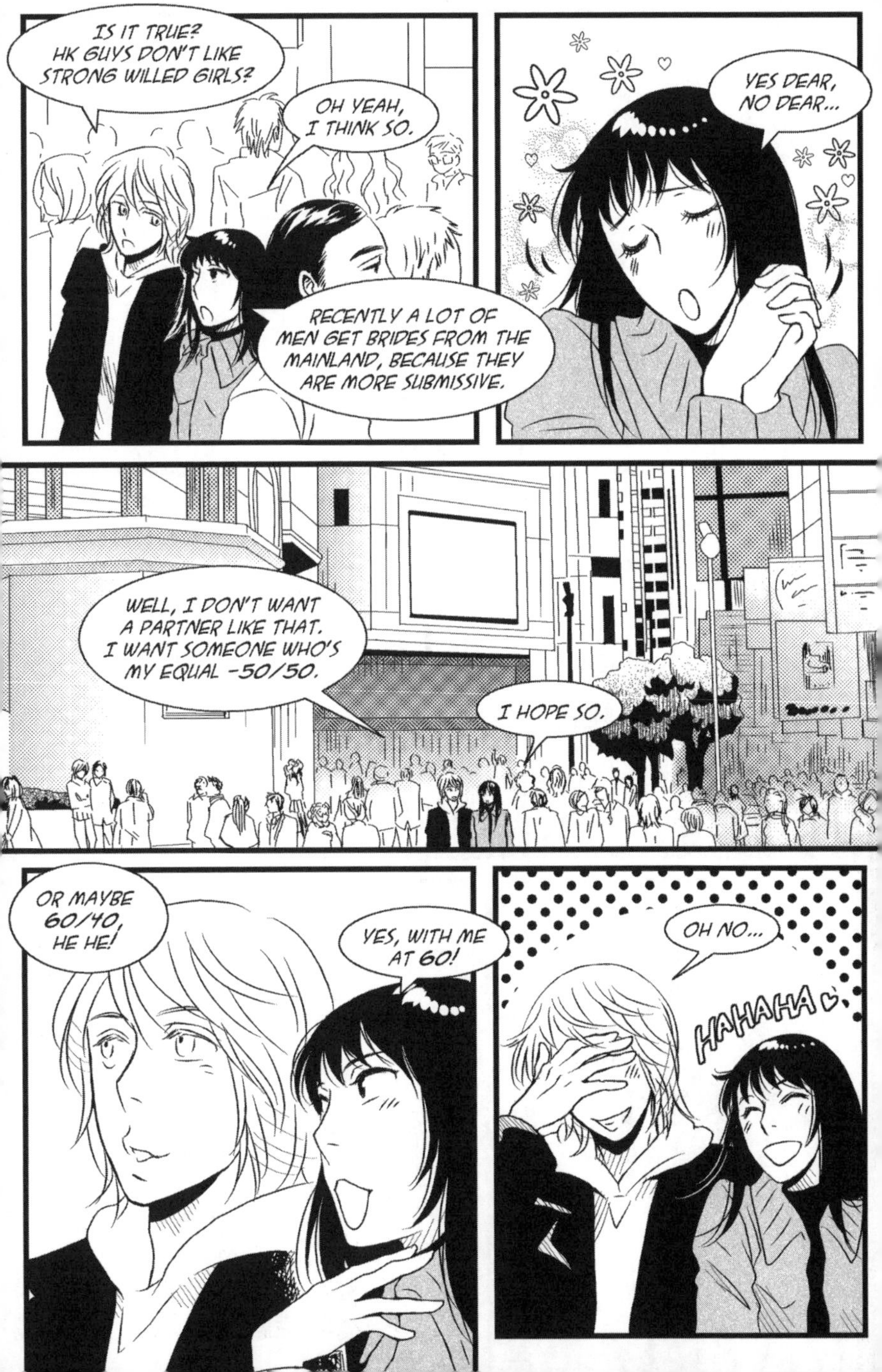
IS IT TRUE?
HK GUYS DON'T LIKE STRONG WILLED GIRLS?
OH YEAH, I THINK SO.
RECENTLY A LOT OF MEN GET BRIDES FROM THE MAINLAND, BECAUSE THEY ARE MORE SUBMISSIVE.
YES DEAR, NO DEAR...
WELL, I DON'T WANT A PARTNER LIKE THAT. I WANT SOMEONE WHO'S MY EQUAL -50/50.
I HOPE SO.
OR MAYBE 60/40, HE HE!
YES, WITH ME AT 60!
OH NO...
HAHAHA

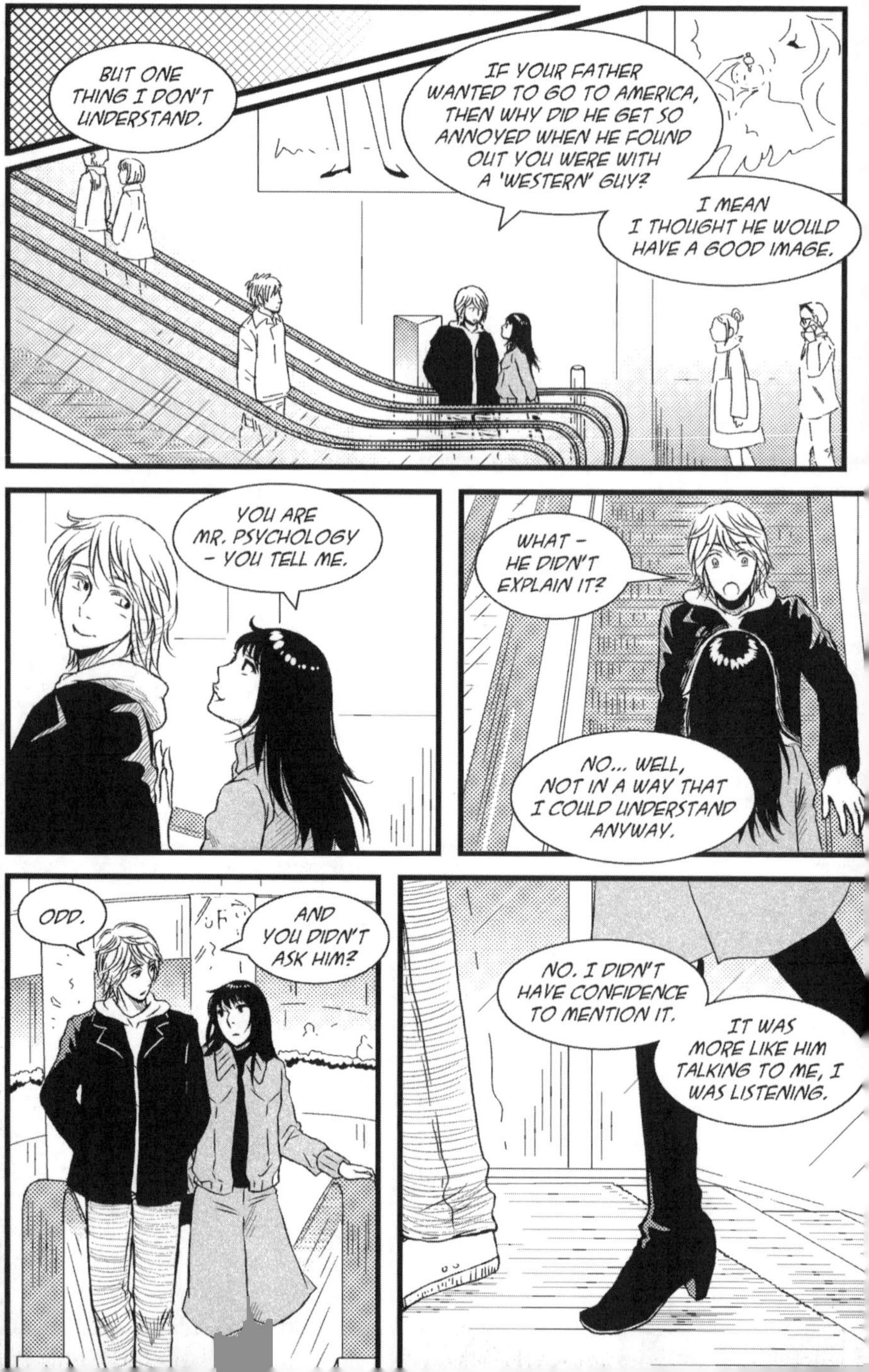
BUT ONE THING I DON'T UNDERSTAND.
IF YOUR FATHER WANTED TO GO TO AMERICA, THEN WHY DID HE GET SO ANNOYED WHEN HE FOUND OUT YOU WERE WITH A 'WESTERN' GUY?
I MEAN I THOUGHT HE WOULD HAVE A GOOD IMAGE.
YOU ARE MR. PSYCHOLOGY - YOU TELL ME.
WHAT - HE DIDN'T EXPLAIN IT?
NO... WELL, NOT IN A WAY THAT I COULD UNDERSTAND ANYWAY.
ODD.
AND YOU DIDN'T ASK HIM?
NO. I DIDN'T HAVE CONFIDENCE TO MENTION IT.
IT WAS MORE LIKE HIM TALKING TO ME, I WAS LISTENING.

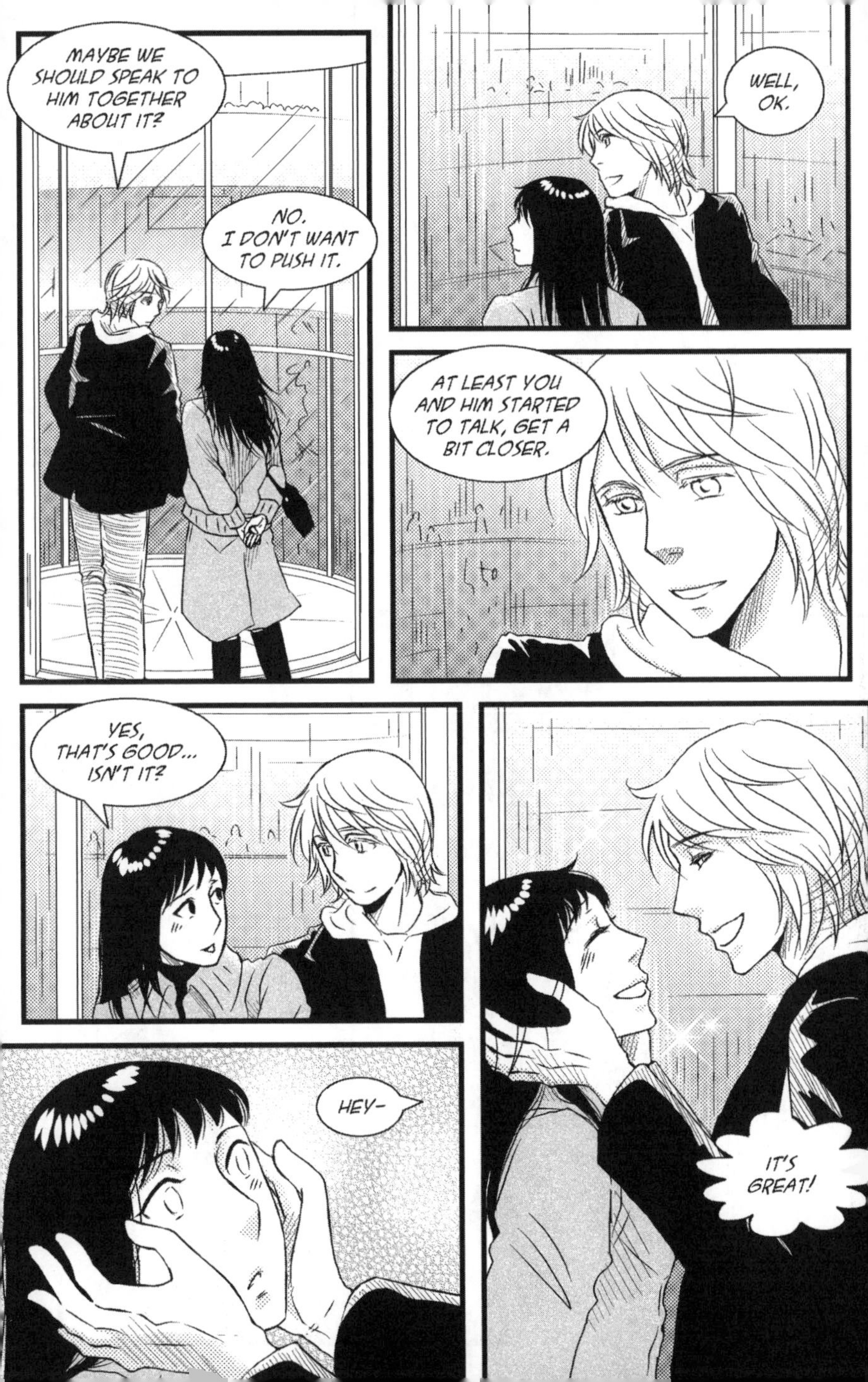
MAYBE WE SHOULD SPEAK TO HIM TOGETHER ABOUT IT?
NO. I DON'T WANT TO PUSH IT.
WELL, OK.
AT LEAST YOU AND HIM STARTED TO TALK, GET A BIT CLOSER.
YES, THAT'S GOOD... ISN'T IT?
HEY-
IT'S GREAT!

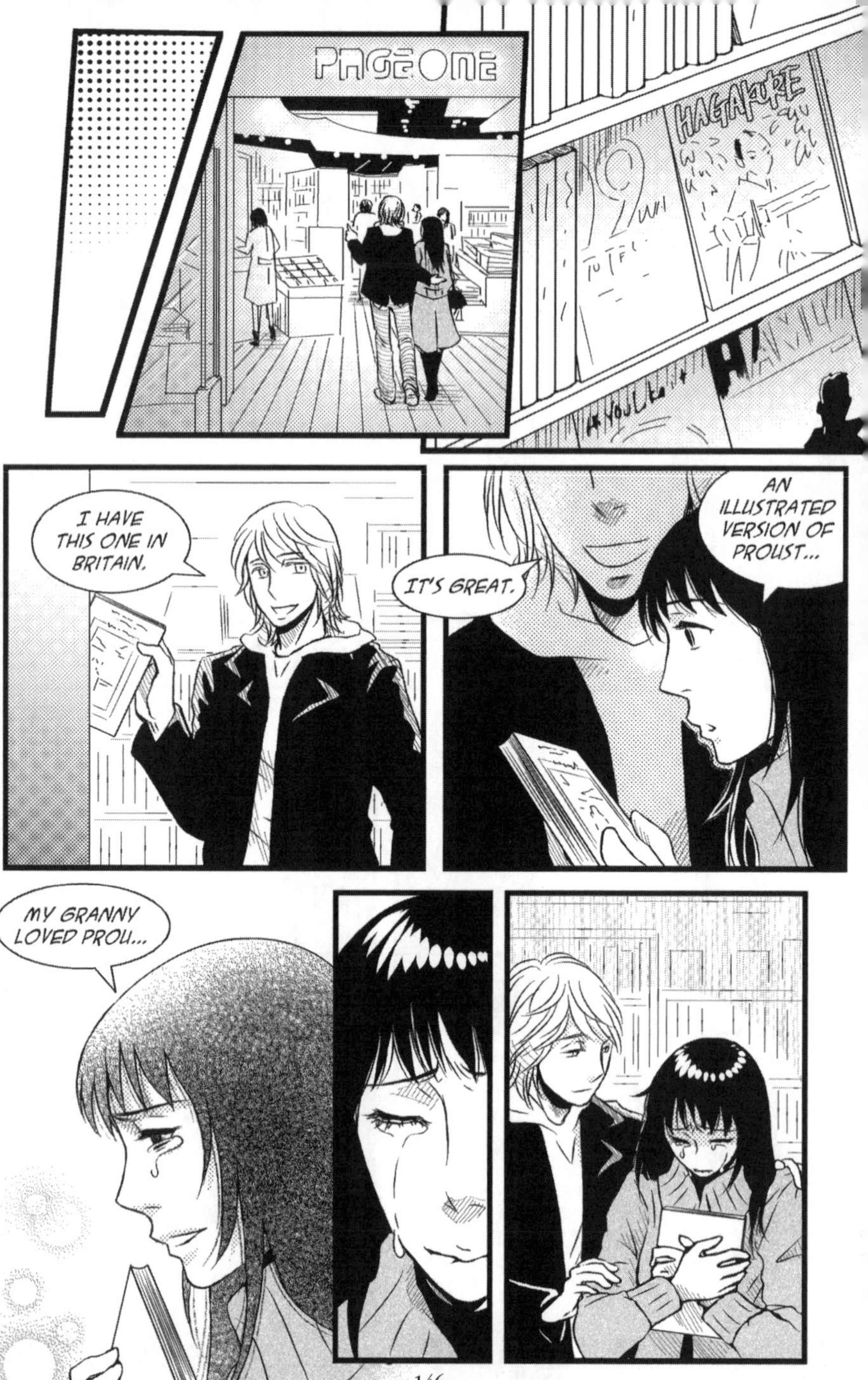
PAGE ONE
HAGAKURE
I HAVE THIS ONE IN BRITAIN.
AN ILLUSTRATED VERSION OF PROUST...
IT'S GREAT.
MY GRANNY LOVED PROU...

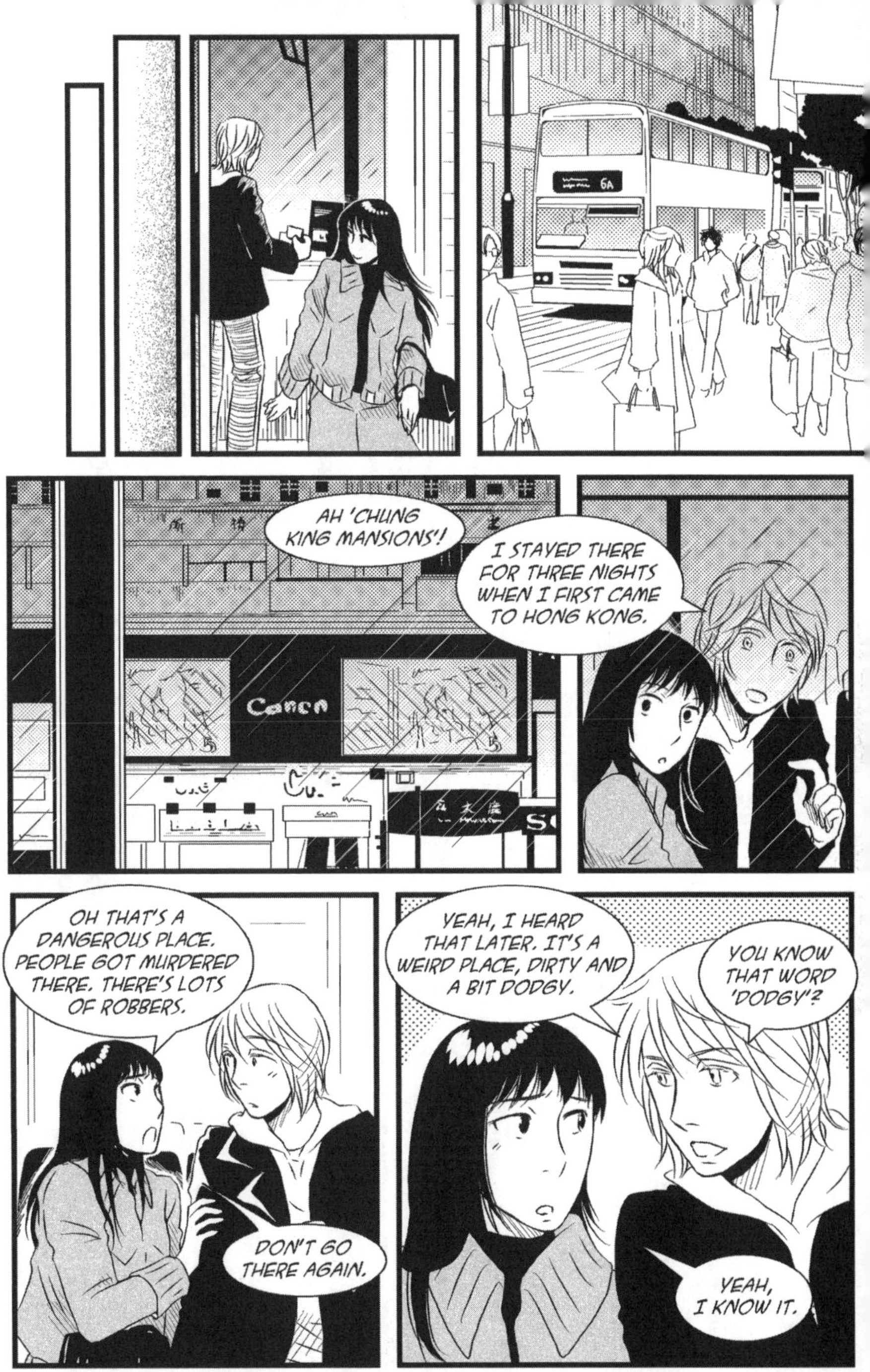
AH 'CHUNG KING MANSIONS'!
I STAYED THERE FOR THREE NIGHTS WHEN I FIRST CAME TO HONG KONG.
OH THAT'S A DANGEROUS PLACE. PEOPLE GOT MURDERED THERE. THERE'S LOTS OF ROBBERS.
DON'T GO THERE AGAIN.
YEAH, I HEARD THAT LATER. IT'S A WEIRD PLACE, DIRTY AND A BIT DODGY.
YOU KNOW THAT WORD 'DODGY'?
YEAH, I KNOW IT.

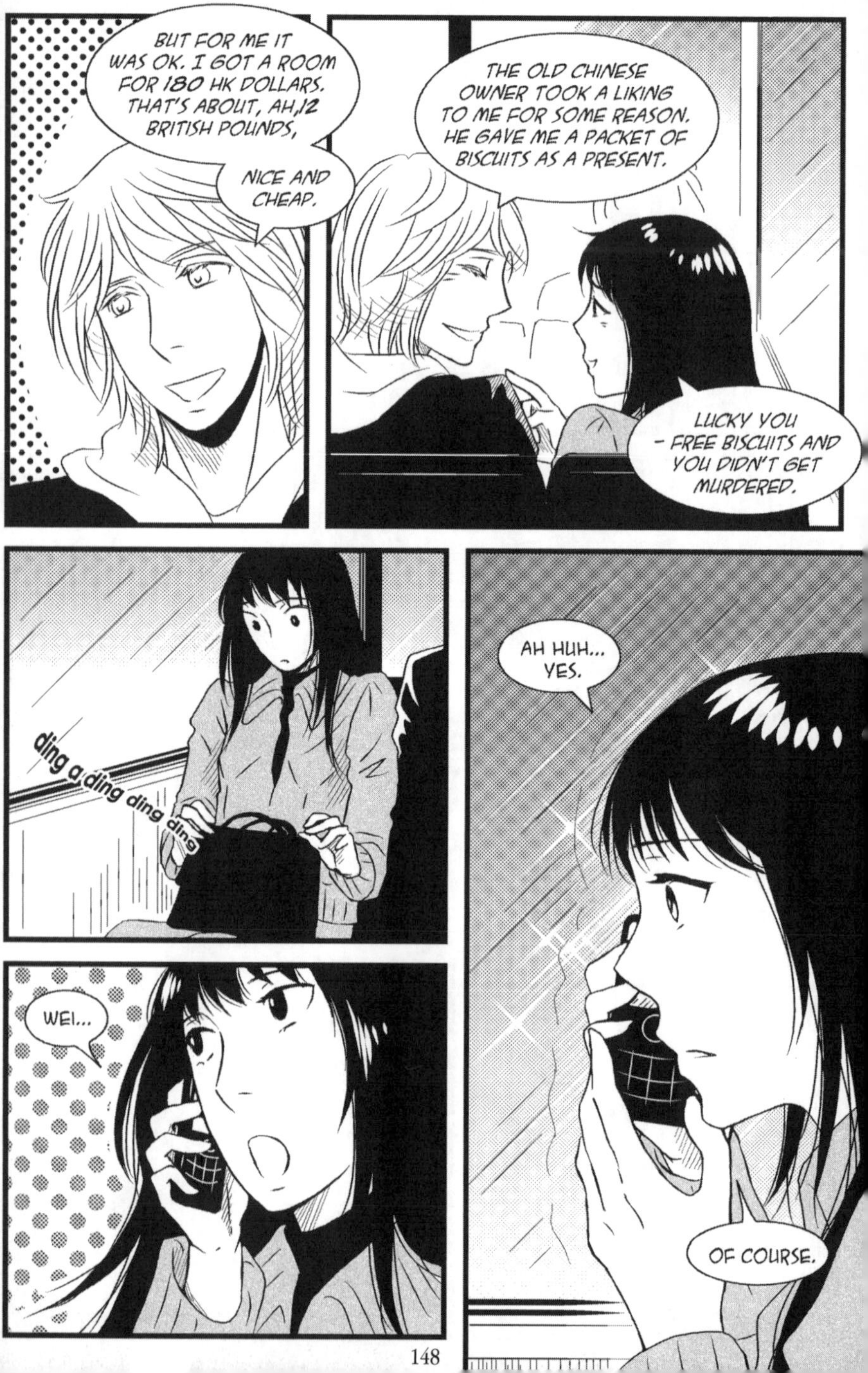
BUT FOR ME IT WAS OK. I GOT A ROOM FOR 180 HK DOLLARS. THAT'S ABOUT, AH,12 BRITISH POUNDS,
NICE AND CHEAP.
THE OLD CHINESE OWNER TOOK A LIKING TO ME FOR SOME REASON. HE GAVE ME A PACKET OF BISCUITS AS A PRESENT.
LUCKY YOU - FREE BISCUITS AND YOU DIDN'T GET MURDERED.
ding a ding ding ding
WEI...
AH HUH... YES.
OF COURSE.

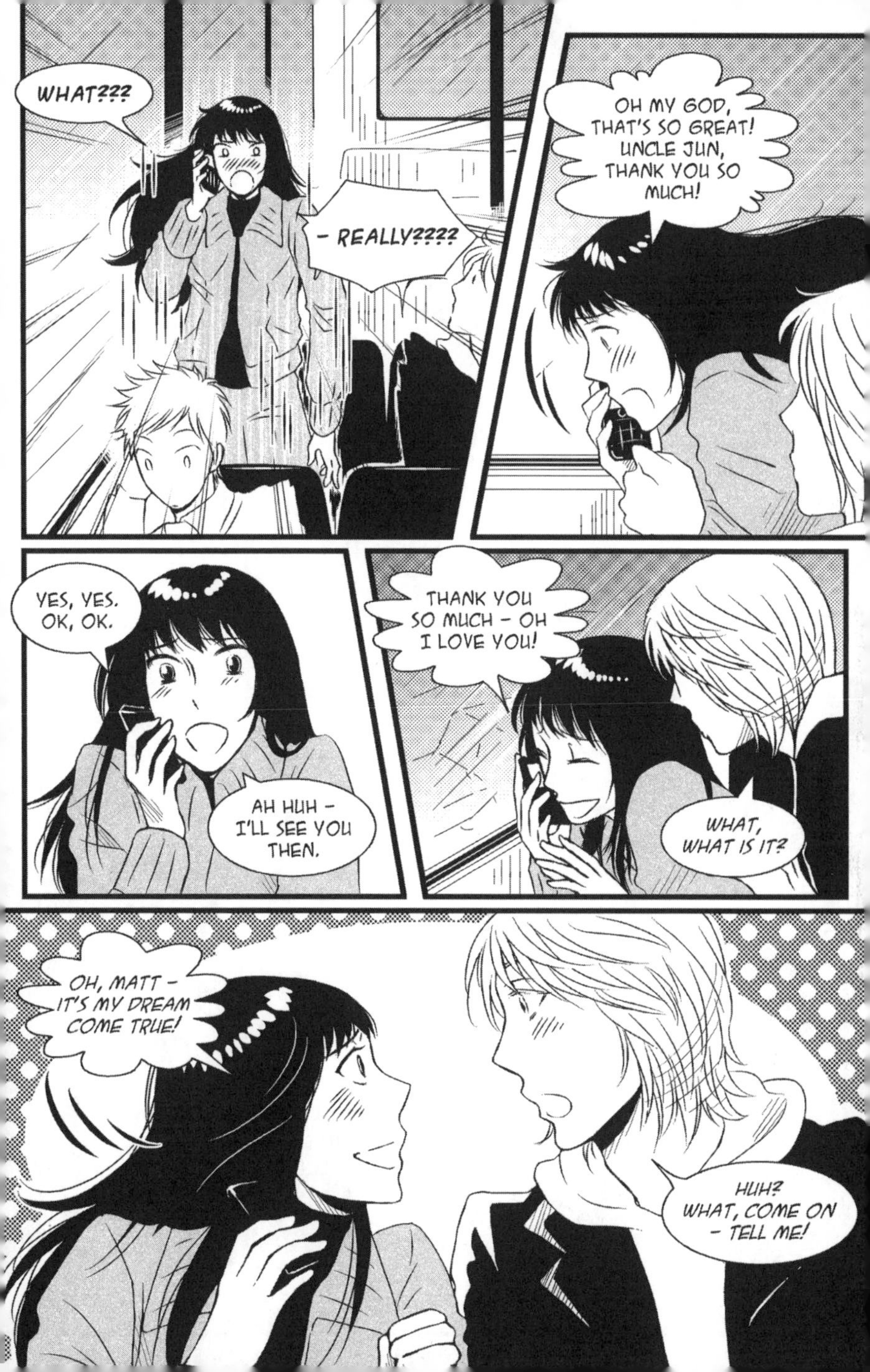
WHAT???
- REALLY????
OH MY GOD, THAT'S SO GREAT! UNCLE JUN, THANK YOU SO MUCH!
YES, YES. OK, OK.
AH HUH - I'LL SEE YOU THEN.
THANK YOU SO MUCH - OH I LOVE YOU!
WHAT, WHAT IS IT?
OH, MATT - IT'S MY DREAM COME TRUE!
HUH? WHAT, COME ON - TELL ME!

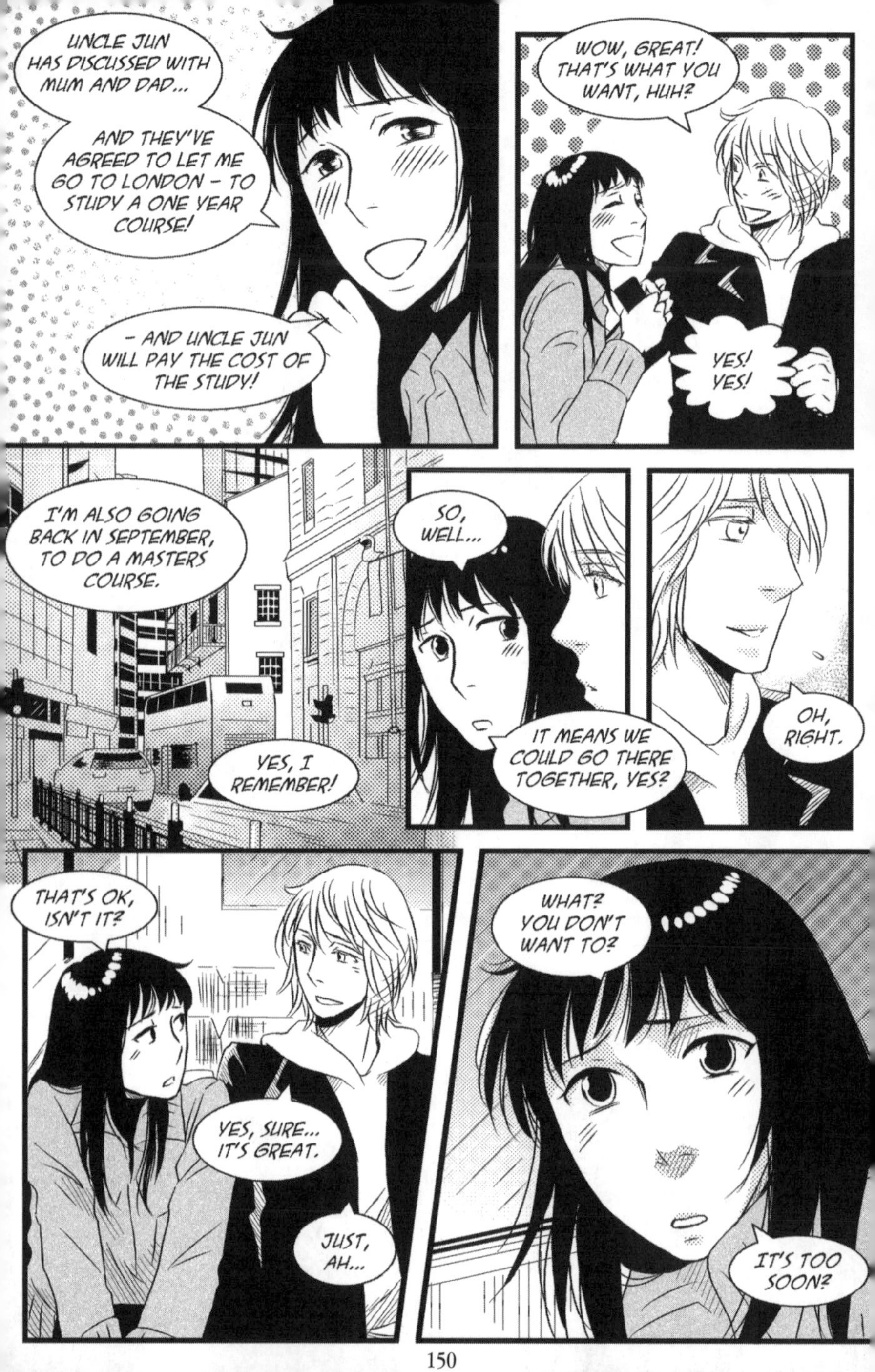
UNCLE JUN HAS DISCUSSED WITH MUM AND DAD...
AND THEY'VE AGREED TO LET ME GO TO LONDON – TO STUDY A ONE YEAR COURSE!
– AND UNCLE JUN WILL PAY THE COST OF THE STUDY!
WOW, GREAT! THAT'S WHAT YOU WANT, HUH?
YES! YES!
I'M ALSO GOING BACK IN SEPTEMBER, TO DO A MASTERS COURSE.
YES, I REMEMBER!
SO, WELL...
IT MEANS WE COULD GO THERE TOGETHER, YES?
OH, RIGHT.
THAT'S OK, ISN'T IT?
YES, SURE... IT'S GREAT.
JUST, AH...
WHAT? YOU DON'T WANT TO?
IT'S TOO SOON?

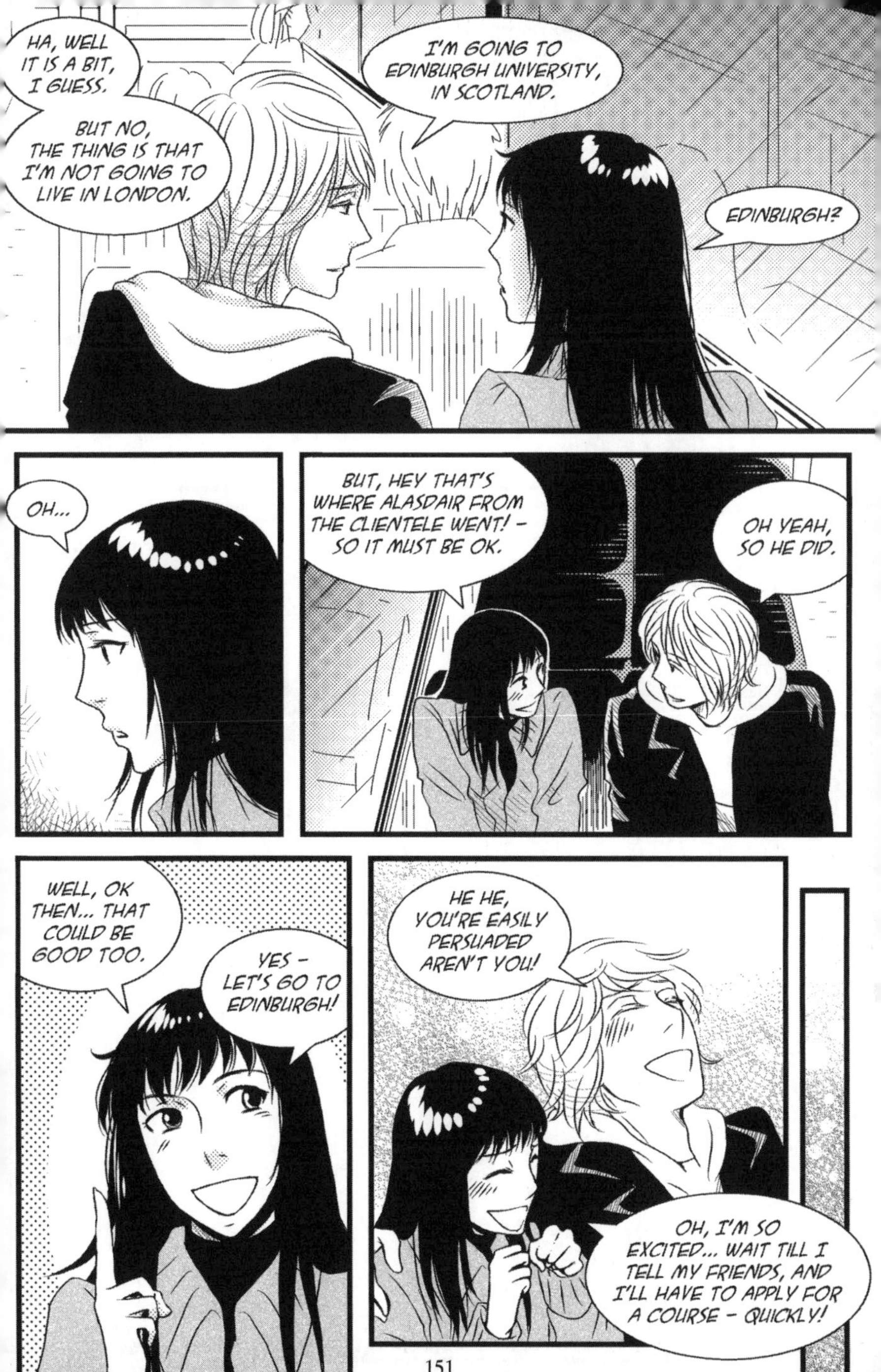
HA, WELL IT IS A BIT, I GUESS.
BUT NO, THE THING IS THAT I'M NOT GOING TO LIVE IN LONDON.
I'M GOING TO EDINBURGH UNIVERSITY, IN SCOTLAND.
EDINBURGH?
OH...
BUT, HEY THAT'S WHERE ALASDAIR FROM THE CLIENTELE WENT! - SO IT MUST BE OK.
OH YEAH, SO HE DID.
WELL, OK THEN... THAT COULD BE GOOD TOO.
YES - LET'S GO TO EDINBURGH!
HE HE, YOU'RE EASILY PERSUADED AREN'T YOU!
OH, I'M SO EXCITED... WAIT TILL I TELL MY FRIENDS, AND I'LL HAVE TO APPLY FOR A COURSE - QUICKLY!

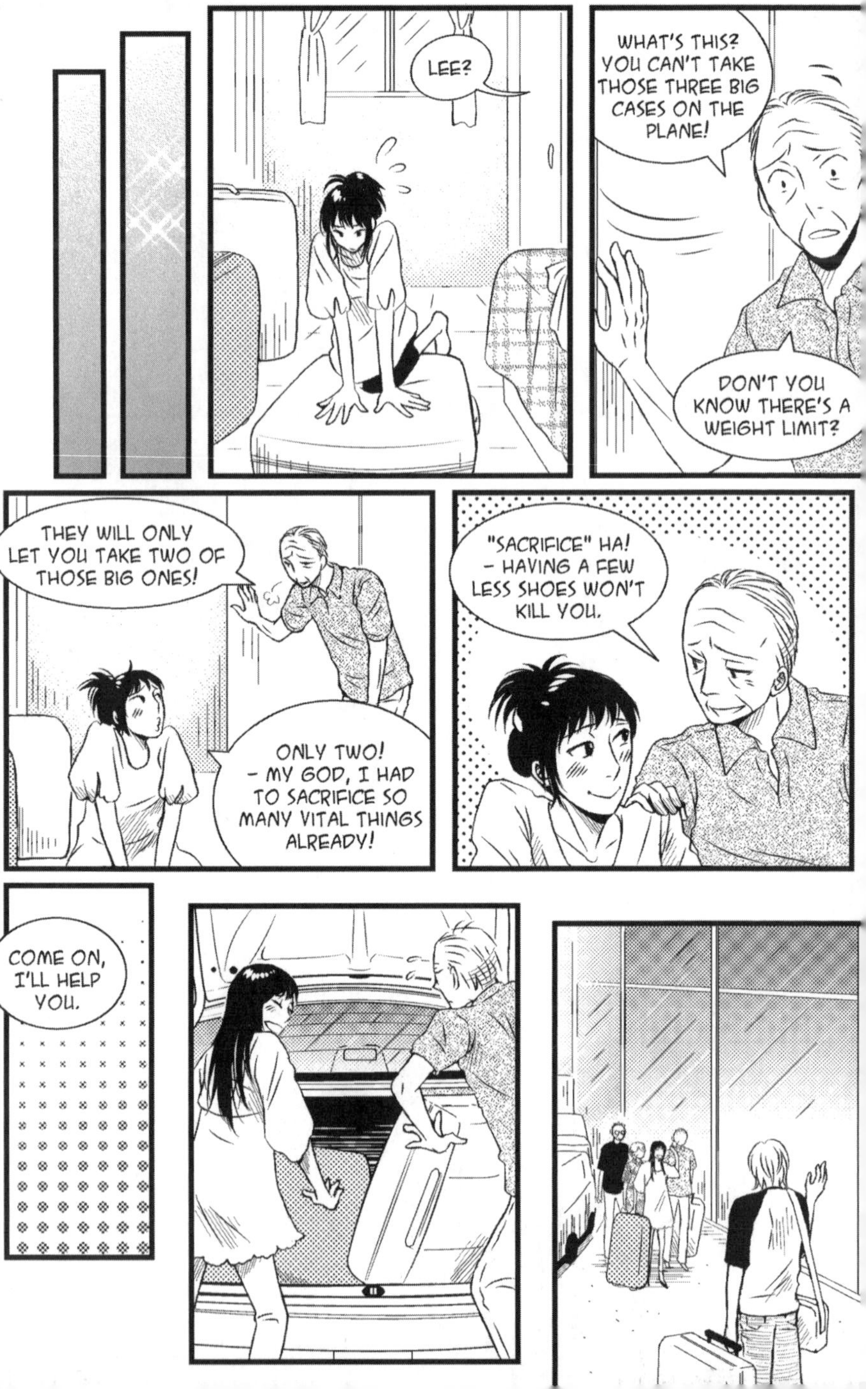
LEE?
WHAT'S THIS? YOU CAN'T TAKE THOSE THREE BIG CASES ON THE PLANE!
DON'T YOU KNOW THERE'S A WEIGHT LIMIT?
THEY WILL ONLY LET YOU TAKE TWO OF THOSE BIG ONES!
ONLY TWO! - MY GOD, I HAD TO SACRIFICE SO MANY VITAL THINGS ALREADY!
"SACRIFICE" HA! - HAVING A FEW LESS SHOES WON'T KILL YOU.
COME ON, I'LL HELP YOU.

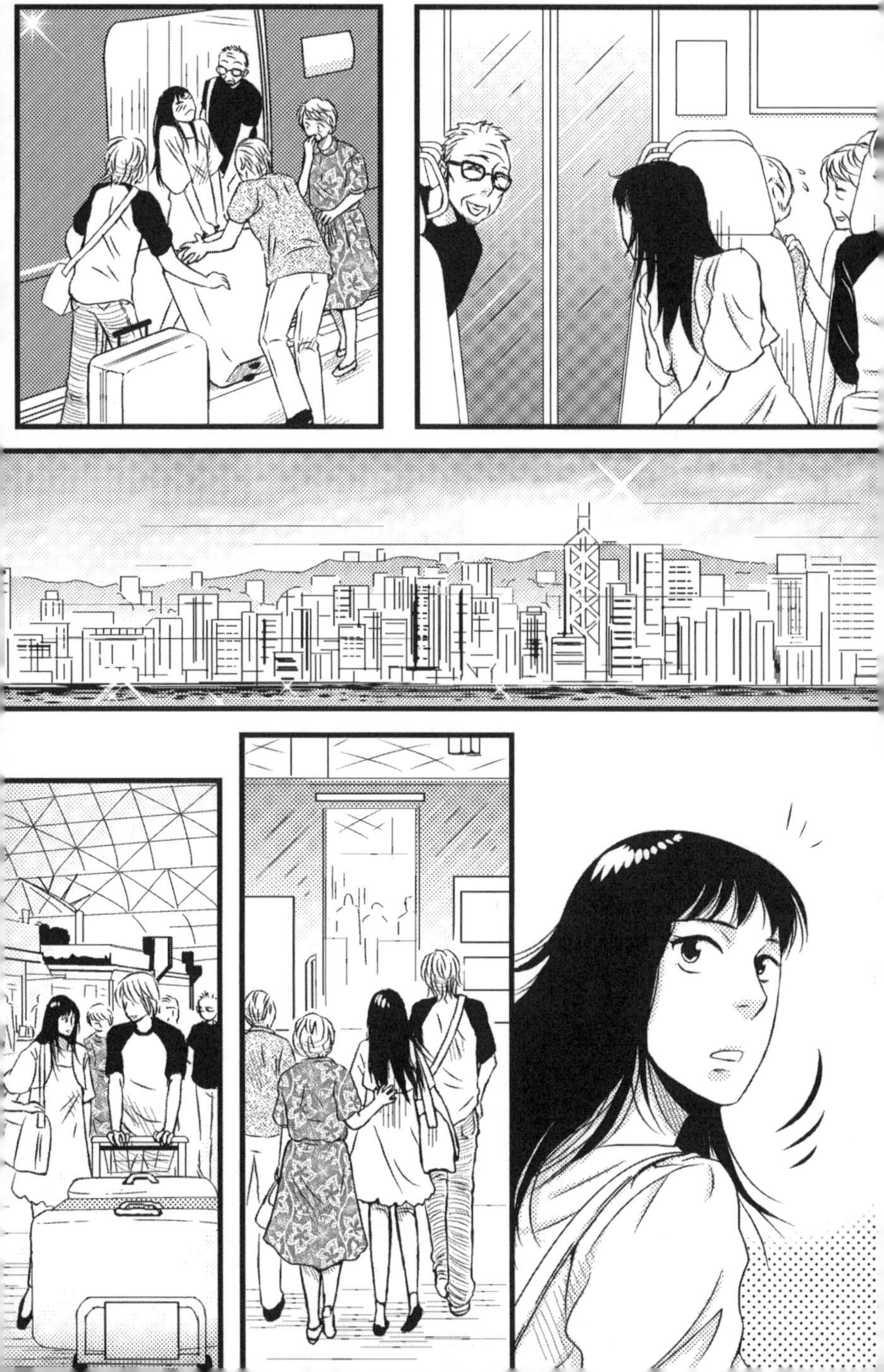

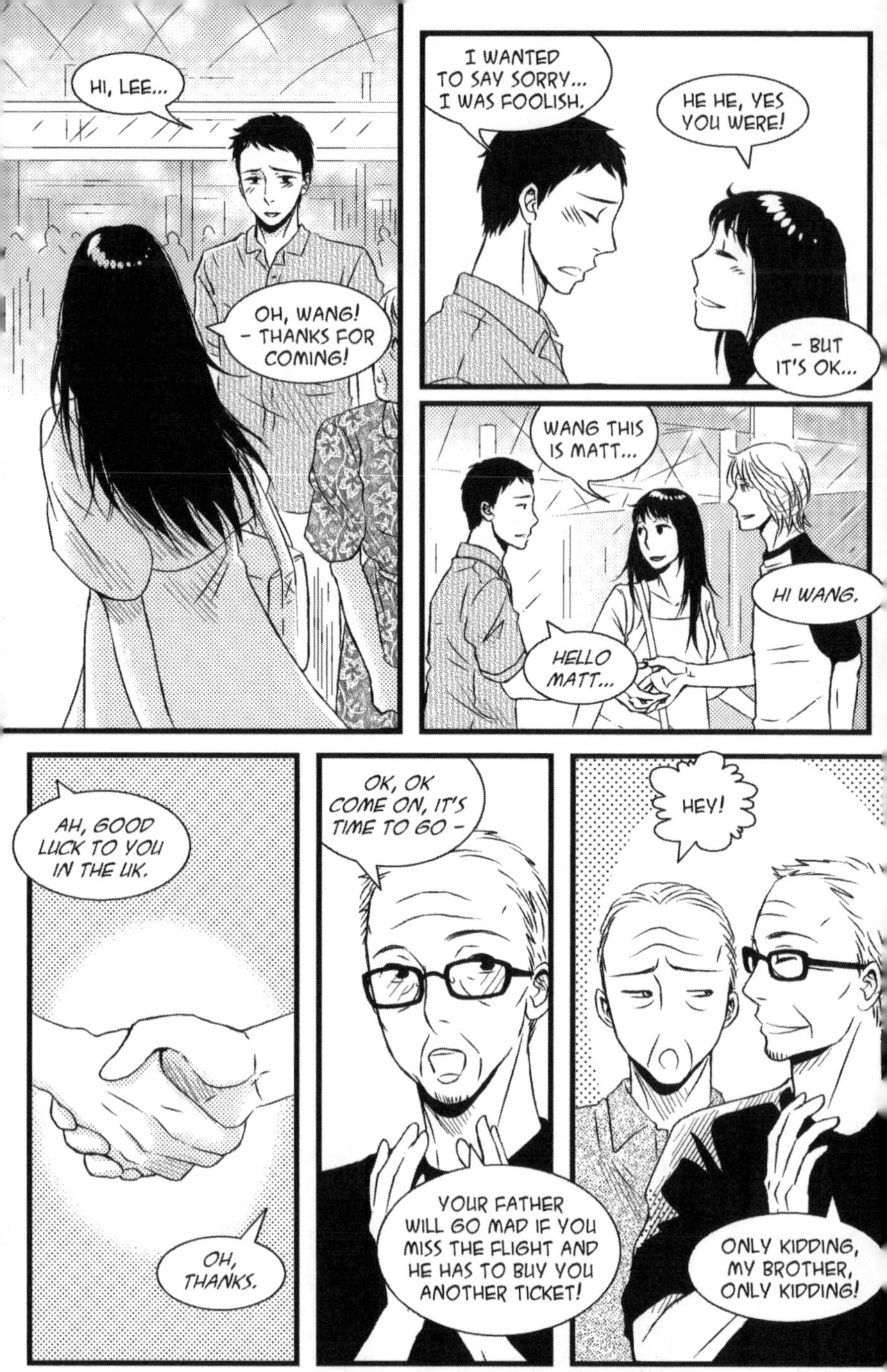
HI, LEE...
OH, WANG! - THANKS FOR COMING!
I WANTED TO SAY SORRY... I WAS FOOLISH.
HE HE, YES YOU WERE!
- BUT IT'S OK...
WANG THIS IS MATT...
HI WANG.
HELLO MATT...
AH, GOOD LUCK TO YOU IN THE UK.
OH, THANKS.
OK, OK COME ON, IT'S TIME TO GO -
YOUR FATHER WILL GO MAD IF YOU MISS THE FLIGHT AND HE HAS TO BUY YOU ANOTHER TICKET!
HEY!
ONLY KIDDING, MY BROTHER, ONLY KIDDING!

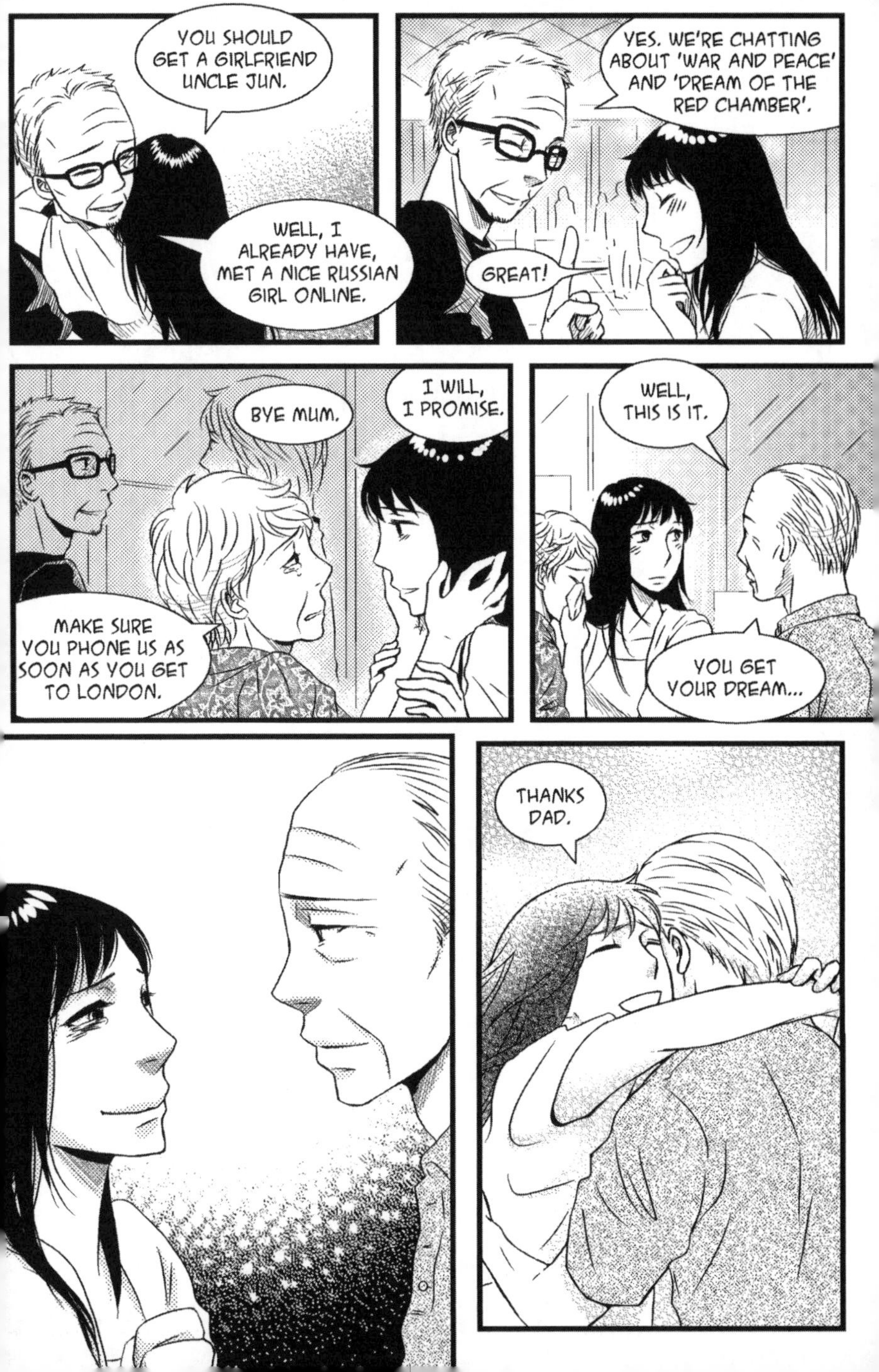
YOU SHOULD GET A GIRLFRIEND UNCLE JUN.
WELL, I ALREADY HAVE, MET A NICE RUSSIAN GIRL ONLINE.
YES. WE'RE CHATTING ABOUT 'WAR AND PEACE' AND 'DREAM OF THE RED CHAMBER'.
GREAT!
BYE MUM.
I WILL, I PROMISE.
MAKE SURE YOU PHONE US AS SOON AS YOU GET TO LONDON.
WELL, THIS IS IT.
YOU GET YOUR DREAM...
THANKS DAD.

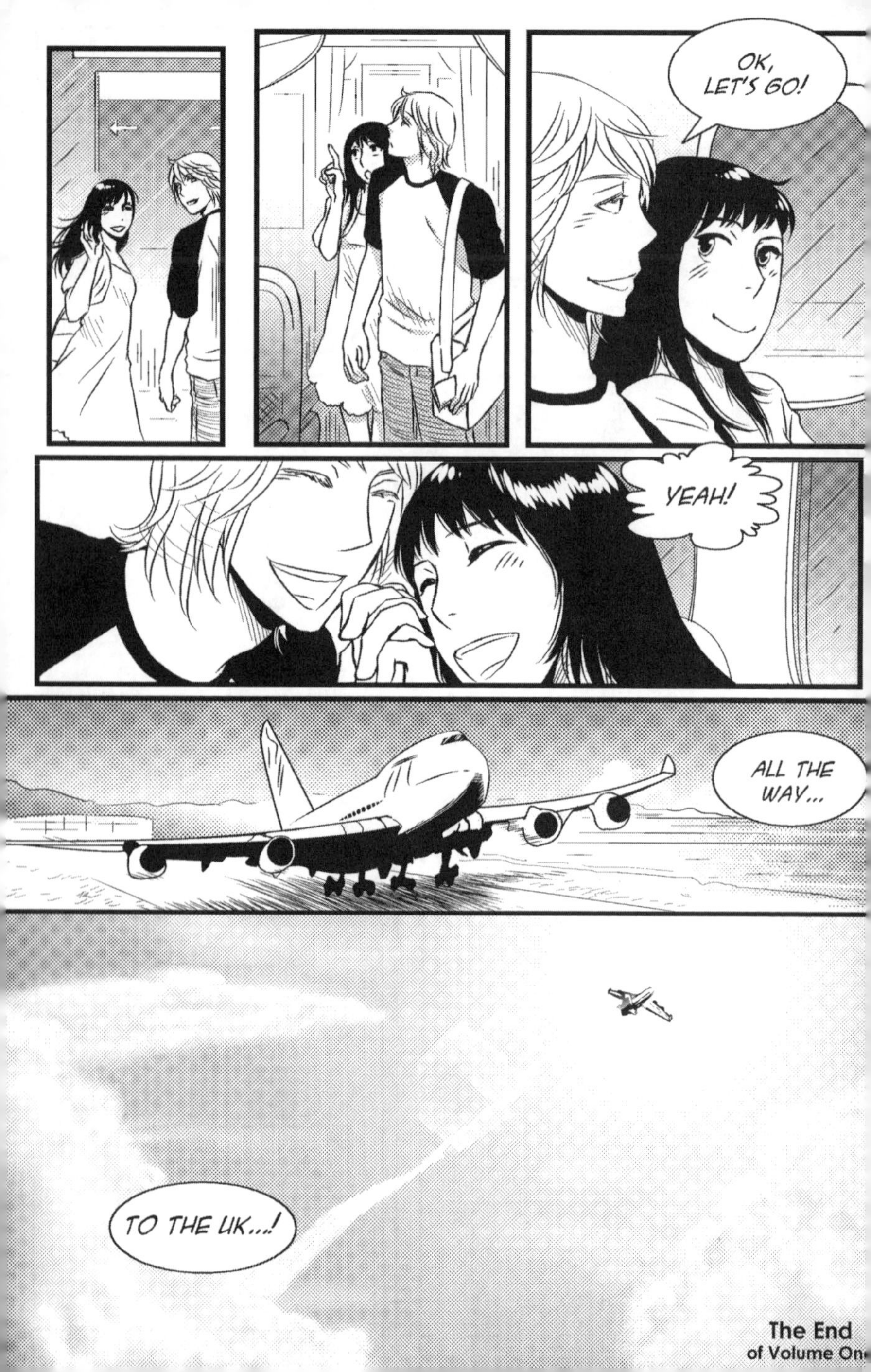
OK, LET'S GO!
YEAH!
ALL THE WAY...
TO THE UK...!

The End
of Volume On

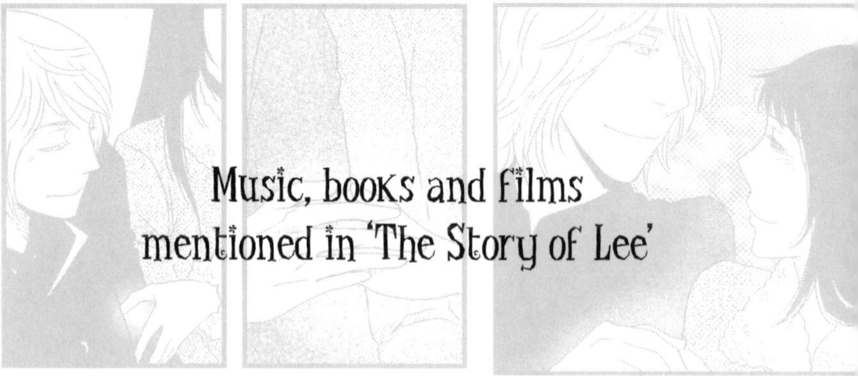

Music, books and films mentioned in 'The Story of Lee'

Music:

The Clientele, 'Losing Haringey', 2005, Merge Records.
The Clientele, '(I Can't Seem) To Make You Mine', 2005, Merge Records.
The Clientele, 'Bookshop Casanova', 2007, Merge Records.
The Birds, 'You're On My Mind',1964, Decca Records.
Scott Walker, 'The War Is Over', 1970, Philips Records.
MC5 - 'Kick out the Jams', 1969, Elektra.

Books:

Jorge Luis Borges, 'Labyrinths', 1964.
Gabriel Garcia Marquez, 'One Hundred Years Of Solitude', 1967.
Rainer Marie Rilke, 'Duino Elegies', 1922.
Marcel Proust, 'Remembrance of Things Past'
(graphic novel), 2001, NBM.
Basho Matsuo, Haiku from 1689 and 1694.
Leo Tolstoy, 'War and Peace', 1869.
Cao Xueqin, 'Dream of the Red Chamber', mid 18thC.

Films:

'On The Town', 1949 (Dir: Stanley Donen) with Gene Kelly, Frank Sinatra.
'Comrade, Almost a Love Story', 1996 (Dir: Peter Chan) with Maggie Cheung and Leon Lai.